John Lydgate, Oscar Lovell Triggs

The Assembly of Gods

Or, the accord of reason and sensuality in the fear of death

John Lydgate, Oscar Lovell Triggs

The Assembly of Gods
Or, the accord of reason and sensuality in the fear of death

ISBN/EAN: 9783337403225

Printed in Europe, USA, Canada, Australia, Japan

Cover: Foto ©Thomas Meinert / pixelio.de

More available books at **www.hansebooks.com**

The University of Chicago

ENGLISH STUDIES

(No. I.)

THE ASSEMBLY OF GODS:

OR

THE ACCORD OF REASON AND SENSUALITY IN THE
FEAR OF DEATH

BY

JOHN LYDGATE.

EDITED FROM THE MSS. WITH INTRODUCTION, NOTES, INDEX OF PERSONS AND
PLACES, AND GLOSSARY.

BY

OSCAR LOVELL TRIGGS, M.A., Ph.D.

CHICAGO
The University of Chicago Press
1895

DEDICATED TO MY MASTER

CHANCELLOR GEORGE EDWIN MacLEAN

WITH HUMBLE AFFECTION.

Reese

PREFACE.

THIS edition of Lydgate's *Assembly of Gods* serves a double pur-
pose. It is, first, a study in literature conducted at The University
of Chicago, a part of the work having been first offered in candi-
dacy for the degree of Doctor of Philosophy ; it is, second, a study
of an English text undertaken for the Early English Text Society
of London. The two institutions are associated in the publication.

The critical and linguistic parts of the work and the notes are as
accurate and comprehensive as I am able to make them with the
materials at hand. The hardihood of venturing to work upon
ancient and foreign matters in a land that has no past at its back,
that neither possesses antiquarian materials nor engenders anti-
quarian enthusiasms, will be appreciated by those who, like myself,
have made the endeavor without what one may call a traditional
training for the event.

The literary discussion of the Introduction maintains the gen-
eral interest that any work of literature is wont to arouse. This
portion represents the reaction which the poem made upon my
mind with its own knowledge of mediæval life and art. While this
part is necessarily somewhat pedantic I have tried to maintain my
natural interest in literature as an exponent of life, as the expression
of the imagination. The study of Allegory is a selection and con-
densation of materials that I have gathered for an extended history
of Allegory.

Every one who works in Lydgate will find himself indebted at
every turn to the investigations of Dr. Schick, now of Heidelberg,
who edited the *Temple of Glas* — indebted not only for matters of
fact but also for judgments of critical and literary insight. Workers
in the same field will bear witness to the value of the edition of
Lydgate and Burgh's *Secrees of Old Philisoffres* by Mr. Robert
Steele, of London. For the facts relating to Lydgate's life and
works, reference may be made to the very accurate and complete
article on Lydgate by Mr. Sidney Lee in the Dictionary of National
Biography.

At home I have every reason to be grateful for the encouragement and assistance given by Dr. George E. MacLean, formerly my teacher in the University of Minnesota; also for kindly help rendered by Professors McClintock, Blackburn, and Tolman, of the Department of English in The University of Chicago. Dr. Klaeber, of the University of Minnesota, has performed the offices of a friend in reviewing the proofs. My brother, Mr. Flloyd W. Triggs, has drawn from old prints the figures of Death for the frontispiece.

To Dr. Furnivall, the veteran Director of the work of the Early English Text Society, every one is indebted.

OSCAR LOVELL TRIGGS.

THE UNIVERSITY OF CHICAGO,
October 2, 1895.

CONTENTS.

CHAPTER VII.

The Poem

INTRODUCTION.

CHAPTER I.

A. The Manuscripts.

1. *Text A=R.3. 19, Trin. Coll. Camb.*—This is a quarto volume, in paper, in handwriting of the second half of the fifteenth century. It contains poems by Chaucer, Lydgate and others (v. Skeat, *Chaucer's Minor P.* p. xliv. Trin: *Legend of Good Women*, p. xl. T. Skeat dates the MS. before 1500). The earliest possible date for the volume is fixed by a poem written by Geo. Ashby, entitled *Prisoner in the Fleet*, and dated 1463. The present poem occupies fols. 68a–98a. A table of *Interpretations* (v. Text p. 1) precedes the poem. The volume belonged formerly to John Stowe and was the source of most of Stowe's additions to Chaucer (Skeat).

This is the earliest and the only authoritative MS. known to me, and its readings are followed with but a very few emendations in the present text. The following are the textual changes made: Eolus is printed for the Colus of the MS.; Morpheus for Morpleus; in feere 166 for feere; Phebe 243, 566 for Phebus; foom 104 for from; presse 256 for preef; she 412 for he; best 634 for bost; ther 635 for the; hys 815 for was; be 875 for he; comparyson 891 for a form not clear in MS.; with 976 for without; fly 1185 for sty; macrocosme 1420 for macocrosme; omnipotent 1467 for omnipotens. The punctuation and the capitalization of proper names are mine.

The orthography is highly unphonetic, the most marked characteristics being the confused uses of *y* and *i*, and the arbitrary doubling of vowels. *Y* is either long or short: wys, whyle, myne; but ys, hys (also his), yn (also in), hyt (also hit), wyth (also with), tyll, wyll, lytyll, shyp, fysshe, sylvyr, knyghtes, syttyng, begynne, etc.; *i* is used in king, philosophres, scisme, idylnesse, Diana, Cirus, Virgyle. The scribe wrote indifferently se or see, fle or flee, fre or free, so or soo, do or doo, wo or woo, mo or moo, whos or whoos, none or noon, hope or hoope, hole or hoole, sore or soore, holy or hooly, wordes

vii

or woorde, god or good, ost oost or hoost, blood or blody, sone or soone ; regularly — deere, leede. seene, seere, reepe, roote, poore, aboorde, stoode, goold, roode, woode, broode, stoon, Ioob, etc. Final *e* (inorganic) is written with no regularity, occurring after short as well as long vowels. The consonants generally follow the rule of doubling after short vowels.

2. *Text B = Bibl. Reg. 8.D. II, Brit. Mus.*—This is written in color on vellum and in two parts. The first part, in a 15th century hand, contains Lydgate's *Siege of Troy* (5 books) and *Siege of Thebes* (illustrated). The second part, beautifully written and illuminated, is early 16th century work and contains a *Treatise betwen Trowthe & Enformacion* by Will Cornish, an Elegy by John Skelton, Stanzas by Lydgate, his *Testament* and *Assembly of Gods*. The latter poem is indexed in the MS. as *Discord between Reason and Sensualitie.* This MS. does not differ materially from the Camb. MS. except in its omission of the table of Interpretations. It is, however, most probably a copy of the print by Wynken de Worde (G.11587), since it follows that print most closely in orthography and in the omission of line 812.

The chief variations of this text from A are given in the following collation. A few variants are given from Print D. To indicate the differences in orthography the variations of the first fifty lines are recorded complete.

---

1. hys | his. 2. toward | towarde; iourne | iourney. 3. speere | spere; begonne | begon. 4. syttyng | sittinge; solytary solitary; alone allone. 5. musyng | musinge; myght might. 6. sensualyte | sensualite: oon one; acorde | accorde. 7. cowde coude: nat not; bryng | bringe; about aboute. 8. long | longe; myght | might; oppresse | oppres. 9. cowde | coude. 10. heede . hede; heuynesse heuynes. 11. myn | myne; habytacle | habitacle. 12. pylow | pilow. 13. dyssese | disease. 14. anone | anon; came | cam. 15. so lay | soo laye; traunse | traunsse. 16. slepyng | slepinge; wakyng wakinge. 17. seyde | saide. 18. gret grete; court | courte; iustyse | iustice. 19. auaylyd auayled; sylogyse | silogyse. 20. hit | it; ys | is; seyde | saide. 21. nedys nedis. 22. when | whan; sy | see; bettyr | better; must muste. 23. seyde | saide: hys his; commaundment commaundemente. 24. whedyr wheder; wold | wolde; leede lede. 25. forthe forth. 26. tyll | till; parlyament parliament. 29. the- dyrward thederward. 30. hys | his. 31. seyde thow | saide thou. 32. seyd | saide. 33. heuen heuyn; outher | either; elles ellis. 34. seyde | saide; myn | myne; abydyng abidinge. 35. ys | is; lytyll | litill; corner cornoure; callyd | callede. 36. these wordys thes wordes; sayd | saide. 37. hys his. 38. raggys | raggis; arayd | arayde. 39. agayn agayne: whom whome; Diana Dyana. 40. seying sayenge; thow thou. 41. yeue | gyue; ageyn | ayen; soo | so.

42. preyse | preise ; lord | lorde. 43. proclamasion proclamacioun. 44. Plutoys Plutos ; co*m*maundyd | commaundede. 45. vppon | vpon ; peyne | payne ; strayte | straite. 46. Diana | Dyana ; myght | might. 47. greefe | gref ; gret | grete. 48. theym | theyme ; done | do ; they | *þ*ei ; compleynyd | co*m*pleyned. 49. begyn | begynne ; Diana | Dyana ; constreynyd | constreynede. 50. whyche | whiche. 56. yef | yf. 57. howe | hou. 70. thorough | thorugh. 71. syngler | synguler. 72. shuld | sholde ; world | worlde. 73. dyspleser | displeasure. 77. yeue | omitted. 94. yow | you. 98. thorough | thrugh. 99. furst | first. 102. ferre | fer. 103. mcrueyle | meruaill. 104. from | come. 107. ebbe | eb. 109. dykes | dyks. 117. oo one. 130. perysshe | perish. 132. pepyll | people. 135. requyreth | req*u*iret. 155. vs | hus. 166. feere | infeere. 183. togedyr | togider. 186. alther | alder. 210. owne wele | one well. 216. pyne | payne. 217. grogyng | grutching (D = grutchyng). 228. eft | oft. 233. lak | lacke. 234. cese | sease. 235. mery | mercy. 248. compaygnably | companably. 256. preef | presse (D = presse). 269. good | god. 283. fawchon | fawcon. 325. frese | frele (D = frese). 337. was then | than was (D = than was). 348. sythe | shithe. 355. chase | chose. 361. Phebus | Pheby. 434. forthe | for. 449. sewerte | suerte. 462. smete | smote. 473. cosdras | coldras. 480. owther | outher. 513. leyte | lightnynge. 520. woll | will. 535. drowthe | drought. 569. I hope shall | I hope I shall. 587. defaute | the faute (D = the faute). 607. at | omitted (D omits at). 634. bost | best. 648. foule rybaudy | foule and rybaudry (D has and). 673. braggars | kraghers. 721. for sowght he | forsoth it. 753. to do a | to a. 763. row | route (D = rowe). 773. wore | were. 812 | omitted. 815. was | and. 825. standardes | standartis. 875. he | be. 966. haue ye lost | haue lost (D omits ye). 970. guytornes | guytors. 974, 981. dubbyd | doubled (D = doubled). 1094. rerewarde | reward. 1113. mervt | might (D = myght). 1161. she | he. 1185. sty | fly. 1201. as they came by Conscience | as thei to C. cam (D follows B), 1243. bende | ben (D = ben). 1358. kept | kepe (D = kept). 1373. menetyme whyle | meanewhill. 1467. omnipotens | omnipotent. 1516. singlerly | sy*n*gulerly. 1537. awter | aulter. 1538. Osee | Ozee (D = Ozee). 1539. Salmon | Salamon. 1591. brayne | barayne. 1701. shall | sall. 1705. nouelte | newelte (D = newelte). 1744. deuyacion | denocyon. 1806. gnawyng | knawi*n*ge. 1854. tryfyl | triphells. 1858. sauns | sauns (D = sannuz). 1975. a a | aha. 2020. dowtys | doubtes. 2062. accusacion | actuacyon. 2103. descendyd | desce*n*deth.

B. THE PRINTS.

3. *Text C = G. 11587. Brit. Mus.*—This is the first print of the poem by Wynken de Worde, a folio dated 1498. It is an unique copy. It contains the *Canterbury Tales* and Lydgate's *Assembly of Gods*. Lydgate's "treatyse" is printed in double columns on the last 15 leaves without pagination. On the recto of the first leaf is a woodcut of the Canterbury pilgrims seated around a table. This print is especially valuable in that it assigns the work to Lydgate in the colophon : "Thus endeth this lytyll moralized treatyse compiled by dan Iohn Lydgat somtyme monke of Bury on whose soule

have mercy." The print has commonly the readings of MS.B. It omits line 812 but has the table of Interpretations.

4. *Text D=C. 13. a. 21. King's Collect. Brit. Mus.*—This print is also by W. de Worde and of about the same date as the first. The Catalogue of the Brit. Mus. and Mr. Lee (*Dict. Nat. Biog.* Vol. XXXIV, p. 313, v.) give the date 1500, but Dr. Schick, on the authority of Mr. Gordon Duff (Brit. Mus.), says it is earlier, perhaps 1498. It contains Lydgate's *Story of Thebes, Assemble de dyeus* and *Temple of Glas* (v. Hazlitt, *Bibl.* p. 358, No. 3 under Lydgate; Schick, *Temp. of Glas*, E. E. T. Soc., p. xxvi, 9). This print exhib-its no notable changes in the text. It follows most closely MS. A.

5. Later reprints by Pynson and Redman, under the title "The Interpretacyon of the Natures of Goddys and Goddesses," show no important textual differences (v. Hazlitt, *Bibl.* p. 358, No. 4 (b) (c) (d). Redman's last edition is dated 1540).

CHAPTER II.

A. THE TITLE.

W. de Worde's second print (D above) has the colophon: "Here endeth a lytyll Tratyse named, *Le Assemble de dyeus.*" This is followed by de Worde's imprint and, on the following page, by the cut of the Chaucer pilgrims seated about a table, also entitled *Le Assemble de dyeus.* Redman's late reprint (1540) ends with the colophon: "Here endeth a lytyll treatyse named *the assemble of goddis and goddesses.*" The catalog of Lydgate's works, probably made by John Stowe for the Chaucer-Lydgate volume, printed by Adam Islip in London in 1598 and 1602, includes the *Banket of Gods and Goddesses with a discourse of Reason and Sensualitie* by Lydgate (ed. 1602 fol. 376 : ed. 1598 fol. 394).

In the Camb. MS. the title, in the handwriting of Mr. Beauprei Bell (Camb. c. 1727), is given as *Assembly of Gods and Goddesses by Lydgate.* The Brit. Mus. MS. is cataloged as *Discord between Reason and Sensualitie.* Lowndes (*Bibl.* Bohn Lib., p. 1419) uses the title *Banquet of the Gods.* Ritson (*Bibl. Poet.*) lists the poem apparently twice, as *The interpretation of the names of goddes and goddesses* (No. 13) and probably confusing it with *Reason and Sensuality* (Fairfax 16), as *Banket of gods and goddesses with a discourse of reason and sensualitie* (No. 113). Bale, probably noticing the list of *Interpreta-tions* prefixed to W. de Worde's print, enumerates among Lydgate's writings, *De Nominibus Deorum.* Collier (*Hist. of Dram. P.* I., p. 30) refers to the poem under the title, *Interpretation of the names of Goddes and Goddesses.* Schick, in his chronology of Lydgate's works (*Temp. of Glas* cix.), adopts the title, *The Assembly of Gods;* and so, following him, Dr. Furnivall in the Early Eng. Text Society's Announcements, Sidney Lee in the *Dict. of Natl. Biog.* (Vol. XXXIV., p. 313, V., 18) and Mr. Courthope in his *History of English Poetry* (I. p. 322). We may suppose, on the authority of W. de Worde's print, that this was Lydgate's own title. It is not, however, a sufficient title as titles go, inasmuch as it does not express the central moral of the story. A truer name would be the *Accora of Reason and Sensuality.*

B. THE AUTHORSHIP AND DATE.

1. *The authorship.* The external testimony is in itself quite suf-ficient to establish the fact of Lydgate's authorship. W. de Worde's first print (C) ascribes the work to our monk of Bury in the colo-phon : "Thus endeth this lytyll moralized treatyse compiled by dan Iohn Lydgat somtyme monke of Bury on whose soule have mercy." All the early lists (of Bale, Dibdin, etc.) agree in the assignment. Collier, in his *History of Dramatic Poetry* (Vol. I., p. 30), printed, for the first time since the black-letter copies, a few stanzas of the poem, referring the work to Lydgate. Dyce, in his notes on Skelton's works (p. 144), makes the same reference. The MS. was not known to Warton or Morley. A definite reference to our poem is found in Hawes's *Pastime of Pleasure* (Chap. XIV.). Hawes was a pupil of Lydgate and recounts as the works of his master, the *Life of St. Edmund, Falls of Princes, Chorl and Bird, Court of Sapience, Troy Book, Temple of Glas:*

> "And betwene vertue and the lyfe vycyous
> Of goddes and goddes[ses] a boke solacyous
> He did compyle."

This must refer to the *Assembly of Gods.*

That Lydgate's name was associated with the battle of the vices and virtues is further indicated by the "extemporal play" of the *Seven Deadlie Sinns*, contrived by Richard Tarleton and performed before King Henry VI. (v. description by Collier, *Hist. Dram. P.,* III., p. 198). Our monk Lydgate (here spelled Lidgate) is supposed to regulate the performance, to deliver the prolog and epilog and to explain the dumb shows.

As to internal evidence Lydgate's finger marks are all here : the monkish piety, the moralization, the allegory, the way in which he dwells upon the themes of death ; then his stock words and phrases, especially those repeated to fill up the lines (v. notes and *Temp. of Glas* p. cxxxvii.) the irregular lines (cf. *Secrees*), the rime-forms, and the peculiar Lydgatian metre (type, C. p. xvi : v. Schick, *Temple of Glas*, lviii); further, the saying of things as if "undir correccioun" (cf. *Secrees*, p. 1, 2), the self-depreciation in confessing his thin brain (text, l. 1591) and thin wit (text, l. 1997) and the request to take the very little wheat from the much chaff of the poem (text, l. 2071–2; cf. *Secrees*, p. xx. and *Temp. of Glas*, p. cxl). Lydgate is one of the easiest poets to detect for his conventional manner.

2. *The Date.* So far as I am able to determine from a study of the contents there is nothing to indicate the exact date of the poem's composition. The allegory of the poem is wholly removed from historical place or time. Dr. Schick conjectures the date 1403. In consideration of the general temper of the work, quite prosaic one must allow, the nature of the allegory, and its domi- nant note of death, I am inclined to assign its writing to Lydgate's second period, that is, after 1412 (the date of the first lines of the *Troy-Book*), as far removed as possible from the genial influence of Chaucer which is so distinctly traceable in the monk's early works. As a youth Lydgate was loath to enter the monastic life, and the poems of his first period have a freshness, a humor, and a love of nature, that belong to the world outside the cloister. But we have the proof of the *Legends* and *Secrees* and the *Testament* that, as he approached age, he grew more pious and more prosaic. The *Assembly of Gods* is the work of a thorough Benedictine both in theory and in practise. And there is a positive lowering of the poetic tone. There are no plaints of lovers, not a word about the "floure of womanhede," not a happy thought of nature. Life is grown serious, and the monk, anxious concerning the battle with Vice and earnest to direct sinners to the Lord of Light, writes in the repentant prayerful temper of the *Testament*.

In arguing for an earlier date it would be true to say that the influence of the *Remaunt of the Rose* is somewhat evident in the alle- gory, and that the work is rather more original and creative than his late riming histories, and it appears in the classification of his works by

Sidney Lee (*Dict. Natl. Biog.*, Vol. XXXIV, p. 313, 314) that most if not all of the poems under the head of "Allegories, Fables and Moral Romances" were written before 1412.

On the other hand the decline in the *Assembly of Gods* in poetic power is, as noted above, very marked, judging from his known early works. In poetic conception and phrasing the poem is in every way inferior to the *Chorl and Bird* and the *Temple of Glas;* the one written before 1400 and dedicated to "his maister with humble affeccioun," the other written about 1403 in imitation of Chaucer's *Hous of Fame.* There is not a line so poetic as these verses from the *Temple of Glas* :

> "A world of beaute compassid in hir face
> Whose persant loke doþ þurugh myn hert[e] race " 755-6;

nor a maxim so unworldly wise as these from the *Chorl and Bird:*

> "Songe and prison have noon accordaunce," Min. P., p. 183,

and

> "Bettir is fredom withe litelle in gladnesse
> Than to be thralle withe al worldly richesse," Min. P., p. 193;

not a moral so manly as

> "When wo approcheþ lat myrþ most habound,
> As manhood axeþ; and þough þou fele smert,
> Lat not to manie knowen of þin hert."—*Temple of Glas*, 1177-9.

The theme also, notwithstanding its place among the allegories, seems to indicate a late date. While Lydgate was always familiar with the thought of change and death, it being his frequent opinion that "all do but show a shadow transitory" and that "all stant in chaunges like a midsomer rose," it is fair to assume that the dread of death would be most dominant after the period of his youth. The *Dance of Macabre*, which is descriptive of the painting of Death's procession on the walls of St. Paul's, belongs to the second period, perhaps to the year 1425 (Schick, *Temple of Glas*, cxii); likewise his translation of De Deguileville's *Pèlerinage de l' Homme*, representing life as a pilgrimage somewhat in the manner of Bunyan's *Pilgrim's Progress*, belongs to this period, the year 1426.

The proof from the metre and from the language is also, I think, on the side of a late date. The measure, very broken and irregular at one's best mending, is nearer the long lines of the *Secrees* than the very good verses of the *Temple of Glas.* There is also a change

in the poetic phraseology, as will be seen by a study of the riming
words, which change compels a date as near as possible to the time
when the final *e* ceased to be spoken. Though, as to this, it is not
impossible that Burgh or some other of Lydgate's pupils rewrote
the poem as we have it in the text. Still it is not probable that
anyone would alter the riming words.

On the whole I should wish to assign the composition of the
Assembly of Gods to about the year 1420 or perhaps, the *Story of
Thebes* being finished, to 1422 or even later. In the absence of
direct testimony, any more exact statement of the date must wait
the publication of Lydgate's other works, which will furnish a surer
basis for poetic, metrical and linguistic tests.

CHAPTER III.

THE METRE.

In the MS. the metre is very irregular. Of course little depen-
dence can be placed upon MSS. of the fifteenth century, written
after the final *e* ceased to be sounded. We know that many little
words were inserted by the scribes, who regarded the lines as imper-
fect. So whether Lydgate himself failed in this poem in his meas-
ures or whether the fault is due to the scribes can not be determined.
However, it does not appear that Lydgate in any of his poems was
especially skillful in the mechanism of his art. He was himself
aware of the imperfections of his verse, and in the *Troy-Book* he
confessedly "sette asyde" truth of metre and took "none hede
nouther of shorte nor longe." Moreover, none of Lydgate's pupils
exhibit any especial grace of form. Burgh, his nearest pupil,
readily acknowledges in continuing the *Secrees* that he is unable to
keep his measures in time and proportion (*Sec.* st. 219). If we take
Chaucer's line as the standard of melody, it is probable that
Lowell's estimate of Lydgate's verse, a "barbarous jangle," is the
correct one. Old French verse with its great variety of lines and
measures (no less than sixteen—Skeat's *Chaucer*, Vol. VI, p. lxxxvii)
and indeed Chaucer's own verse forms, may have given Lydgate his
license to vary his metres at will. If we forego a fixed metre and
read the lines with their natural accentuation, a fairly good rhythm
is secured.

Our present poem, *The Assembly of Gods*, is written in the common seven line stanza, which came to be known as the Rhyme Royal, riming *ababbcc*. The scheme of the Chaucerian stanza cannot be rigidly applied. Every liberty in respect of length of line and character of measure is taken by Lydgate. Some lines are bald prose.

Type A. In the first place examples will be given of lines which seem to have five iambic measures with the cæsural pause after the second measure. This may be called the standard-line form.

> 43: Then was there made a proc ' lama | sion.
> 45: Vppon | the peyne of strayte correc | cion.
> 57: Remem ' bre furst howe I ' a godd | esse pure.
> 163: For hys | excuse came yn | a mess | ynger.
> 750: And bade hem come in all | the haste | they myght.
> 816: He semyd a lorde of ryght | gret ex cellence.
> 980: To wynne | theyr spores they seyde | they wold | asay.
> 1026: Whyche made ' the grounde as slep | yr as | an yele.
> 1086: But all ' the tyme whyle Ver | tew was away.
> 1146: And fro thens forth to Sat | ysfac | cion.

1. The cæsura in the standard line falls generally after the second measure, but Lydgate shifts its position at liberty. He has more freedom than Chaucer in this respect, though the latter is by no means regular in his pauses (v. Skeat's *Chaucer*, Introd. sec. 107). The examples here given to illustrate this variation include lines of different types (see below). The pause may fall

(*a*) after the first measure :
> 566: To compleyn than Phebe styrt vppon her fete.
> 1504: Sate & Scrypture was scrybe to theym all.

(*b*) after the third :
> 18: To the gret Court of Mynos the iustyse.
> 782: But the felde was clene defaute ' fonde he none.

(*c*) after the fourth :
> 621: Pryde was the furst þat next hym roode || God woote.
> 879: And made hem be caryed toward Vyce y wys.

(*d*) twice or thrice in a line :
> 603: Wherfore þow Cerberus I now the dyscharge.
> 1231: Ys he soo quod Vertu well he shall be taught.
> 1210: Well quoth Feythe || for hys sake ! I shall do that I may do.
> 1377: Now Prayer ' efte Fastyng & oftyn tyme Penaunce.

Type B. An extra syllable may occur before the cæsura and at the end of the line. Two such syllables may also occur before the cæsura (v. ll. 38, 390, 808).

(*a*) Before cæsura :

    38: Brought theder Eolus   in raggys euyll arayd.
  160: Shape vs an answer   to thyne accusement.
  305: Rewler of knyghthode   of Prudence the goddese.
  390: There was sad Sychero   and Arystotyll olde.
  456: Thus haue I dewly   with all my dilygence.
  808: Next whom came Pacyence   that nowhere hath no pere.
  908: Well menyng merchauntes   with trew artyfyceres.

(*b*) At end of line :

The form is comparatively infrequent (v. Chap. IV, c).

    9: So ponderously   I cowde make noon obstacle.
   12: To rowne with a pylow   me semyd best tryacle.
   60: Thys traytour Eolus   hath many of my places.
  946: In thys mene tyme   whyle Vertu thus preuyded.

Type C. The thesis may be wanting at the cæsura.

    8: For long er I myght   slepe me gan oppresse.
   68: So that the deere   shall haue no resort.
   85: Thow knowest well   that I haue the charge.
   87: No shyp may sayle   keruell boot ner barge.
  233: For lak of shade ;   I dar vndyrtake.
  279: And next by her   sate the god Saturne.
  600: No maner of thyng   can hym hurt nor dere.
  618: Hard as any horn   blakker fer then soot.
  806: Roody as a roose | ay he kept hys chere.

1. This is a form almost peculiar to Lydgate (v. Schick, *Temp. of Glas*, p. lviii. C.), though Chaucer occasionally employed it (Skeat, *Chaucer*, Vol. VI. Introd., sec. 110). It is easy however to read some of these lines with four accents : thus line 85 may read : "Thou knówest wéll that I háue the chárge." Other lines, however, as 618. 87. etc.. can have no other reading than that given.

Type D. A thesis may be wanting in the first measure.

    17: For he seyde   I must yeve attendaunse.
  106: Secundly   whereas my nature ys.
  124: That to theym   shuld fall opon the see.
  197: Madame ye shall haue all your plesere.
  251: To be had   wherfore ye may nat let.
  557: Walewyng with hys wawes   & tomblyng as a ball.
  640: Malyce   Frowardnesse   gret Ielacy.
  645: Wrong   Rauyne   sturdy Vyolence.
  654: Heresy   Errour   with Idolatry.

Type E. A trochee may take the place of an iambic in the first measure. These measures are best read, however, with "hovering accent," as Ten Brink (*Chaucer's Sp.*, p. 182, sec. 316) and Gummere (*Handbook of Poetics*, pp. 186, 187, 206, 224) read similar lines in Chaucer and other English poets.

> 5: Musyng | on a maner .| how that I myght make.
> 374: Cryspe was | her skyn ,| her eyen columbyne.
> 418: Seying to | her sylf ,|| that chere should þey repent.
> 472: Iason ne | Hercules ||| went they neuer so wyde.
> 631: Slówthe was | so slepy ||' he came all behynde.
> 648: Boldnes | in Yll .| with Foule Rybaudy.
> 747: Pepyll | to reyse || hys quarrell to menteyn.
> 760: Gaderyd | to Vertew | in all that they mowte.
> 1174: Hauyng | in her hande ||| the palme of vyctory.

Type F. There may be a double thesis in any measure. In many cases the extra syllable may be slurred over. But the trisyllabic measure was without doubt an accepted poetic form (v. Ellis, *Early Eng. Pron.*, ch. iv, p. 334; ch. vii, p. 648. Ellis cites 69 examples in the Prolog. See Skeat, ed. of *Prioresses Tale*, etc., Introd. p. lxiii).

> 7: But I cowde | nat bryng | about | that mon | acorde.
> 66: He breketh | hem asondre ,| or rendeth ,| hem roote | & rynde.
> 98: For hurt | of my name .| thorough | thys gret | offence.
> 126: With a sod | eyn pyry .| he lapp | yd hem | in care.
> 139: The more gre | uous peyne '| and hast | y iug | ement.
> 199: But furst | I yow pray ,| let me | the mat | er here.
> 361: And ones | in the moneth ,| with Phe | bus was | she meynt.
> 383: That he ther | with glad | yd all | the com | pany.
> 410: But there was | no rome | to set | hyr in | that hous.
> 472: Iason | ne Hercules ,| went | they neu | er so wyde.
> 487: To the dynt | of my dart .| for doole | nor des | tyny.

Type G. Lydgate frequently expands the normal pentameter line to six measures. Mr. Steele, the editor of the *Secrees*, remarks that the greater part of that poem might be scanned on a six-beat basis. If such lines were of sporadic occurrence they might be slurred over, but there are so many lines with the longer rhythm that the acceptance of the Alexandrine is rendered imperative. It is possible, of course, to read some of these lines with four accents, as if they were formed on the model of the alliterative four-beat measures as found in the Mystery Plays (v. *York Plays*, ed. by Smith, Introd., p. li), certain ballads (v. *King John and the Abbot of Canterbury*) and the contemporary alliterative poems. The long doggerel lines in Shakespeare may be reduced to this form (v. *Quell. u. For.*, vol. 61, p. 119, 3). But the use of the Alexandrine was now established both by itself and in association with other metres (v. Schipper, *Engl. Met.*, I, Kap. 5, 8, 13, and cf. its later usage by

Wyatt, and see *Mirror for Magistrates*, ed. by Haslewood, p. 123, for mixture of pentameter and Alexandrine), and Lydgate would naturally adopt the form at a time when every irregularity in verse was permissible. He himself was most attracted to the French forms, though the English alliterative principle still had some force in his verse. I think there can be no question about Lydgate's Alexandrines.

Mr. Ellis (*Early Eng. Pron.*, ch. vii. p. 649) thought that Chaucer made use of this variation and noticed four instances in the prolog of the *Canterbury Tales* of what seemed to him to be a six-measure line (ll. 148, 232, 260, 764), all of which have the justification of the best MSS. Zupitza and Skeat in their critical texts of the *Prologue* reduce these lines to the normal (l. 764 by slurring).

```
  4: Syttyng ' all sol ! ytary   alone  besyde  a lake.
 54: Accord | yng to ' the offence   that he | to me ' hath do.
161: And ellys  I most | procede   opon ! thy iug ' ement.
253: And when ! Apol | lo sy " hit wold ! noon oth ' er be.
267: Lyke ' as she | had take   the man ! tell & | the ryng.
298: The pal | eys ther | of shone   as though ' hit had | be day.
325: Clad | in rus   set frese   and brech | ed lyke ' a bere.
327: A shepe | crook in | hys hand   he spar ' yd for ! no pryde.
340: Aboute ' hym in | hys gyr   dyll stede   hyng fyssh | es man   y a score.
347: She lok | ed eu | er about   as though ! she had | be mad.
359: Fat | she was ' of face   but of ' complex | yon feynt.
364: And on ' hyr hede | she weryd   a crowne | of syl.| uyr pure.
367: He had | a gyld   yn tong   as fyll   for hys   degree.
372: By   hym sate | Dame Venus   with col ! our erys | tallyne.
385: In sygne   that he ' was mastyr   & lord   of that   banket.
```

So I read lines 401, 404, 420, 421, 422, 462, 476, 490, 495, 496, 497, 500, 504, 525, 542, 560, 634, 656, 817, 864, 937, 949, 952, 962, 995, 999, 1048, 1050, 1093, 1097, 1106, 1113, 1120, 1167, 1204, 1210, 1225, 1239, 1240, 1267, 1344, 1589, 1792, 2099, 2100, 2106, 2107. Lines 61, 102, 128, 130, 131, 338, 343, 578, 672, 856, 1000, might be read either as Alexandrines or as pentameters of type F.

Type II. There are occasional four-measure lines.

```
 232: So that | your game ! shall nat   dyserese.
 307: Safe on ! her hede   a crowne   ther stood.
 444: All ye   gret goddys ' yeue at ! tendaunce.
 693: Getters   chyders   causers | of frayes.
 758: To Ver ' tews frendys ' thus all | aboute.
 979: These four | tene knyghtes   made Vyce ' that day.
1659: Wherfore ' ar chyl ' dren put   to scoole.
1834: Of eu | ery mans | oppyn | yon.
```

In this manner may be read lines 16, 17, 22, 27, 28, 47, 50, 94, 134, 182, 204, 530, 550, 703, 722, 916, 1065, 1243, 1506, 1654, 1655, 1740, 1839, 2004, 2035, 2046.

2. Of course many lines can be scanned in more than one way. Other prosodists will probably not agree with the scansion of the examples given. It is difficult and often impossible to determine the pronunciation of many words. I think the final *e*'s are often, if not generally, mute. The rhythm of many lines would be broken by the requirements of the Chaucerian scheme of inflections. It is evident that during Lydgate's lifetime the language was undergoing transformation. The general irregularity of the metre, the intrusion into Chaucer's carefully constructed seven-line stanza of the four and six-beat lines, and the frequent alliteration, suggest the influence of the older English metrical forms. But it is further obvious that Lydgate used in composition the principles both of metre and of stress.

This mixture in his measures of free and regular stress, seems to confirm the opinion[1] of Professor Gummere (v. *Amer. J. of Phil.* Vol. VII, I, p. 46) that the English iambic is not merely the French measure introduced by a *tour de force*, but a "harmonizing of two great systems, the Germanic and the Romance, the rhythmic and the metric, on the basis of two representative measures," the heroic pentameter line being the "result of forcing the iambic movement upon some late form of our old four-stress verse." The conditions are thus stated by Professor Gummere: "On the one hand, four stresses, fixed pause, indeterminate amount of light syllables; on the other, five stresses, shifting and slighter pause, strict ordering and number of light syllables." Proofs of such compromise are furnished by Chaucer, the majority of whose pentameter verses are formed, to some extent, on the plan of the O. E. line of four stresses; by the Mystery and Morality Plays, whose irregular measures very plainly display the continuance of the English traditions; by Skelton, whose peculiar metre seems to be due to the splitting of the O. E. long line and the riming of the parts; by Spenser in his

---

[1] Little attention has been given hitherto to this view of Professor Gummere, but the trend of opinion now seems to favor it. See Courthope's treatment of Lydgate's verse in his recent *History of English Poetry*, I., pp. 326–33. Cf. the statement of Mr. I. Gollancz in his edition of Cyn. *Christ*, p. xvii: "The secret of Marlowe's discovery (the secret of blank verse) lies in this that he Teutonized the 'versi sciolti' imported from Italy."

Shepherd's Calendar, which combines free and regular stress in a remarkable manner; and again by the heroic verses of Shakespeare and Spenser and of Dryden and Pope, many of which have rhetorically but four stresses.

On the whole Lydgate followed his French models, or more strictly his Chaucer. The many alliterative phrases in his poem illustrate, however, the traditions of the older poetry; such a line as 66b

"or *r*endeth hem *r*oote & *r*ynde"

indicating the "*rum ram ruf*" principle of composition. The variable measure and line reveal the confusion into which English verse had fallen after Chaucer, it being still uncertain whether free or regular stress would prevail. Had Lydgate been favored with Chaucer's literary environment and gifted with his genius and ear for rhythm it is probable that he might have maintained the master's delicate Normanized literary English, but the influence of the vulgar Suffolk tongue with its accentual principles of verse and its rapidly disappearing inflections was too strong for the monk. Chaucer's regular measures — regular because artificial — were given over to confusion. The oral, in the rude times of the fifteenth century, superseded the literary. From Chaucer to Spenser no one was able to give permanency to the forms of English verse.

That the metre is at best extremely irregular is shown by counting the syllables. In the first one thousand lines, slurring wherever possible and omitting, except where forbidden by the rhythm, the final *e*'s, the following result is given:

2	14-syllable lines.			See 66, 340.
5	13	"	"	See 404, 525.
47	12	"	"	
210	11	"	"	
546	10	"	"	
179	9	"	"	
11	8	"	"	See p. xvii, Type F.

Types B and F make up the 11-syllable lines and D and C the 9-syllable lines. G has frequently but 11 syllables (v. line 359).

CHAPTER IV.

The Rime.

1. *End-rime:*—The rime is generally pure throughout. Correct masculine rimes are the rule. The most numerous rime-endings are -ace, -ake, -all, -aunce,- ay, -e, -ence, -ent, -ere, -esse, -y, -yde, -yght, -o, -on, -ore, -ought, -ow, -ure (*v.* Rime Index).

(a) *Identical rimes* occur in a number of cases. By identical rimes I mean here those in which the riming syllables coincide in sound throughout. These syllables may be etymologically different. Acorde 6: monacorde 7; malapert 503: pert 504; dyscharge 603: charge 605; ouerse 772: see 775; take 1388, 1409: vndyrtake 1390, 1411; become 1406: welcome 1407; serue 1408: descrue 1410; goon 1836: ouergoon 1838; before 1871: therfore 1874; hande 1912: hande 1914; dyffuse 1955: refuse 1957; dyscorde 2015: monacorde 2016; alone 923: euerychone 924 (14 cases). *Identical suffix-rimes:* (a) *with initial consonant:*—iugement 139: auysment 140; resystence 228: sentence 229; satysfaccion 834: dysposicion 836; sadnes 1380: glad-nes 1382; royally 268: sykerly 270; herytykes 678: scismatykes 679; pycture 1514: creature 1516; (b) *with initial vowel:*— varyaunce 244: ordynaunce 245; conuenyent 249: expedyent 250; precious 790: vyctoryous 791; swerers 702: morderers 704 etc. (about 140 cases of such rimes (b) and (a).

(b) *Imperfect rimes* are occasional:—am 86: man 88; strong 260: hand 262; came 785: man 787; came 862: than 864; doon 1217: com 1218; come 1336: oblyuyone 1337; came 1702; woman 1704 (7 cases of *assonance*); beste 1056: lyste 1057 (v. lyst 1297: myst 1299); neere 1616: desyre 1617 (v. desyre 1870: wyre 1872,—cf. *Schick* Intro. lxi); bedde 2038: vnderstande 2040; crysmatory 1444: sanctuary 1446; *probably imperfect:*—syt 191: yet 193 (perhaps=yit as in Chaucer); fete 566: yete 567 (cf. yet 193: syt 191); ende 1777: mynde 1778 (mynde 1923: ende 1922: spende 1920; ende 1931: mende 1932; but cf. mynde 1784: behynde 1785).

(c) *Feminine rimes* occur in the following instances:—obstacle 9: habytacle 11: tryacle 12; chases 58: places 60: manaces 61; philosophres 272: cofres 273; centre 769: entre 770; seuyn 821: heuyn 823: steuyn 824; euer 1203, 1974: neuer 1204, 1973; ? reson 1259: seson 1260; crysmatory 1444: sanctuary 1446: tary 1447; story 1513: memory 1515; fable 1686: acceptable 1687; ymages 1731: stages 1733: passages 1734; nother 1807: brother 1809; parable 1987:

fable 1988; ? compleynyd 48: constreynyd 49 (cf. herde 498: con-
queryd 500=masc.); grauntyd 118, 874: hauntyd 119, 875; prom-
ysyd 482: dyspysyd 483; preuydyd 946: guydyd 948; aqueyntyd 1345:
peyntyd 1347; deuydyd 1765: prouydyd 1767; ? declaryd 736: sparyd
738; ? retornyd 1119; mornyd 1120; ? excusyd 1399: dysvsyd
1400; *probably:* — requyreth 135: expyreth 137: desyreth 138 (but
cf. gooth 426: wrooth 427 =masc.); sygnyfyeth 2010: applyeth 2012;
chaungeth 2094: estraungeth 2096.

    Doubtful cases are:—colowres 321: shoures 322 (but cf. embas-
satours 1016: shoures 1018): oonys 499: boonys 501: noonys 502;
goddys 491: pesecoddys 493; dremes 1854: stremes 1855 (but cf.
astronomers 1696: speres 1698: yeres 1699: laborers 911: freres
913); *the final e's are perhaps pronounced in these words:* — releuë
(inf.) 13: sleuë (obl. sng.) 14; kepë (inf.) 107: depë (adj. pl.) 109:
crepë (inf.) 110; morë 149: storë (obl. sng.) 151: sorë (adv.) 152;
Saturnë 279: mornë (inf.) 280: hedë (obl. sng.) 286: leedë (obl. sng.)
287: cornë (obl. sng.) 293: hornë (obl. sng.) 294: leuë (obl. sng.)
520: foryeuë (inf.) 522: myscheuë (inf.) 523; carrë (obl. sng.) 554:
marrë (inf.) 556; wydë (obl. sng.) 664: abydë (inf.) 665; hertë (obl.
sng.) 1451: aduertë (inf.) 1453: stertë (inf.) 1454; foolë (obl. sng.)
1658: scoolë (obl. sng.) 1659: pylgremagë (obl. sng.) 1779: passagë
(obl. sng.) 1781; holdë 1821: oldë 1823; sonnë (obl. sng.) 1896:
tonnë (obl. sng.) 1897.

    (d) Medial *gh* (O. E. *h*), already weak in Chaucer, has ceased to
be pronounced in the cases following, and probably therefore in all
cases:—abont 261: fought 263: mought 264 (cf. aboute 386: route 388:
mowte 760: dowte 761; abowte 1124: showte 1122: withowte 1125):
ryght 489: saf condyght 490: ipocrytes 701: ryghtes 703: sodomytes
708: syghtes 710: cyrcute 757: myght 759: trypartyte 1031: lyght
1033: wyght 1034; syght 1037: wyght 1039: fyght 1112: meryt 1113:
bryght 1367: whyte 1369: myght 1370 (cf. infynyte 1605: myte 1607:
whyte 1608; myte 1814: appetyte 1816): myght 1801: dyspyte 1803:
lyte 1804.

RIME INDEX.

A

–ade 69, 70; 1560, 1561.
–adde 1415, 1417; 1875, 1876; 1982, 1984.
–aff 2071, 2072.
–aft 1133, 1134.
–age 1779, 1781; 1889, 1890; 1899, 1901, 1902; 1906, 1908, 1909.
–ages 1731, 1733, 1734.
–ak 366, 368, 369.
–ake 2, 4, 5; 233, 235, 236; 608, 609; 722, 724; 1014, 1015; 1052, 1054, 1055;
   1220, 1222, 1223; 1388, 1390, 1391; 1409, 1411, 1412; 1420, 1421; 1457,
   1459; 1812, 1813; 1905, 1907; 1947, 1949; 2043, 2044.
–ale 358, 360.
–ales 685, 686.
–all 114, 116, 117; 153, 154; 230, 231; 246, 248; 435, 437; 555, 557, 558; 776,
   777; 1007, 1008; 1072, 1074; 1226, 1228; 1443, 1445; 1504, 1505; 1588, 1589;
   1597, 1599; 1612, 1614, 1615; 1707, 1708; 1819, 1820; 1898, 1900.
–am 86, –an 88, 89. See –an.
–ame 132, 133; 589, 591; 713, 714; 785, –an 787; 862, –an 864; 1238, 1239; 1702,
   –an 1704.
–an 925, 927; 1395, 1397, 1398; 1518, 1519. See –am, –ame
–ane 2011, 2013, 2014.
–and 262, –ong 260 ; 370, 371; 1177, 1179. See –ang.
–ande 128, 130, 131; 1084, 1085; 1161, 1162; 1562, 1564; 1574, 1575; 1651, 1652;
   1912, 1914; 1959, 1960.
–ape 524, 525; 1315, 1316.
–ard 601, 602.
–are 125, 126; 723, 725, 726; 807, 809, 810.
–arge 85, 87; 545, 546; 603, 605; 1632, 1634.
–arke 937, 938.
–arpe 400, 402.
–arre 554, 556.
–art 876, 878; 1940, 1942.
–ary 1446, 1447, –ory 1444.
–aryd 736, 738.
–as 274, 276; 611, 613, 614; 1065, 1067; 1339, –ase 1341, 1342; 1878, –ace 1880,
   1881. See –ase, –ace.
–ase 314, 315; 461, 462; 513, 515, 516; 632, 634, 635. See –as.
–ases 58, 60, 61.
–ast 72, 74, 75; 127, 129.
–aste 1045, 1047, 1048.
–ate 27, 28; 422, 424, 425; 1483, 1484; 1546, 1547; 1639, 1641.
–ates 706, 707.
–aught 1231, 1232.
–aunce 244, 245; 335, 336; 398, 399; 407, 409; 442, 444; 659, 661; 797, 798; 835,
   837, 838; 954, 956, 957; 989, 991, 992; 1094, 1096, 1097; 1147, 1148; 1374,
   1376, 1377; 1430, 1432, 1433; 1450, 1452; 1507, 1509, 1510; 1598, 1600,
   1601; 1660, 1662; 1714, 1715; 1835, 1837; 2003, 2005; 2060, 2062, 2063.
–aunge 1402, 1404, 1405.
–aungeth 2094, 2096.

-aunse   15, 17; 996, 998, 999.

-aunt   883, 885; 1254, 1256; 1294, 1295.

-auntyd   118, 119; 874, 875.

-ause   134, 136.

-aute   587, 588.

-ay   29, 31; 282, 284, 285; 296, 298, 299; 548, 550, 551; 666, 668; 715, 717; 727,
       728; 729, 731; 743, 745; 813, 815; 958, 959; 965, 966; 979, 980; 1028, 1029;
       1086, 1088; 1245, 1246; 1276, 1278, 1279; 1324, 1326; 1464, 1466; 1590,
       1592; 1661, 1663, 1664; 1828, 1830; 1968, 1970.

-ayd   36, 38.

-ayde 164, -eyde 162; 207, -eyde 205.

-ayed 1998, -eyde 1996.

-ayes 692, 693.

-ayll 615, 616; 751, 753, 754; 1219, 1221; 1969, 1971, 1972.

-ayn   1567, 1568.

-ayne 1668, 1670, -eyne 1671. See -eyne.

-awe   559, 560; 1227, 1229, 1230.

E

⎰ -e (gen. = -y) 121, 123, 124; 198, 200, 201; 253, 255; 271, -y 270; 457, 459,
│   460; 492, 494, 495; 519, 521; 552, 553; 617, 619; 650, 651; 772, 774, 775;
│   804, 805; 811, -ee 812; 828, 830, 831; 842, 844, 845; 919, 921, 922; 933,
│   935, 936; 1002, 1004; 1010, 1012, 1013; 1080, 1082, 1083; 1105, -ee 1106;
⎨   1261, 1263; 1280, 1281; 1329, 1330; 1416, 1418, 1419; 1423,
│   1425, 1426; 1700, 1701; 1800, 1802; 1868, 1869; 1926, 1928; 1945, 1946;
│   1980, 1981; 1994, 1995; 2017, 2019; ? 2038, 2040; 2057, 2058; 2067, 2069,
│   2070.
⎱ -ee 365, 367; 505, 507; 995, 997; 1136, 1138, -e 1139; 1961, -e 1963.

-eare 421, -ere 423.

-ecte 895, 896; 1847, 1848.

⎰ -ede 286, -eede 287; 569, 571, 572; 755, 756; 832, 833; 1000, 1001; 1035, 1036;
│   1129, 1131, 1132; 1360, 1362, 1363; 1378, 1379.
⎱ -eede 1023, 1025; 1583, 1585; 1815, 1817, 1818.

-eet   1064, · et 1063.

-eft   562, 564, 565.

⎰ -elde 667, 669, 670; 932, 934; 1044, 1046; 1095, 1093 -eelde.
⎱ -eelde 1093, -elde 1095.

⎰ -ele 55, 56; 1026, 1027, -eele 1024; 2068, -eele 2066.
⎱ -eele 1024, -ele 1026, 1027; 1637, 1638; 2066, -ele 2068.

-ell   30, 32, 33; 433, 434; 590, 592, 593; 1331, 1333; 1532, 1533.

-eme   1609, 1610.

-emes 1854, 1855.

-ence 44, 46, 47; 76, 77; 79, 81, 82; 97, 98; 174, 175; 228, 229, -ense 226; 456
       458; 639, 641, 642; 645, 647; 814, 816, 817; 1135, 1137; 1163, 1165; 1436,
       1438; 1490, 1491; 1611, 1613; 1863, 1865; 2001, 2002; 2025, -ens 2027,
       2028; 2106, 2107. See -ens, -ense.

-ende 737, 739, 740; 1623, 1624; 1665, 1666; 1777, -ynde 1778; 1798, 1799; 1920,
       1922, -ynde, 1923; 1931, 1932. See -ynde.

—ykes 678, 679.

—yll 120, 122; 575, 577; 916, 917; 1058, 1060; 1079, 1081; 1990, 1992, 1993.

—yme 953, 955.

—yn 1049, 1050; 1857, 1859, 1860.

—ynde 64, 66; 393, 395; 512, 514; 631, 633; 1343, 1344; 1387, 1389; 1542, 1544, 1545; 1647, 1649, 1650; 1756, 1757; 1778, —ende 1777; 1784, 1785; 1923, —ende 1922. See —ende.

—yne 265, 266; 372, 374; 1225, —ygne 1224; 2018, 2020, 2021.

—yng 267, 269; 1366, 1368; 1528, 1530, 1531; 1535, 1537, 1538; 1618, 1620.

—ynges 687, 689.

—ynke 2052, 2054.

—ynne 947, 949, 950; 1997, 1999, 2000.

—yre 1617, —eere 1616; 1870, 1872. See —eere.

—yreth 135, 137, 138.

—ys 106, 108; 877, 879, 880; 1310, 1312.

—yse 16, 18, 19; 225, 227; 447, 448; 568, 570; 826, —yce 825; 865, —yce 863; 1115, 1117, 1118; 1352, 1354; 1780, 1782, 1783; 1962, 1964, 1965. See —yce.

—yst 1297, 1299, 1300.

—yste 1057, —este 1056.

—ysyd 482, 483.

—yt 191, —et 193, —yte 194; 1113, —yght 1112. See —et, —yte, —yght.

—yte 211, 213; 1031, —yght 1033, 1034; 1369, —yght 1370; 1605, 1607, 1608; 1803, —yght 1801; 1814, 1816. See —yght.

—ytes 701, 703; 708, —yghtes 710.

—yue 517, 518; 939, 941; 1849, 1851.

—yues 20, 21.

O

—o 22, 24; 41, 42; 51, 53, 54; 142, 144, 145; 169, 171; 195, 196; 218, 220; 295, 297; 471, 473, 474; 496, 497; 1210, 1211; 1248, 1250, 1251; 1322, 1323; 1353, 1355, 1356; 1527, 1529; 1539, 1540; 1563, —oo 1565, 1566.

—oo 41, —o 42; 92, 94; 1565, —o 1563.

—ood 307, 308; 1126, 1127; 1311, 1313, 1314; 1422, 1424; 1569, 1571.

—oode 540, 542; 799, 801; 1038, 1040, 1041.

—oddys 491, 493.

—oft 99, 101.

—ook 1142, 1144; 1455, 1456; 1724, 1726, 1727.

{ —oke 181, 182.
{ —ooke 1303, 1305; 1885, 1887, 1888.

—olde 387, 389, 390; 428, 430; 1766, 1768, 1769; 1821, 1823; 1934, 1936, 1937; 1983, 1985, 1986; 2059, 2061; 2073, 2075.

—oole 1394, 1396; 1658, 1659; 1952, 1953.

—ome 190, 192; 1336, —one 1337; 1406, 1407. See —one.

{ —on 43, 45; 90, 91; 636, 637; 643, 644; 834, 836; 849, 851, 852; 974, 976; 988, 990; 1103, —owne 1101; 1108, 1110, 1111; 1143, 1145, 1146; 1178, 1180, —own 1181; 1205, 1207; 1301, 1302; 1413, 1414; 1429, 1431; 1619, 1621, 1622; 1646, 1648; 1681, 1683; 1721, 1722; 1737, 1739; 1744, 1746; 1751, 1753; 1772, 1774; 1833, 1834; 1842, 1844; 1864, 1866, 1867; 1910, 1911; 1913,

–ow	762, 763; 1149, 1151; 1164, 1166, 1167; 1191, 1193; 1241, –owe 1243, 1244; 1317, 1319; 1371, 1372; 1401, 1403; 1954, 1956; 2024, 2026.
–owe	484, 486; 1243, –ow 1241. See –ow.
–own	1181, –on 1180.
–ownd	508, –ound 506. See –ound.
–ownde	1688, –ounde 1689. See –ounde.
–owne	379, 381; 1101, –on 1103, 1104. See –on.
–owre	1077, –our 1078. See –our.
–owres	321, –oures 322. See –oures.
–owte	760, –oute 758; 1087, 1089, 1090; 1122, 1124, 1125; 1318, 1320, 1321; 1439, –out 1437; 1861, 1862; 1924, 1925; 1948, 1950, 1951; 1976, 1978, 1979.

U

–u	1121, –ew 1123. See –ew.
–ude	890, 892; 1703, 1705, 1706.
–ure	57, 59; 83, 84; 100, 102, 103; 363, 364; 414, 416; 454, 455; 477, 479; 860, 861; 931, –ewre 930; 1268, 1270; 1325, 1327, 1328; 1448, 1449; 1514, 1516, 1517; 1520, 1522; 1693, 1694; 1723, 1725; 1770, 1771; 1773, 1775, 1776; 1877, 1879; 1884, 1886; 2088, 2090, 2091. See –ewre.
–urre	328, 329.
–urne	279, –orne 280.
–us	177, 179, 180; 1168, 1169; 1469, 1470; 1938, 1939.
–use	1917, 1918; 1955, 1957, 1958.
–ust	1098, 1099; 1275, 1277.
–usyd	1390, 1400.
–ute	757 –yght 759. See –yght.
–uy	1720, –y 1719.
–uydyd 948, –ydyd 946.	

2. Alliteration is a marked feature of the verse. As is well known, the usage of combining alliteration and end-rime, which became conspicuous in western and northern England about the middle of the fourteenth century, grew in favor through the fourteenth and fifteenth centuries, reaching its highest popularity in Scotland during the second half of the fifteenth century (v. *Scottish Allit. Poems*, ed. by Amours in Scot. Text Soc.). The alliterative phrases record, clearly enough, the influence of the Old-English method of verse. In this poem alliteration occurs chiefly in formal phrases, as an ornament of the verse, rarely having any constructive significance. Lydgate followed no fixed method, though of course accent most often determines the phrase. For Chaucer's usage consult Ten Brink, *Ch. Sp.* p. 196, *et. seq.*, and *The Alliteration of Chaucer*, a thesis by Dr. C. F. McClumpha (Univ. of Minn.). I cite a few of the most notable instances:

4: *s*yttyng all *s*olytary a*l*one be*s*yde a *l*ake.　5: *m*usyng on a *m*aner how that I *m*yght *m*ake.　13: so *l*eyde I me *d*owne my *d*yssese to re*l*eue.　35: ys in a lytyll corner *c*allyd Fantasy.　66: *r*oote and *r*ynde.　127: *b*oystous *b*last.　261: *f*lame of *f*yre.　270: full sad and wyse he semyd sykerly.　303: *w*orldly *w*ysdom.　320: hyr gowne was of gawdy *g*rene chamelet.　345: in *c*uras *c*lad.　354: *c*lad in *c*lustres.　372: *c*olour *c*rystallyne.　379: *c*opyr *c*rowne.　382: *b*eames *b*ryght.　425: *d*euyll's *d*ate.　487: *d*oole nor *d*estyny.　501: *b*oody, *b*lood and *b*oonys.　557: *w*alewyng *w*ith hys *w*awes.　556: *m*ake and *m*arre.　631: *s*lowthe so *s*lepy.　673: *b*osters, *b*raggars and *b*rybores.　675: *sh*amefull *sh*akerles, *s*oleyn *sh*aueldores.　684: *m*alycious *m*urmurers.　688: *r*obbers, *r*euers, *r*auenouse *r*yfelers.　690: *m*arrers of *m*aters and money *m*akers.　806: *r*oody as a *r*oose.　848: *r*efuse of *r*ychesse.　890: *p*erpetuell *p*restes.　902: *f*ysshers of *f*owles.　907: on *p*eynfull *p*oore *p*yteous com*p*assioners.　912: *h*ooly *h*eremytes.　913: *m*onasteriall *m*onkes.　996: *ch*aunger of the *ch*aunse.　1166: *p*eyne *p*erpetuell.　1362: *w*ylde *w*antones *w*ede.　1603: *c*oloryd *c*rystall *c*lere.　1743: *f*eynyd *f*ables.　1886: *d*aryng as a *d*astard.　2071-2: Try out the *c*orne *c*lene from the chaff And then may ye say ye have a sure staff.

CHAPTER V.

The Rime and the Final e.

See Paul's *Grund.* II. p. 1034, sec. 24.—The language and metre of the poem seem to be in such confusion that evidence either for or against the pronunciation of the final *e* is rarely conclusive.　So far as I am able to judge from a study of the metre and of the riming words the final *e* is quite generally mute.　Double forms were evidently permissible, especially in words of Old-English origin.　Still the riming words show a very considerable loss of the final *e*, and a consequent change in poetic phraseology, as compared with the *Chorl and Bird* and the *Temple of Glas*, which conform much more closely to the phraseology of Chaucer.　On this latter evidence I should argue for the later date of the *Assembly of Gods*.　For while a skillful copyist, by the addition of monosyllabic words, might make the measure run without the *e*'s, he would not change the riming words themselves.

1. A study of the common riming words from Chaucer to Spenser will illustrate the changes in operation during the fifteenth century which affected the final *e* sound.　It will be observed that the adverbial suffix -ly (O. E. *lic*), which in Chaucer[1] and contemporary works rimed only with itself, -y or the pronoun I, rimes in Lyd-

---

[1] The *Romaunt* has cases of -y and -ye rime; but the date of the MS. is late, c. 1450 (Skeat).

gate's *Assembly of Gods*, King James' *Quair* and in other poems suc-
ceeding these, with endings of Romance nouns such as company
(O. F. companie, M. L. compania), melody (O. F. melodie, L. L.
melodia, Gk. μελῳδία), etc., and of infinitives as testify, multiply, spy,
etc. The usage of riming the ending -y and -ye became customary
before the middle of the fifteenth century. Chaucer rimes regu-
larly -yē with -yë. Thus companye rimes with maystrie, ielousye,
hye, espye, envye, hostelrie, dayesye, etc.; ielousye with maystrie,
folye, espye, maladye, etc. So -ly rimes regularly with itself, -y
or I. Thus I rimes with properly, utterly, verraily, trewely, wik-
kedly, boldely, certeynly, by; utterly rimes with trewely, esely,
sikerly; why rimes with casually. Chaucer has no exception to these
rules.

Gower in his *Confessio Amantis* (1386–1393), Hoccleve in his
Minor Poems (c. 1425) have Chaucer's usage very strictly. I find
no instance in Lydgate's *Temple of Glas* (c. 1403) of the -y -ye rime.
In the *Assembly of Gods*, however, the rule is no longer maintained.
Thus company rimes with pleasauntly 380, feruently 382, melody 401,
ly 404, chyualry 463, by 663, Apostasy 977, vyctory 1190, Sodechy
1549, Sophony 1551. Ey rimes with enuy 622, Pawmestry 870,
deny 872, fly 1185, sodenly 1187, foly 1631, generally 1729. Hy
rimes with testyfy 104, thereby 1461, certeynly 1495, I 1496, glory-
osly 1572, by 1570, naturally 1691, glory 1841. magnyfy 2102,
Mary 2105. Multyply rimes with indyfferency 846, deyfy 1719.
Comonly rimes with Fantasy 35. Curtesy rimes with innocency 841.
Memory rimes with glory 848, story 1513. Victory rimes with
party 1009, glory 1789, occupy 1787. Spy rimes with pryuyly 1021,
cry with sodeynly 1075 and myghtyly 1073; stody with espy 1989;
occupy with testyfy 452 and deny 453.

In Lydgate and Burgh's *Secrees* (c. 1446) the latter usage obtains.
The final *e* is there rarely sounded (Steele, *Intro. to Sec.* p. xx. § xvii.).
Applye rimes with partye 1516, fantasye 303. Victorye rimes with
pryncipally 2181, prudently 2182, hastely 2445, remedy 2448.
Remedy rimes with hevyly 1735, specially 2008. Hastily rimes with
denye 1846. Partye rimes with streyghtlye 2131. Mallady rimes
with specially 1700; foly with discretly 2281, angry 2652; leccherye
with fynally 2503 and velony 2504.

The change had already been accomplished in the *Quair* (1423)
of King James I., who rimed armory with contynually, ielousye with
melancholye and quhy (N. E. why), philosophye with properly, partye

with I, quhy with companye, ielousye, folye, onely, I with humility,
gye, supplye, etc.

In the *Pastime of Pleasure* (c. 1506), the work of Stephen Hawes,
the pupil of Lydgate, and in Spenser's poems and in other sixteenth
century works, the new usage is completely established. The period
of transition would seem to be from about 1415 to 1450. Lydgate's
own works exhibit the change, and very likely his poems can be
approximately dated by reference to his treatment of this -y rime.

2. *The infinitives among the riming words* present the phenomena
given in the following word list. The inflectional ending has dis-
appeared in most cases. It is maintained somewhat in verbs of English
origin but is almost completely lost in verbs of Romance origin. I
use ĕ to indicate the conjectural pronunciation of the infinitive end-
ing. In the table the first word in each series is the infinitive,
which is followed by the words with which it rimes:

(a) *Of Teutonic Origin.*

abydë: wyde 664: tyde 718: ryde (inf.) 719: pryde (obl. sng.) 928: syde (obl. sng.)
929: gyde (inf.) 703: hyde (inf.) 894.

arysë: iustyse (obl. sng.) 18: sylogyse (inf.) 19.

astert: hert (obl. sng.) 468.

awakë: take (inf.) 1015: shake (inf.) 2044.

be: perplexyte (obl. sng.) 200: se (inf.) 201: me 255: pyte (obl. sng.) 921: vnyte
(obl. sng.) 910.

beware: care (obl. sng.) 126.

blyn: syn (inf.) 1857: wyn (inf.) 1859.

borow: sorow 1166: folow (inf.) 1164.

bow: how 2026.

call: fall 1008: wall 1898.

crepë: depe (obl. pl.) 109: kepe (inf.) 107.

decëë: wele (obl. sng.) 2068.

do: so 144: to 145.

dwell: tell (inf.) 585: rebell 583.

fall: shall 231: all 246.

farë: care (obl. sng.) 809: bare 807.

feelë: yele 1026: dele (obl. sng.) 1027.

fet: banket (obl. sng.) 167: met 1154: get 1678.

fly: sodenly 1187: ey (obl. sng.) 1188.

folow: sorow 1166: borow (inf.) 1167.

forsakë: take (inf.) 1052: make (inf.) 1055.

foryetë: entrete (inf.) 241.

foryenë: lene (obl. sng.) 520: myscheue (inf.) 523.

fulfyll: wyll (obl. sng.) 575.

fyght: myght 993.

fyndë: rynde (obl. sng.) 66: behynde 514.

gete: conterfete (inf.) 212: entrete (inf.) 214: whete 1334.

go: fro 24.

herë: fere (obl. sng.) 52 (nere 396: Omere 397): daungere (obl. sng.) 96: prysonere 93: apere 157: plesere 197: offycere (obl. sng.) 446.

hy: redely 767: ny 768.

hydë: syde (obl. sng.) 891: abyde (inf.) 893.

kepë: depe (obl. pl.) 109: crepe (inf.) 110: wepe (inf.) 1257: slepe (inf.) 1258.

lerë: geere (obl. sng.) 886: were 884.

lowte: rowte (obl. sng.) 1087: dowte 1090: abowte 1924.

ly: company 403: melody (obl. sng.) 401: Pyromancy 869.

makë: lake (obl. sng.) 4: take (inf.) 2.

markë: parke (obl. sng.) 938.

metë: shete (obl. sng.) 420.

mornë: Saturne 270.

mys: wys 879: thys 877.

nedë: spede (inf.) 571: dede (obl. sng.) 572.

ouerse: meyne (obl. sng.) 774: see (inf.) 775.

rydë: wyde 626: tyde 718: abyde (inf.) 716.

say: day 1830: deley (obl. sng.) 1858.

se: perplexyte (obl. sng.) 200: be (inf.) 198: meyne 774: ambyguyte 1012: lyberte 1013: benygnyte 1426.

shakë: awake (inf.) 2043.

slepë: wepe (inf.) 1257: kepe (inf.) 1255.

spedë: nede (inf.) 569: dede (obl. sng.) 572.

steuyn: heuyn (obl. sng.) 823: seuyn 821.

syn: wyn (inf.) 1859: blyn (inf.) 1860.

syt: yet 193: abyte 194.

takë: lake (obl. sng.) 4: make (inf.) 5: awake (inf.) 1014: forsake (inf.) 1054.

tell: dwell 32: hell (obl. sng.) 33: fell (obl. pl.) 434: rebell 583.

wepë: kepe (inf.) 1255: slepe (inf.) 1258.

wynne: ynne 949: synne 950: syn (inf.) 1857: blyn (inf.) 1860: thynne 1997: theryn 1050.

wythstandë: hande (obl. sng.) 1084.

(b) *Of Romance Origin.*

acorde: monacorde (obl. sng.) 7.

apelë: wele (obl. sng.) 56.

apperë: herbere (obl. sng.) 1935: fere (obl. sng.) 2006: here (inf.) 2004.

asaute: defaute (obl. sng.) 587.

asay: day 979: may 1278: nay 1276.

assent: content 172: iugement (obl. sng.) 170.

aualë: pale (obl. sng.) 358.

auaunce: puruyaunce 956: daunce (obl. sng.) 957.

auowë: bowe (inf.) 486.

carpe: harpe (obl. sng.) 400.

cese: dyscrese (inf.) 232: doutlese 1754: prese (obl. sng.) 1755.

chastyse: dispyse (inf.) 448.

compleyn: tweyn (obl. pl.) 146.

conclude: multitude 890.

confound: drownd 508: fownd 509.

counterfete: entrete (inf.) 214: gete (inf.) 215.

cry: sodeynly 1075: myghtyly 1073.

daunce: penaunce (obl. sng.) 1148.

deny: testify (inf.) 452: occupy (inf.) 450: Pawmestry 870: ey (obl. sng.) 873.

depart: cart (obl. sng.) 878.

depryue: lyue 518.

dereygne: cheyne (obl. sng.) 610.

deyfy: multyply 1717: guy (inf.) 1720.

dyscrese: cese (inf.) 234.

dyspyse: chastyse (inf.) 447.

dysusë: muse (inf.) 1917.

endure: mesure (obl. sng.) 102: nature (obl. sng.) 100: creature (obl. sng.) 2088: sure 2091.

enhaunse: remembraunse 998: chaunse (obl. sng.) 996.

enlumyne: discyplyne (obl. sng.) 2018: Doctryne 2021.

entrete: counterfete (inf.) 212: gete (inf.) 215: foryete 239: banket 1654: gete (obl. sng.) 1657.

escape: iape (obl. sng.) 525.

eschew: Vertew (obl. sng.) 963: sew (inf.) 964.

espy: stody (obl. sng.) 1991.

exorte: reporte 1486: sorte 1489.

fade: shade (obl. sng.) 69.

greuë: leue (obl. sng.) 429: meue (inf.) 431.

gydë: tyde 795: abyde (inf.) 796.

magnyfy: hy 2104: Mary 2105.

menteyn: peyn 746: ageyn 744.

meuë: leue (obl. sng.) 429: greue (inf.) 432: sleue (obl. sng.) 2033.

multyply: guy (inf.) 1720: deyfy (inf.) 1719.

musë: disvse (inf.) 1918.

myscheue: leue (obl. sng.) 520: foryeue (inf.) 522.

occupy: testyfy (inf.) 452: deny (inf.) 453: hy (obl. sng.) 1173: vyctory (obl. sng.) 1174.

oppresse: heuynesse 10: neuerthelesse 1059: duresse (obl. sng.) 1062.

peruert: hert 1786: desert (obl. sng.) 1843: smert 1845.

promyse: wyse (obl. sng.) 225.

rebell: tell 502: well 503.

recompense: audyence (obl. sng.) 1249.

refusë: diffuse 1955: vse (inf.) 1958.

reherse: werse 405.

releuë: sleue (obl. sng.) 14.

repent: went 417: inconuenyent (obl. sng.) 415.

resorte: comforte (obl. sng.) 1152: porte (obl. sng.) 1153.

sew: Vertew (obl. sng.) 963: eschew (inf.) 961.

sylogyse: iustyse (obl. sng.) 18: aryse (inf.) 16.

tary: sanctuary 1446: crysmatory 1444.

testyfy: hy 105: occupy (inf.) 450: deny (inf.) 453.

vsë: diffuse 1955: refuse (inf.) 1957.

CHAPTER VI.

The Language.

A. Vocabulary.

The modern character of Lydgate's language has often been remarked. Warton long ago gave his judgment to the effect "that Lydgate made considerable additions to those amplifications of our language in which Chaucer, Gower and Occleve led the way : and that he is the first of our writers whose style is clothed with that perspicuity in which the English phraseology appears at this day to an English reader" (*Hist. of Eng. Poet.*, II., 270). The influence of French and Latin is more apparent in his vocabulary than in that of any other East Midland writer (v. *Dict. Natl. Biog.*, XXXIV., p. 310 ; Skeat *Prin. Engl. Ety.*, II., ch. viii). The *Assembly of Gods* is especially rich in words of Romance origin, and, as compared with contemporary writings, in words of recent adoption from the French. The poem is therefore especially helpful in tracing the gradual assimilation of foreign words into the language. In the Prolog to the *Canterbury Tales* in 303 words in the first 42 lines, Chaucer used 263 native English words, leaving 13 *per cent.* of foreign words. In 84 lines of the *Assembly of Gods*, of 669 words, the total number employed, 153, or nearly 23 *per cent.*, are foreign : of the 305 different words used in the same lines, 107 are of foreign origin. As Lydgate was popular long in the reign of Elizabeth, his service in naturalizing the foreign vocabulary was considerable. It will be seen that the number of obsolete words is comparatively small, the proportion of such words being less than in Chaucer or Wyclif or Pecock (Lee, *Dict. Natl. Biog.*).

B. Grammar.

Lydgate's grammar has been well treated by Dr. Schick in his Introduction to the *Temple of Glas* (chap. vi. p. lxiii). This MS., being of a late date, can aid but little in the construction of Lydgate's own speech. In the main, it is probable that Lydgate's phonological and inflexional system did not differ much from that of Chaucer. There was, however, in the case of Lydgate a much less certain use of inflexional endings. In the present MS. the pronunciation of many endings is purely conjectural, the metre, owing to its irregularity, being seldom conclusive. The language

is seen to be in a state of greatest confusion about the year 1450.
I note below a few of the grammatical forms of this text.

I. Declension. Nouns. *In Substantives of English origin, the
final e of the sng. nom. is maintained in some cases :* tymë 137, 1751;
namë 132; erthë 535. *Inorganic e occurs* in frendë 1798, 1807;
wyttë 1887. *Genitives have regularly the endings (e)s, ës, ys:* whalës
1535; foës 1126; feldys 1451: the genitive form ladyes is found
in 1178.

The dative and accusative maintain the ë in crabbë 1 : ërthe 67,
1627; tymë 69; hedë 271 (: sykerly) 286, 356, 384 (perhaps hede
379): tydë 334; feldë 959: endë 1799; sonnë 1896; tonnë 1897;
tylthë 1710; and others. *Plurals commonly end in (e)s, ës, ÿs; other
plurals are found, as* deere 65, 68; thyng 1064; eyen 220; men 759;
foon 1762; chyldren 1659.

*In Substantives of Romance origin the final ë in the sng. nom. is
found in only a few cases:* hoostë 1124; bandë 1162; cherë 375;
gownë 320. *The genitives end regularly in (e)s, ës. With proper names
hys is sometimes used to indicate the genitive,* as Vertew hys men 1072;
Vyce hys quarrell 1055. *The dative and accusative are most often
without endings, though a final ë occurs in* pesë 238; charë 792;
scorgë 1170; scoolë 1396, 1659. *Plurals are regularly found in (e)s,
ës, ÿs.*

II. *The Adjectives are generally without case endings. The final
ë appears, however, in all cases, sng. and pl.: as nom. sng.* foulë,
dymmë, 313; oldë 390, 1749; *pl.* oldë 294; *in oblique cases sng.*,
derkë 310; crystallynë 372; rewdë 438; foulë 648; hoolë 1172; *pl.*,
sagë 389; blakë 1412.

III. *The Pronouns have the common M. E. forms;* ye *is used as
singular in* 32, 95, *as plural in* 150; she *is found in* 378, se *in* 376;
hit *occurs regularly;* theym *is used in* 48, 415, hem *in* 66, 126; her
(their) *is used in* 47, 65, 123, 867, *and regularly. The indefinite*
som, *without ending, occurs in* 865, 1196, 1198, 1199. *For relatives,*
which that *and* who (rare), *are used;* by hem that lyues 20; he
that 21; poetes whyche 1743: [he] who 769.

IV. *Adverbs are found with endings ë, ës or ys, ly and without
endings:* sonë 36, 461, 721, 1345; while 181, 72; ferrë 1627; newë
562: nedys 21, 1372; nedës 1245; ellës 33, 1033; ellÿs 1614, 1385;
eftsonës 1007.

V. *Conjugation of Verbs.* The formation of the tenses of the
verbs, strong and weak, is the same as in Chaucer. *Infinitives end*

in ë, though perhaps more often they are without endings, as fall 230, riming with shall; syt 191 riming with yet; fly 1185 riming with sodenly; bow 2024 riming with how; tell 30 riming with hell, etc. *The third person, indicative, present, has regularly the ending eth, ëth. The northern es is found in two places:* dryues 21, manaces 61 *(in pl.* lyues 20). *The past participle is without a prefix ge-, i- or y-: the strong verbs end commonly in en and ë, the weak in yd, ed, t:* knowën 1141; beholdyn 1866; takën 501; takë 59, 267, 547, 722, 725; tane 2013; brokë 182; spokë 181; ronnë 1; drevën 1080; cropyn 1953; ouerthrow 1149 rimes with know (inf.) and 1191 with low. The form beene occurs in 2047 riming with seene, also bene 420, 1343, ben 627, byn 1798, be 115, 298, 460; bee 1136. So occur the forms goon 757, go 1396; done 48, 563, doon 84, do 195, 1248 (riming with lo), 496,; scene 545, seyne 1671.

CHAPTER VII.

THE POEM.

A. LITERARY ANALYSIS.[1]

A. *Introduction (stanzas 1–5).* The time: when Phœbus had nearly finished his course in the Crab. The place: I was sitting alone beside a lake. The theme: musing how I might make Reason and Sensuality to accord. The framework of the action: a dream. The director of the dream: Morpheus.

B. *The Action of the Dream: the Theme illustrated (6–291). Act I. The case of Eolus (6–87). Scene I. At the Court of Minos in Hell* (6–26).—Characters at the Court: Pluto, Ruler of Hell; Minos, the Justice; Cerberus, the Constable; Diana and Neptune, plaintiffs; Eolus, the defendant; Morpheus and Lydgate, spectators. (*a*) Eolus led in by Cerberus (6). (*b*) Silence proclaimed by Pluto (7). (*c*) The complaint of Diana: Eolus had destroyed her forests with his blasts wherefore the deer were without shelter (8–11). (*d*) The complaint of Neptune: Eolus had disputed with him the jurisdiction of the sea and had caused him to turn against his natural course and to labor far out of measure, making him to ebb and flow out of his season. Moreover, Eolus had destroyed those to whom he had granted protection (12–20). (*e*) The case in judgment (21–23).

---

[1] I have analyzed the poem according to its dramatic divisions as if it were a Moral Play.

(*f*) The court dismissed, without action, at the invitation of Apollo to a banquet (24–27). *Scene II. At the palace of Apollo* (27–87). (*a*) Apollo sues for Diana's forgiveness of Eolus (27–34). (*b*) Neptune accepts Phebe as arbiter of his case (35). (*c*) The banquet (36–59): Apollo seats his guests at the table, Aurora and Apollo, Diana and Mars, Juno and Jupiter, Ceres and Saturn, Othea (Athena) and Cupid, Fortune and Pluto, Isis and Pan, Minerva and Neptune, Phœbus and Bacchus, Venus and Mercury. The waiters were philosophers and poets. Orpheus and Pan made music. Of dainties and meats there was a plenteous store. (*d*) Discord enters but is denied a place at the table (59–60). (*e*) Discord departs in wrath and meets with Atropos (60). (*f*) Atropos takes her part and enters the palace (61–62). (*g*) He rudely salutes the Gods (63); recites his services to them in destroying Hector, Alexander, Cæsar, etc. (64–69); charges them with assisting one whom he can not destroy (70); refuses to serve them longer (71). (*h*) The Gods in dismay swear to help Atropos and to confound this rebel. But Eolus will not help them (72–75). (*i*) Excursus: how Eolus came into the power of Pluto (76–80). (*j*) Eolus, forgiven by Neptune at the request of Phebe, promises to afflict the rebel if he be in the air (81–84). (*k*) The name of this rebel is Virtue (85–86). Pluto sends for his son Vice (87).

Act II. The Battle between the Vices and Virtues in the field of Microcosm (88–210). Scene I. The gathering of the hosts (88–133). (*a*) Vice and his head-captains, Pride, Envy, Wrath, Covetousness, Gluttony, Lechery, Sloth (88–91): inferior captains, Sacrilege, Simony, etc., a great company (91–95); such a host of commons man never beheld they were led by Idleness (95–102). (*b*) Virtue and his head-captains, Humility, Charity, Patience, Liberality, Abstinence, Chastity, Good-Business (103–118): inferior captains and common soldiers numbering a tenth of Vice's host (119–133). *Scene II. The preparation for the combat (134–138).* The field is Microcosm. It is entered by five highways. Conscience is judge of the battle. Freewill is Lord of the Field. (*a*) Vice and Virtue dub fourteen knights each (140–142). (*b*) They send ambassadors to Freewill (143–146). (*c*) Sensuality sows the field with wicked seeds (146–147). *Scene III. The battle (148–162).* (*a*) Virtue tarries under the Sign of the Cross and wards off the shots by the Shield of the Holy Trinity (149–150). (*b*) Virtue, abandoned by Freewill, retreats (151–154). (*c*) Other captains hold the ground and Perseverance brings reinforcements (155–159). (*d*) Vice is overthrown (160–162). *Scene IV. The result.* (*a*) Freewill repents (163–164). (*b*) Vice is met by Despair (165). (*c*) Prescience drives Vice and his host through the gates of Hell (166–167). (*d*) Predestination gives Virtue the palm of Victory and to all a heavenly habitation (168–170). (*e*) Some of Vice's host repent (171–174). (*f*) Freewill recompenses Virtue. Freewill is made bailiff in Microcósm under Reason. Sensuality is guided by Sadness. To Morpheus are given the five keys of the highways (178–187). (*g*) Atropos, angry at the Gods, seeks another master. He is called Death and given possession of Microcosm (188–209). (*h*) Virtue is exalted above the firmament to receive the Crown of Glory (210).

Act III. The School and Lessons of Doctrine : The Doubt Solved (211–290). The place, a garden with four pictured walls ; the porter, Wit ; the teachers, Doctrine, Holy Text, Gloss and Moralization ; the scribe, Scripture. *Scene I.* (*a*). *The Interpretation by Doctrine of the dream and of the four " Times" pictured on the walls (211–275).* First, the imprisonment of Eolus signifies that wealth increases misrule. Every man is judged by Minos according to his wickedness. The complaint of Diana and Neptune signifies the folly of fools in seeking to bring the winds to correction. When they came to the banquet of Apollo like fools they gave up the matter to oblivion. The Gods resemble false idols. In the beginning the people slept in pagan law. The poets feigned many fables which were given places and names. Idolatry was the rule during the Time of Deviation from Adam to Moses. With Moses began the Time of Revocation which endured to the Incarnation of Christ. The New Testament opens the time of Reconciliation. The Time of Pilgrimage or War is signified by the battle between Vice and Virtue. As for Atropos his complaint signifies the constraint of friendship. Discord must needs be avenged by Death. The battle betokens the moral struggle in the soul. Microcosm is the world of man. Perseverance betokens the continuance of virtuous living. Prescience and Predestination are the rewarders of Vice and Virtue. The five keys are man's five wits. The return of man to sin is prevented by Reason and Sadness. *Scene II. The reconciliation of Reason and Sensuality: the theme completed (276–288). a.* Death, Reason and Sensuality enter. Of Death Lydgate is afraid. Reason argues that Death ought to be shunned. In this sentiment Sensuality accords. (*b*). Doctrine vanishes (289–290).

C. *The Conclusion (292–301).* (*a*). The dream broken (291–293). (*b*). Lest fault be found with me I record the vision (294–296). (*c*). The exhortation (297–301): Gentle Reader, walk alway in the path of Virtue. Fight daily against the World, the Flesh, and the Devil. Thine shall be the glory and the heavenly mansions. Let us pray that the Lord of Glory give us grace. Let us magnify his name. To you may Jesus grant eternal joy.

B. Literary Studies.

1. *The Religious Character of the Poem.*—The *Assembly of Gods* is one of Lydgate's numerous moral treatises so sounding in virtues that Bishop Alcock of Ely (b. 1430), in sermons addressed to the generation succeeding the poet, might praise it as leading to "the encrease of vertue and the oppression of vyce."[1] It is a sermon in verse, only the moral truth is "cloked," as Stephen Hawes phrases it, "with cloudy fygures." By this time Lydgate at Bury St. Edmunds must have become an excellent ecclesiastic. In the poem he freely employs the vocabulary of mediæval monasticism. The explanation by Doctrine, for instance, of the pagan deities, and indeed the whole discourse of Doctrine, is in the manner of the early theologians and schoolmen. Thus the writings of Fulgentius, the grammarian (c. 480–550), notably his *Mythologiarum (Mythologicon) Libri,* which explains the pagan names and legends, may be cited as the far source of that portion of the poem which interprets the deities, and the *Hamartigenia* and *Psychomachia* of Prudentius, the Christian hymn writer, a little earlier than Fulgentius, may be consulted for the origin of that part which contains the battle of the vices and virtues. Lydgate's immediate masters in opinion and sentiment were the compilers of the *Gesta Romanorum.*

The definite teachings of the treatise might indeed be gathered into a system.[2] The one God is thought of as a Supreme Judge, Alpha and Omega omnipotent, standing above the firmament and apportioning infinite rewards and punishments. Life is a pilgrimage, a war with the sins. Sin is the parent of all woe. Death

[1] *Sermo* on Luke viii., printed c. 1496. "Frendes I remembre dayes here before in my youthe that there was a vertuous monke of Bury called Lydgate, whiche wrote many noble histories and made many vertuous balettes to the encrease of vertue and oppression of vyce." Brydges' *Brit. Bibliog.,* iii, p. 533.

[2] That Lydgate knew his creed well is shown by *London Lackpenny,* Minor Poems, p. 106.

is the supreme object of dread. Salvation is sacramental and sacer-
dotal. Remedies against sin are found in the Seven Blessings of
the Gospel, the Seven Virtues of God, the Ten Commandments, the
Twelve Articles of the Faith, the Seven Sacraments, Veneration of
the Cross and the Saints, the Doctrine of Unity and the System of
Redemption in Christ. The necessity of penance is especially
enjoined. The chief sacraments are Baptism and the Eucharist, the
one being regarded as the sacrament of the new birth, the other as
the sacrament of sanctification which maintains the new life. Of
course the church is built on the stone of Peter who keeps the keys
of Heaven. In all the poem there is not the least suggestion of
the coming Reformation or of the work of Wyclif. A digression
is made at one point to notice the error of Origen (st. 227.) And
circumcision is held in derision (st. 173.). The work closes appro-
priately with a prayer to the Son of the Virgin Mary.

Of the artistic merits of such a treatise little can be said. The
poem is simply one of the many moral poems which were so popular
during the Middle Ages throughout Europe and which were calcu-
lated to gratify the almost universal taste for poetry of a serious and
didactic nature. We can now consider these works hardly other
than monuments of the bad taste that accompanies a low literary
culture. Such writings belong however to the history of literature
and without their consideration that history would be incomplete.

The *Assembly of Gods* is worthy of special attention for its complex
allegory, which is one of the best of its kind. I admit at the begin-
ning that it will furnish no pleasure to those who seek in literature
for originality and imaginative power. No one today would think of
echoing the praise of Lydgate's poet-friends, or of placing Lydgate's
name by the side of Chaucer, though he may be fair companion for
Gower and Hoccleve. That Burgh should think his master knew the
muses well (*Secrees*, st. 226), that Stephen Hawes should maintain that
Lydgate was the "most dulcet sprynge of famous rhethoryke"
(*Pastime of Pleasure*), that Dunbar should write that Lydgate had
with his "mellifluate" speech illumined the English language, and
that before his coming the English Isle was "bare and desolate of
rethorike or lusty fresch endyte" (*The Golden Targe*)—that this
chorus of eulogy should be at all received only illustrates the
imperfect literary sense of the late Middle Ages in England, that
period which Taine calls appropriately, for its almost utter lack alike
of the "grand style" and any high imagination, the Dark Age. Lau-

reate Skelton, alone among these early writers, has a bit of discerning criticism of Lydgate's work in his *Phyllyp Sparrowe* (ll. 804-12):

> "It is dyffuse to fynde (difficult to understand)
> The sentence of his mynde,
> Yet wryteth he in his kynd,
> No man that can amend
> Those maters that he hath pende;
> Yet some men fynde a faute,
> And say he wryteth to haute (loftily)."

But while we cannot greatly admire a poem of this moralizing kind, it must be remembered that the work is no worse than very much of the prose and poetry of the Middle-English period, nearly all of which is ethical if not distinctly religious in character, and which might be assigned with propriety to the alcoves of the theological library. Chaucer is almost the only writer apud the multitude of preachers and satirists who obeyed his artistic rather than his moral conscience. The moral and artistic blend happily, it is true, in Langland who, although a reformer, was gifted with such Dantean earnestness and strength as to elevate his noble *Piers the Plowman* into a true and poetic allegory of the soul. Beautiful too is the poem of the Pearl in its perfect union of religious earnestness and deep and delicate poetic feeling, the lyric gem of all this period. Still on the whole it must be said that while England was ready ripe for an artistic literature in the period of the Renaissance, during the Middle Ages the secret of art was wanting. For literature with the artistic stamp we must go to the continent, especially to Italy. To Provençal poetry England presents no counterpart save perhaps the people's ballads and songs of Robin Hood. Not until the advent of the "courtly makers" of the reign of Henry VIII. was there any sign of change to an artistic literature. Religion and not Art, in short, was the "Time-spirit" of the age. So prevalent is the moral motive, indeed, that it is not surprising to find even Chaucer professing himself in his last years to be more thankful that he had translated the Consolation of Boethius and repeated Saints' Lives and religious homilies than that he had written the great works of his artistic imagination, the worldly vanities of which filled his senile mind with concern. As Mr. Lowell observes in comparing Chaucer and Dante, the main question with the former was after all the conduct of life. The conduct of life this concern has been the characteristic English trait from Cædmon to Browning. That Lydgate's life tended to moral good if not to artistic purpose is evidenced by the prayer of Hawes in his Excusation of the *Pastime of Pleasure*, who prayed God to give him grace to compile books of "moral vertue"—

> " Of my maister Lidgate to folowe the trace,
> His noble fame for laude and renue,
> Whiche in his lyfe the slouthe did eschue ;
> Makyng great bokes to be in memory,
> On whose soule I pray God have mercy."

2. *The Fear of Death and the Scorn of the World.*—It is now quite generally acknowledged that the mediæval conception of life is very accurately signified by a line in Dante's *Purgatorio* (xxxiii, 54–5) : "To those who live the life that is a race to death." It is notable that the same sentiment is repeated in almost the same words, though in broad Scotch, by William Dunbar, whose death year was just two centuries after the passing of Dante, his daily sombre line running : " Quhat is this lyfe bot ane straucht way to deid ?"

These lines expressly point to what was the most characteristic feature of mediævalism, the almost universal dualism of thought. In art there was developed during the early Christian era a complete system of allegory and symbolism. A world of sense images on the one hand was set over against a universe of analogical and mystical meanings on the other, the former being strictly subordinated to the latter. This exaltation of the spiritual at the expense of the natural characterized the religious life of the whole people. As Mr. Kidd makes clear, the first fourteen centuries of our civilization were devoted to the growth and development of a stupendous system of otherworldliness. The supernatural became the object of the popular faith. And the conception of a future life simply overshadowed every consideration of the present. During the two centuries that I have noted, reckoning roughly from Dante to Dunbar, this faith in the other-world reached its culmination. Before Dante the boundaries of the dual realm had not been perfectly limned ; the construction of the circles of the supernatural was the work of the poet in whom thirteen centuries of Christianity actually came to expression. After Dunbar the spirit of the Renaissance is working, introducing into this divided universe the principle of unity. It is certain that in Shakespeare unity is well nigh established. The development of the English drama away from the supernaturalism of the Miracle Play and the abstraction of the Moralities and towards a more or less consistent realism indicates the breaking-up of dualistic thought. Shakespeare having seen that men and women arrive at judgment in the world could disregard the life to come. Taking then into our view the dramatic realm of Dante, the other-world, and of Shakespeare, the present world, we discover in the centuries intervening between the life-work of these two artists the incidents of a remarkable transition in thought, the break-up of a dualistic system. In the art of the 16th century, which was more immediately the product of the Renaissance, the new principle of unity is seen to be confirmed. Naturally the tradition of religion continued longer in force. Still the Reformation church destroyed one feature of supernaturalism, the belief in Purgatory, and though it was under the necessity of maintaining the theory of Paradise and Hell, it laid greater stress than before upon the actual life of men upon the earth. It was after all a problem of the earth that Milton tried to solve—the justification of the ways of God to men.

Following the rise of the system of otherworldliness there grew in the heart of man, century by century from the founding of the church, an ever present fear, a fear that for sinful men was only increased by the joy of the martyrs, the fear of Him who was called Death, the Foeman, the invincible Archer. During the 14th and 15th centuries this dread of death was at its uttermost. On the physical side the fear at this period was heightened by the helplessness of all Europe before the ravages of the Black Plague, at the approach of which householders could only cry, "The Lord have mercy upon us." Spiritually the Day of Doom with its attendant terrors was a fully realized conception, and no man was so sure of victory that he did not tremble on the verge of the grave.

By reference to the homiletic and didactic literature of the 14th and 15th centuries in England the fear of death is found to be part and parcel of the religious feeling of the time. In the *Pricke of Conscience*, which contains the religious meditations of that strange hermit and visionary, Richard Rolle of Hampole, most of whose life was contemporary with that of Dante and who bore about with him a certain Dantean mysticism, we learn of the Unstableness of the World, of Death and why it is to be dreaded, of Purgatory, Doomsday, and the Pains of Hell. Dan Michel's *Ayenbite of Inwyt*, contemporary with Hampole's work, and illustrative likewise of the teachings of the church, takes a similar view of the present and future life. Comparing these and other typical treatises with reference to the report which they make upon death, it is seen that they accord in assigning to Death, who is invariably heralded by Dread, the execution upon all creatures of the awful sentence of doom.

It was taught, to be sure, that to good men death may be the end of evils and the beginning of every blessing. Yet the righteous could not escape from the terrors that attend death — the death that might be eternal. On the day of Doom even angels and archangels shall tremble. In a parable it was written that at the door of the house of the Spirit, Dread, the messenger of Death, should knock and demand entrance. He comes from Hell, the torments of which surpass the picturing of the imagination : in a great deep below Hell yawns, bottomless and frightful. Out of the stench and dark- ness rise the songs of sorrow from loathsome fiends in chains. Rest- less are the souls encumbered there, that are tormented by hunger and thirst, that are driven by heat and cold and bathed in burning pitch, withal feeling the turnings of the worm of conscience. Satan is there with his rake, having horns upon his head and knees, yawn- ing with his mouth, venting fire from mouth and nostril and eyepits. This was the background of terror upon which were pictured the glories of heaven. By hopeful ones it was remembered that Christ had descended into Hell and broken the gates asunder. Gentle spirits taught that " Loue is more stranger *þanne* drede " (*Aly. of Inw.* p. 75) that "Love of God driveth out fear" (*Sawles Warde, O. E. Hom.* p. 259). Yet upon the foundation of fear the mediæval church was erected. The church then seemed to have been established for little else than to harass the human race.

The homiletic treatment of death and doom precedes the poetic by about a century. The characteristic utterance on these themes in English poetry is subsequent to 1400 and well along in the 16th century.[1] Yet Langland's great poem (about 1362–1393) has a con- tent typical of the century to which it belongs. Perhaps the most striking and vigorous passage in all his Vision of the World at work is the one descriptive of the procession of Death amid the " field full of folk " :

> " Elde *þe* hore he was in *þe* vauntwarde,
> And bare *þe* banere bifor deth by righte he it claymed.
> Kynde come after with many kene sores,
> As pokkes and pestilences and moche people shente ;

[1] See Sackville's picture in the Induction to the *Mirrour for Magistrates* and Southwell's *Image of Death*, and many others of like import even in the days of the Renaissance.

> So kynde þorw corupciouns kulled ful manye.
> Deth cam dryuende after and al to doust passhed
> Kynges & knyghtes, kayseres and popes ;
> Lered ne lewed he let no man stonde,
> That he hitte euene þat euere stired after.
> Many a louely lady and lemmanes of knyghtes
> Swouned and swelted for sorwe of dethes dyntes."
>
>   — *P. Pl.* Pas. xx.ll. 94–104.

So in the fear of death, Dunbar, a characteristic melancholy figure of the 15th century, wrote his startling and horrible *Dance of the Sevin Deidly Synnis.* For "This fals warld," he said, "is bot transitory." When Beauty won her victory over the poet—so ran his allegory—he was consigned to the custody of Grief. Youth and loveliness, bravery and wit, all come to an end :

> " Onto the ded gois all estatis,
> Princis, prelates, and potestatis,
> Baith riche and pur of all degre ;
>   Timor mortis conturbat me."—*Lament.*

The poets, "the makers" themselves, for all their sweet service cannot escape the end ; " I see the makers among the rest."

> " He hes done petuously devour
> The noble Chaucer, of makaris flour,
> The monk of Bery, and Gower, all thre;
>   Timor mortis conturbat me." [1]—*Lament.*

At length the man that feared not Death found a place in Barclay's *Ship of Fools* (85th), the author knowing well :

> "There never was man of so greate pryde ne pompe
> Nor of such myght, youth nor man of age
> That myght gaynsay the sounde of dethes trompe.
> He makes man daunce and that without courage
> As well the state as man of lowe lynage
> His cruell cours is ay so intretable
> That mannys myght to withstand is nat able."
>
>   - Barclay, *Ship of Fools*, II. p. 110.

In this manner the Fool who thought to escape Death became a prominent character in the spectacle-plays. The Fool always ended by becoming perforce Death's servant. Shakspeare refers to the action in *Measure for Measure* (Act. III. Sc. i.):

[1] This line occurs in one of Lydgate's poems and forms the burden of more than one of the popular songs of the day, indicating the rather "sad sincerity" of English life. And cf. Villon's ballad with the refrain : "Où sont des neiges d'antan ? "

> "Merely, thou art death's fool;
> For him thou labour'st by thy flight to shun,
> And yet runn'st toward him still."

There were many sides, of course, to mediæval life. The monks often forgot their professions of sanctity and, living for the moment for the world, incurred — rightly, no doubt — the satire of the poets and preachers. Chaucer's gay, worldling monk who "loved vene-rie," and the churchman who knew rimes about Robin Hood better than his prayers and could hunt a hare in the fields better than a clause in a Saints' Lives, were not, perhaps, uncommon types. Dunbar said, after all, "best to be blyth" in the face of the false world, and to his verses he often gave, like Villon, the sweetness of melancholy. Among the poems of the Percy MS. (Vol. III. 56) is one entitled *Death and Life* and thought to be late Middle-English work. It contains a gracious picture of Lady Dame Life, brighter than the sun, redder than the rose, ever laughing for love, awakening life and love in grass and tree, in bird and beast and man, as she speeds, with Comfort, Hope, Love, Courtesy, Honor, Mirth, Mercy and Disport in her train, in her conquest over Death. The sense of the piece, despite the intrusion of the "ugly fiend Dame Death," is that of gladness in the thought of life. Still the ballad shines by con-trast. It was most common, it appears, to scoff at the world—that was vanity and mockery. Where there was one like Chaucer who could take a calm, sane delight in life, seeing too deeply into the nature of things to despair, there were many like Pope Innocent III. to enu-merate without a gleam of hope the miseries of human conditions.[1] "þe worlde ycleped þe dane of tyeeres," expresses Dan Michel's judg-ment. Langland, the English Mystic, had likewise an austere and frowning face, and, having in his view the "field full of folk," burned with indignation at the worldlings there that Chaucer loved, the latter poet's sunny and sensuous tales being regarded as mortal sin. Death it was that made the world a mockery. When Graund Amoure, in Hawes' *Pastime of Pleasure*, became eager to heap up the world's riches it was Death that stood by to warn that these are valueless. So it was Death that rendered Nature unlovely. In the *Example of Virtue* Hawes brought Lusty Juven-tus within the glorious mansion of Dame Nature, whose perfect loveliness the youth admired; but Discretion, as was his part, led

---

[1] *De Contemptu Mundi sive de Miseria Conditionis Humanæ.*

to a place where the goddess's back was seen, which was all marred
by an image of Death.

Taking now into consideration these two sentiments of mediæval
life, the scorn of the world, and the fear of death, it is noteworthy
that Lydgate represents most fully the religious attitude. In his
youth he loved the pleasures of the world. In his *Testament*, refer-
ring to his wayward youth, he tells how he was converted:

> "When Ver is fresshest of blosmys and of flourys.
> An vnwar storm his fresshnesse may apayre.
> Who may withstande the sterne sharp shourys
> Of dethys power, wher hym list repayre?
> Thouhe the feturis fresshe, angelik and fayre,
> Shewe out in childhood, as any cristal cleer,
> Dethe can difface hem witheyne fyfteene yeere.

> "Which now remembryng in my latter age,
> Tyme of my childhood, as I reherse shal.
> Witheyne fifteene holdyng my passage,
> Mid of a cloistre depict vpon a wal ;
> I sauhe a crucifix, whos woundys were nat smal,
> With this woord VIDE writen ther besyde,
> ' Behold my mecknesse, O child, and lefe thy pride.'"

From various sources we have the outward aspect of the monk
in this "latter age" revealed. In a Shirley MS. (Addit. 16,165 Brit.
Mus.) reference is made to "Lydgate the Monk clothed in blakke."
Douglas, mentioning Lydgate among the poets in the Court of the
Muses, witnesses that he "raid musing him allone" (*Palice of
Honour.*) In the prolog to the *Story of Thebes*, written by Lydgate
to complete the Canterbury Tales, he describes himself as looking
pale and bloodless and wearing a cape of black — no fit companion
for Chaucer's gayer pilgrims one would think. But the most per-
fect description is given by William Bullein in his *Dialogue against
the Fever Pestilence* (Lond. 1573). Having spoken of Homer,
Hesiod. Ennius and Lucan as favorites of the Muses, Bullein adds
to the list of beneficiaries Gower. Skelton, Chaucer, and Lydgate.
The last he thus describes: "Lamenting Lidgate. lurking emong
the lilies with a bold skons, with a garland of willowes about his pate ;
booted he was after Sainct Benet's guise, and a black stamell robe,
with a lothly monsterous hoode, hanging backwarde : his stoopyng
forward, bewayling euery estate, with the spirite of prouidence for-
seyng the falles of wicked men. and the slipprie seates of Princes,
the ebbyng and flowyng, the risyng and falling of men in auctoritie,

and how vertue doth aduaunce the simple, and vice ouerthrowe the most noble of the worlde." (Bullein's *Dialogue*, E. E. T. S., p. 17.)

Of these accounts there is every justification in Lydgate's writings. The dominant themes are without question those connected with the thought of death and change. The painting at St. Paul's of the procession of Death seemed to impress his mind deeply. Beside his translation of the French verses of the Dance Macawbre more than one reference occurs in his lyrics to the "Daunce of Poules" (*Minor Poems*, p. 34, 77). Often he pictures life as a hard pilgrimage, "in which there is no stedfast abyding." He harps recurrently upon the wretchedness of human affairs — the note being taken, he affirms, from his master Chaucer! One of his favorite topics is to show the greatness of mankind and how they are brought low: "All do but show a shadow transitory."

> "Stabilnesse is founde in nothyng,
>   In worldly honour who so lokithe wele;
> For dethe ne sparithe emperour ne kyng,
>   Thoughe they be armed in plates made of steele;
> He castithe downe princes from fortunes wheele,
>   As hir spokes rounde about goo,
> To exemplifye, who that markithe wele,
>   How this world is a thurghfare ful of woo."
>   *On the Wretchedness of Worldly Affairs*, M. P., p. 126.

> "Considre and see the transmutacioun,
>   How the sesoun of greene lusty age,
> Force of juventus, hardy as lioun,
>   Tyme of manhood, wisdom, sad corage,
> And how decrepitus turneth to dotage,
>   Al cast in ballaunce, bewar, forget nothyng,
> And thu shalt fynde this lyff *a pylgrymage*,
>   In which there is no stedfast abydyng."
>   —*On the Mutability of Human Affairs*, p. 198.

The *Daunce of Poules* or the *Daunce Macawbre* consists of verses spoken by Death to the various persons he is leading to the grave and of their responses. All must go upon this dance, the Pope, the highest in the land, the Emperor, the Cardinal, the Empress, the King and all the lower ranks — there is none escape.

> " In this myrrour every man may fynde
>   That hym behoveth to gon upon this daunce
> Who goth to forne or who schal go behynde
>   Al dependeth in goddes ordynaunce.

> Wherfor eche man lowly take his chaunce.
> Deth spareth not pore ne blode ryal,
> Eche man therfor haue this in remembraunce
> Of on matere God hath forged al."

The *Assembly of Gods* is the consummate expression of Lydgate's fear of death. Death is here the central figure throughout. In the fear all accord—Lydgate, Reason and Sensuality. Very appropriately the last recorded line written by this somewhat sombre monk, line 1491 of the *Secrees of Old Philisoffres*, is of Death :

> "Deth al consumyth which may nat be denyed."

3. *The Conventional Materials.*—The *Assembly of Gods* in respect to its materials, its machinery, so to speak, is anything but original. The poet is thrown into the conventional sleep by a lake side, on the hackneyed spring morning. At once we expect the poem to be crammed full of stereotyped theology, mythology and allegory. Indeed the work as a whole is merely a mosaic of current traditions, the different parts being fitted together with more or less perfect skill. When, then, we come to estimate the literary effects of compositions of this sort, their origins and history must be taken into account. Mediæval ideas had always a definite pedigree. While modern romantic literature is most characterized by its personal element, mediæval literature may be divided rather into impersonal classes, as romances, chronicles, lays, etc. Individuality rarely appeared as an element of poetic composition. Each writer, being under no compulsion to originate or invent, simply threw what he had to say into the prevailing form. The genius of poetry, both with respect to form and materials, was conventionality.¹ An artist was held in estimation according to his skill in plagiarizing from the world's literatures. It was sufficient that he could wisely quote, that he had won a reputation for scholarship, and that the epithet "learned" be attached to him. It is characteristic of the age that Dante, after a youth spent in writing love songs, should plan a *Convito*, to be a vast encyclopædic work, so anxious was he that the title of "learned" might offset the reproach of a youth misspent in composing love sonnets. So Chaucer was called with approbation "learned" and

¹This feature of mediæval literature is commonly spoken of by readers slightingly and with meagre patience. But a traditional literature is cumulative, so to speak, in its effects. Repetition is then a virtue and not a weakness. Traditions are most effective at the moment of most common use. A later age is quite incapable of giving full and due credit to conventions that have passed; it should at least exercise charity.

the "great translator." In his case, by reason of the blending in
his works of his own stream of romantic fancy and feeling with this
remote traditional tide, often strange anomalies of thought were
produced. In fact Chaucer was differentiated from the writers of
the period by his originality which worked with new results upon
the materials that tradition had given him. Yet it was for his learn-
ing that he was most admired. It is not necessary to disprove the
extent or accuracy of Chaucer's attainment in this respect.[1] Like
other writers of the period he was learned enough to refer sugges-
tively to matters more or less familiar to his readers, who held their
own knowledge loosely, and in the manner of all middle-age erudi-
tion, without critical accuracy. A work of this period is not then to
be interpreted by itself but by the class of literature to which it
belongs by virtue of associated themes and *motifs*. When one first
reads the opening stanzas of the *Assembly of Gods* he exclaims
that it is a dream like *Piers the Plowman*, like the *Poem of the
Pearl*, like the *Roman de la Rose* and the *Divina Comedia*. These
poems and many more add their several contributions to one's
delight. A phrase here, a thought there, the dream, the allegory,
the pictured walls, the theme of death, in one way or another
serve to recall pretty much the whole of mediæval literatures—just
probably as the author intended. Only by thus recovering the past
and setting a work in the historical current, can we understand the
pleasure and profit with which a poem of this kind was read by
contemporaries and by those of a later time to whom its literary
traditions were familiar. We must remember that to Lydgate,[2] for
a century after his death, the distinction was given of belong-
ing with Gower and Chaucer to the great triumvirate of letters.
Not alone for his "sugurit lippis and toungis aureate" was this
fame acquired, though for these he seems to have been most admired
by Hawes, the Scottish poets, the critic Webb, and the poet Gray;
but his praise was in the mouth of his nearest disciple, Benedict
Burgh, for that "ye have gadred flouris in this motli mede,"—in the
literature, that is, of the past—and on this account "to yow is yeven
the verray price of excellence." Of course a succeeding age, intent
upon the Reformation and the New Learning, forgot the mediæval
traditions, the dream, the allegory, the teachings of Doctrine, and

[1] Cf. Lounsbury *Studies in Chaucer*, ch. v.

[2] For the subject of Lydgate's literary fame v. Sidney Lee's summary in *Dict.
of Natl. Biog.* XXXIV., p. 309-10.

Lydgate and his school were relegated to obscurity. Chaucer survives now not for his learning but because of the perrennial charm of his native genius.   No one of us cares much for Boethius or Fulgentius or Prudentius, or even Dante in his doctor's robes, dead, all of them, to modern comprehension.

No one will question Lydgate's learning or the extent of his reading.   He was more or less familiar with ancient and mediæval literatures, especially that written in Latin and French.   His library contained much the same books that Chaucer, Gower and Langland read.   He is as pedantic as they in filling his pages with the names of authors and famous men.   He illustrates, as they, the influence exercised in poetry by the scholastic and encyclopædic training of the Church and School.   Mr. Lee's statement on this point is sufficient :

"Lydgate mentions familiarly all the great writers of classical and mediæval antiquity.   Of Greek authors he claims some aquaintance with 'grete' Homer, Euripides, Demosthenes, Plato, Aristotle and Josephus.   Among Latin writers he refers constantly to Ovid, Cicero, Virgil, and his commentator Servius, Livy, Juvenal and 'noble' Persius ; to 'moral' Seneca, Lucan, Statius, Aulus Gellius, Valerius Maximus, Prudentius, Lactantius, Prosper the 'dogmatic' epigrammatist, Vegetius, Boethius, Fulgentius, Alanus ab Insulis, and Guido di Colonna.   Dante, Petrarch, and Boccaccio are repeatedly commended by him among Italian writers, and he was clearly acquainted with the 'Roman de la Rose,' with French fabliaux, romances, and chronicles."—*Dict. Natl. Biog.* XXXIV., p. 309.

The mosaic of the *Assembly of Gods* is made up of the following materials, all of which are traditional and common.

Introduction with the season *motif.*

The dream.

The painted walls.

The School of Doctrine.

The pagan Divinities.

The court scene and the banquet of the Gods.

The Nine Worthies and the learned men of antiquity.

The allegory.

Proverbial phrases.

The teaching of the Church.

The Seven Sins and Virtues.

The battle of Antichrist.
The Liberal Sciences.
The five Wits.
The fear of Death.
The romance of Paris and Helen.

4. *The Season Motif.*[1] The introduction of Middle-English poems by reference to the season of the year and the position of the planets seems generally to have been merely a part of the machinery of composition—a happy way of getting started. The same prelude is met with in the Provençal, French and German lyrics of the period with wearisome regularity. The May landscape especially was stereotyped into set forms that could have had but a rhetorical significance. With Chaucer and most of the Scottish poets, the nature-prelude was, one feels, something more than derivative. Chaucer, King James, Dunbar, and Douglas especially appear to draw quite directly from nature with a heartfelt feeling for the season. They write with an unction and an eye for delicate effects never exhibited in the purely conventional prelude. Chaucer's love of nature amounted almost to a passion. Whatever he touched broke into full blossom. Reading him, as Lowell says, is like brushing through the dewy grass at sunrise. Poets with Chaucer's spirit had naturally a sense for nature as a dramatic background for their compositions. Thus it was agreed that May[2] was the "mirthful month," the "quicking" season, the month of "joy and disport," the one that "among months sittith like a queen"—the time, therefore, for beginning love-poems and romantic allegories. Chaucer tells us that in the Spring he would say farewell to his books and walk out in the meadow; this was the time to compose "Seyntes Legends of Cupid." The association of the romances with the Spring was so common that there came to be a saying that "Arthur is the man of May." Where the dramatic motive was present other seasons would be employed as the occasion required. *The Pearl* occurred in the high season of August when the reapers' sickles were in the corn. Lyndesay's *Dreme* opens appropriately with a

[1] See McLaughlin, *Studies in Mediæval Life and Literature*, ch. i.; also Veitch, *Nature in Scottish Poetry*.

[2] There is a primitive feeling among poets that Spring is the season of delights. Keats had this sense in a large degree when he began to write *Endymion* "while the early budders are just new," hoping that no wintry season should find his work incomplete.

dreary winter's night in January. Dunbar's horrible *Dance of the Sinns* is seen in February. Sackville's *Mirrour for Magistrates*, which harks back to the Chaucer School, begins in the "wrathful winter." In one instance Chaucer opens a poem, the *Hous of Fame*, modelling his work upon Dante, with the December season. In Henryson's melancholy story of Troylus and Creseyde there is an open effort to construct a dramatic background, for the poet says in beginning:

> "*Ane doolie sesoun to ane cairfull dyte*
> *Suld correspond, and be equivalent:*
> Richt sa it wes quhen I began to write
> This tragedie, the wedder richt fervent,
> Quhen Aries, in middis of the Lent,
> Schouris of haill can fra the north descend,
> That scantlie fra the cauld I micht defend."

But there are other cases, as Langland's *Piers the Plowman*,[1] where no æsthetic value in the prelude can be determined. The last of these derivative forms, as in Skelton's *Bowge of Court*, or Fletcher's *Purple Island*, seem but rhetorical. The conventional aspect of the introduction is well displayed by Lyndesay when he begins his doleful *Monarchie* with the May morning, as if he were unable to get started in any other way, but realizing that his purpose is to describe mortal miseries, he calls a truce to his vain descriptions and turns to the matter in hand.

In the minds of some writers there may have been a thought of the planetary influences that ever streamed down from the heavens upon the earth. Astrology is known to have been an attractive theme to the mediæval poets. "It was the delight of Dante," says Dean Church, "to interweave the poetry of feeling and of the outward sense with the grandeur of order, proportion, measured magnitudes, the relation of abstract forces displayed on such a scene as the material universe." Chaucer constantly makes a literary use of astrology though personally skeptical of the pretentions of the science. This perception of the starry forces at work in the lives of men must have been present in the first of the preludes. Thus the introduction served almost the function of an invocation to the Muses. King James, indeed, invoking the Muses Nine, passes at once to consider the Spring "that full of vertu is and gude." In one of the very earliest of the poems containing the typical season

---

[1] Langland seemed to have had Mapes' Golias satire in mind when he began to write. Note Mapes' "Inter prodigia plebem innumeram."

motive, the *Apocalypse of Golias,* written toward the close of the 12th
century, the astronomical allusion is prominent·

> "A Tauro torrida lampade Cynthli
> Fundente jacula ferventis radii
> Umbrosas nemoris latebras adii,
> Explorans gratiam levis Favonii.
>
> Aestivae medio diei tempore,
> Frondosa recubans Jovis sub arbore,
> Astantis video formam Pythagorae :
> Deus scit, nescio, utrum in corpore."

May was the month of life because the planets at that season had
special power of hot and moist.[1]

With Lydgate and his immediate pupils, as Hawes in the *Pastime of Pleasure,* the astronomical introduction is apparently a
matter of pure literary habit. The vision of the *Temple of Glas*
takes place in December, after its model the *Hous of Fame.* The
opening of the *Assembly of Gods* — the only reference to nature in
the work — is conventional. It is barely possible that in the monk's
scholastic mind there was in the reference to the spheres the suggestion of the harmony to be achieved by Reason and Sensuality.

5. *The Vision.*[2] In the psychology of the Middle Ages the
vision is perhaps the most remarkable phenomenon displayed. The
records of dreams constitute in Europe and England an entire literature with features peculiar to the kind. Some of this dreamwork is in imitation of the revelations of Scripture ; some works
are clearly due to the hallucinations of an ascetic life ; some are as
plainly the results of adoration, the fruits of "contemplative life,"
in the exercise of which men passed from the knowledge of things
of sense to knowledge of things eternal ; others reveal the passion
for dogmatic definition that characterized the schoolmen however
mystical the theme ; other forms are secular and merely a part of
the higher rhetoric of poetry as then conceived and developed.
After the Bible, the head sources of the mediæval visions seem to
have been the "Dialogues" of St. Gregory, a compilation of many
religious dreams, the *De Consolatione Philosophiæ* of Boethius, and
the *Somnium Scipionis* in Cicero's treatise on The Republic. In

[1] For the effects of the seasons upon the lives of men see Lydgate's *Testament,
The Mutability of Human Affairs,* and the *Secrees.*

[2] See Lecky's *History of European Morals,* II., pp. 116 *et seq.,* 220. For further references to the literature of the vision see Schick's Intro., p. cxviii.

general, two types of vision are distinguishable, in accordance with
their monastic or worldly origin. In the visions of one class the
dreamer takes into his view the circles of the supernatural, and
reports as man may of the revelations accorded him either of
Heaven or Hell or the intermediate states. In the other class the
objects of contemplation are in the "wilderness of this world," and
the dream may be but a poetical device, a kind of framework for
any secular action or incident, as the experiences of a lover
in the *Romaunt of the Rose*. In English literature illustration
of the first type is furnished by *The Pearl*, with its view of the
heavenly city; Dunbar's *Dance of the Seven Deadly Sinns*, with its
vision of Hell; and Lyndesay's *Dreme*, which gives the reader sight
of all the circles of the Infinite. Probably the earliest instance in
England of this kind of dream is the *Apocalypse of Golias*, written
in Latin by Walter Mapes (b. 1143), a work which enjoyed an
extraordinary popularity during the 13th and 14th centuries. The
chief examples of the second type are Langland's *Piers the Plow-
man*, Chaucer's several dreams, King James's *Quair*, Dunbar's
Golden Targe, Skelton's *Bowge of Court*, etc.

The *Assembly of Gods* is in its scope a vision of the first order,
though the battle takes place in Microcosm. Probably Lydgate
did not have any very real sense of the other worlds, nor could he
ever loose his imagination so that he really saw visions—at best he
asked but for dogmatic definition as the schoolmen before him.

6. *Proverbial Phrases.* Like other writers of the period Lyd-
gate makes a conspicuous use of conventional phrases and pro-
verbial sayings. A considerable body of proverbs, rhetorical figures,
and phrases may be gathered from his works, some of which are
peculiar to his own usage and style, while others are the common
property of literature. On a later page is given a list of the prov-
erbs and phrases employed in this poem. The manner of the
employment of a stock simile by writers is well illustrated by the
history of the phrase "hair like gold wire" which seems to have been
given currency by Lydgate. The simile first occurs in Layamon's *Brut*
(ll. 7047–8), where it is employed to describe King Pir who was so
wondrous fair. By Lydgate it was first used to characterize the
feathers of a bird in the *Chorl and Bird*. In the *Temple of Glas*
and the *Assembly of Gods* (l. 373) the reference is to Venus with her
ever sunnish hair. In the *Troy-Book* it occurs no less than seven
times being applied both to men and women. The larger compari-

son "hair like gold" is often found in European literature before Lydgate as in the *Roman de la Rose,* but this special phrase is Lydgate's own. From this time to the close of the sixteenth century the figure is in constant employment[1], generally descriptive of women of ideal beauty. Its force is partly spent in Shakespeare's time, for the reverence for gold hair is satirized by the saying of Benedick in *Much Ado about Nothing* (II., 3, 36): "Her hair shall be of what colour it please God." In sonnet cxxx. reference is made to Lydgate's simile in the line, "If hairs be wires, black wires grow on her head."

7. *The Painted Wall.*[2] The pictured wall was another rhetorical device common to mediæval poetry—an elastic framework into which any subject could be made to fit. It was a convenient means of extending indefinitely the scope of one's work. To such an extent was the method carried that a secondary poet like Stephen Hawes cannot mention a wall without covering it over with pictures. Instances of the usage will be found in Boccaccio's *Thesiad,* in the romance of *Guigemar* by Marie de France, Lorris's *Roman de la Rose,* Chaucer's *Boke of the Duchesse,* Lydgate's *Temple of Glas* and *Assembly of Gods,* Hawes's *Pastime of Pleasure,* Dunbar's *Dream,* Barclay's *Towre of Vertue and Honour,* etc. In the romances the stories depicted are commonly those of love. In *Guigemar,* for instance, the walls are painted with images of Venus and scenes from Ovid's Art of Love, and in the *Boke of the Duchesse* the imagery is that of the *Roman de la Rose.* In descriptions of the temples of Mars and Diana scenes of war and the hunt will appear. The siege of Troy or Thebes was a favorite theme for the walls of palaces. Scriptural scenes occur in cathedrals and cloisters. Dunbar saw on his chamber walls

> "All the nobill storyis old and new,
> Sen oure first father formed was of clay."

[1] For many instances of its usage see Schick's *Temple of Glas,* notes, pp. 88–90; and Kölbing, *Bevis of Hamtoun,* notes, pp. 244–5; and for a full discussion of its usage and æsthetical meaning see a paper by the present editor read before the English Club (Chicago) and reported in outline in the *University Quarterly Calendar* (May, 1895), p. 80.

[2] See Warton, *Hist. of Eng. Poetry,* II., pp. 131, 275, 402; III., p. 63; on page 402, Vol. II., is reprinted a passage from an Itinerary written in 1322 describing Westminster palace; see Longfellow's *Golden Legend* for instances of picture and play; a description of convent walls is given in *Piers the Plowman's Crede,* ll. 186, *et seq.*

While this method is an open piece of machinery when viewed as rhetoric, quite ludicrous too when as elaborate as Lydgate's arbor walls which reveal the history of the world in small, yet it should be remembered that during the Middle Ages the picture was the favorite means of conveying story and doctrine. It is a remarkable feature of mediæval art that often no positive line of division can be drawn between literature and picture or spectacular show. The paintings on royal palaces of the scenes of war, the weaving on ladies' tapestries of the incidents of romance, the picturing on cloister walls of the saints and scenes from Scripture, the depiction in public places as on the bridge at Lucerne and in the churches in France and England of such instructional processionals as the Dance of Death, the scenic representation of sacred things in liturgies, and pageants and street plays—these constituted the popular literature of the period, of far greater influence than the written page that issued from the scriptorium of the monastery. Allegory, the written picture, necessarily adopted the scenic method for which the mind was already prepared. This interplay of imagery between picture and allegory contributed much to the later establishment of an independent literature. But for the present the pictorial was the literary. Even Chaucer was not freed from the necessity of "drawing of picture."

8. *The Admixture of Pagan and Christian Traditions.*—One characteristic of the *Assembly of Gods* is the curious admixture in it of pagan and Christian traditions. The pagan deities are all ranged on the side of the Vices of Christendom. The Christian Vice is represented as the son of Pluto, who is the Lord of the Christian Hell. The ancient Fateful Atropos, who cut with shears the thread of pagan life, is transformed into Death with a lance, the dread of the Christian Church.

It was the almost universal practice of the poets of late Middle English to confound the mythology of all peoples and to mix up incongruously the pagan myths and Christian allegories, constituting in fact a veritable mythology of their own. Gower in his *Confessio Amantis*, Douglas in his *Palice of Honour*, King James in his *Quair*, and others of the allegorical school display their learning in this manner. Such usage points to the renaissance of paganism, accompanying the temporary decay of Christianity in the 14th century, and to the rise of a new mythology, and foreshadows the new learning of the next century. The results of this renaissance in Europe a century later are well exhibited by Browning in his poem, *The Bishop Orders his Tomb*, where Pans and Nymphs, symbols of Delphic wisdom and Bacchic revels, the Saviour on the Mount, St. Praxed in his glory and Moses with his tables are brought into juxtaposition on the sculptured tomb. We know too that in Italy Plato was called the second Moses and Orpheus, Empedocles, Parmenides and others were placed on a level with David and the prophets.

In some cases there seems to be more than a poetic use of the machinery of mythology—as if some profound meaning was read into the ancient myths. Always when traditional currents from different sources blend, the underlying human meanings are transferred and commonly understood. When Angelo painted in the Last Judgment an Herculean Christ he was clearly not irreverent. Dante wrote Olympus for Paradise (*Purg.* c. xxiv. l. 15). He spoke of Christ as "Sommo Giove" who was crucified for us (*Purg.* c. vi. l. 118). In canto xxix, the Grifon naturally symbolizes the Christ. In a like spirit Milton and others have spoken of Christ as the "mighty Pan," and Milton's Deity, as Lowell observes, was a Calvanistic Zeus. Even Bunyan introduces, into his *Holy War*, Cerberus, who swears by St. Mary, and the Furies, Alecto, Megaera and Tisiphone, and the incongruity of their presence there seems to have escaped his attention. Chaucer in calling one of his works the *Seintes Legend of Cupyde* must have entered into the spirit of the heathen pantheism as a real form of religion.[1]

It is not so clear that Lydgate entered very deeply into the spirit of mythology. His usage is not very consistent. In the *Assembly of Gods* Cupid is counted among the vices. But in another piece attributed to Lydgate (Fairfax MSS. xvi. Bibl. Bodl.) the rubrics of the missal are applied to the god Cupid for whose sake many were martyrs. In the *Life of Our Lady* the beauty of the Virgin Mary is compared with that of Helen, Polyxena, Lucretia, Dido, Bathsheba and Rachel. The clearest case of insight is in his *Testament* where Jesus is spoken of as

> "Our Orpheus that fro captyvyte[2]
> Feit Erudice to his celestial tour."

In the present instance Doctrine is under the necessity of explaining away the heathen worship.

[1] Cf. Mr. Jephson's remark, Skeat's ed. *Pr. Tale.* notes p. 136.

[2] Jesus was frequently represented in early Christian paintings in the form of Orpheus, who overcame death.

9. *The Allegorical Type.*—Middle-English literature exhibits two types of allegory : the one religious and scholastic, having its origin in the exegetical and homiletic literature of the monks and leading on to the literature of the Reformation ; the other secular and profane, embodying the spirit of romance, personifying especially the God of Love, who was the central object of the song and worship of the continental minnesinger and troubadour, leading on in its turn to the literature of the Renaissance. The two types, differing thus in origin, while often confused with respect to form, are always distinguishable in motive.

The original *Roman de la Rose* represents in one composition the double type already established on the continent. The first part, being conceived in a love of beauty and composed with the fancy and imagination actively at play, is pure poetry. Lorris, though a belated *trouvère*, was true at heart and sang as the impulse prompted him. The second part of the *Roman*, written forty years after the first by a reformer and moralist, Jean de Meung, not to be mistaken for a poet, is didactic, satirical, and metaphysical. By the aid of Lorris's personification, Meung was enabled to expound and popularize his ideas of reform, but his impersonations recall nothing so well as the entities of the schoolmen. The personifications and materials of the didactic system were adopted by the poets whose purpose was moral or satirical, by Langland, Gower, Lydgate, Lyndesay, Skelton and Barclay, and by the Moral-plays so soon as personification became necessary in the advance of the drama from scenic representation to dramatic characterization.

Upon the model of the *Roman de la Rose*, which was translated into English with amplifications of the first part and omission of much of the second part, were formed the love allegories and romances which, being all in the "May morning" style, with sunny gardens and birdies manifold, contain whatever of poetic inspiration the later Middle Ages in England possessed. The new *Romaunt of the Rose* provided the staple model for the poets of the court. It directed the composition of the *Court of Love*, and was the chief influence that entered the *Dreme*, Chaucer's *Boke of the Duchesse* and perhaps his *Hous of Fame*. To the list we may add Lydgate's *Temple of Glas*, which was modeled upon Chaucer's *Hous of Fame*, and probably Hawes's *Pastime of Pleasure*. To the same family of romance allegory belongs much of the literature of Scotland written during the 15th century, that at least of most refinement and delicacy, notably Dunbar's *Thissil and the Rois* and the *Golden Targe*, and the beautiful *Quair* by James, "the best poet who ever was a king." In the romantic vein Gawain Douglas wrote his *Palace of Honour*, a more serious style appearing in *King Hart*, which allegorizes the progress of human life. This stream of romantic allegory flows on to Spenser, forming in the *Faery Queene* the supreme type of poetic allegory. Though Spenser was an artist of the Renaissance he was yet the literary descendant of Chaucer and the mediæval romanticists, of those who were too great as artists to be ever dominated by the moralities.

As for the rest of the allegorical literature in late Middle-English the tendency is to sermonize. In the case of Langland and perhaps of Lyndesay their seriousness is of such a nature as to claim our attention as artistic. Gower might have been a romancer if he had not seen behind every tale some hidden form of Vice. John Skelton, laureate of Henry VII, the last of the school which called Chaucer master, while writing some pieces in the romantic spirit, yet is more pleased to satirize follies and vices as in his *Bowge of Court*. Characteristic of the times now that the Reformation was near at hand is the *Ship of Fools* (1508), a satirical allegory after the model of Brandt's Swabian poem, by Barclay who caught up for the purpose of satire the idea of a navy of practical vices sailing out presumably into the ocean of ruin. Erasmus in a corresponding spirit wrote his satirical *Praise of Folly*. The allegory of the Reformation culminates at length in Bunyan's Visions.

To this now primary and now secondary stream of moral and allegorical literature Lydgate's *Assembly of Gods* belongs. This is not, however, satirical or very serious concerning reform, and it strives after certain effects of the *Romaunt of the Rose*. But so far as Lydgate is concerned the romantic tide has ebbed—he is a monk with the interest of the church at heart.

10. *The Relationship between the Allegory and the Moral Play.*— The close relationship between the moral plays and the *Assembly of Gods* is clearly seen. In an earlier period[1] such poems as the *Cursor Mundi* and the contemporary miracle plays exactly corresponded, the only difference being that one was recited and the

---

[1] It is conjectured with good reasons that the demon frolics in Dante's *Inferno*, c. xxi and xxiv, were reproduced from some dramatic mystery plays of which the performances on the Ponte Carraia at Florence in 1304 are conspicuous instances (Plumptre).

other acted. The same correspondence existed later between the
moral plays, which represented the natural dramatic evolution from
the miracle plays, and the allegories, which exhibit a like advance in
dramatic expression. This interaction between the two forms of
art is important to observe. The moral play involved allegory as
an essential part of its artistic apparatus. In the very earliest
pageants and plays, allegorical characters, taken from both profane
and sacred writings, played a more or less important part. The
miracle plays required the introduction of such characters as Sin
and Death, Faith, Hope and Charity. Among the first innovations
were representations of Veritas, Justitia, Pax and Misericordia, as in
the "Parliament of Heaven" in the English Coventry series (XI).
As early as Henry VI., whose reign may be fixed upon as the epoch
of the permanent adoption of the moral play (Collier, *An. of the
St.*, p. 32), personification of the Sciences, Nature, Grace, Fortune,
and the moral qualities was well known. The World, Flesh and
Devil appeared in character in *Originale de Sancta Maria Magdalena,*
a play of the time of Henry VII. The play of *Everyman,* belong-
ing perhaps to the time of Edward IV., is one of the most perfect
allegories ever given form. In the Vices and Virtues especially
there was something inevitably dramatic in the very nature of con-
trast. So that with few exceptions the allegory of the Moral-plays
is based on the contest between good and evil in the mind of man ;
of this character is the allegory of the *Castle of Perseverance, Min
Will and Understanding, Nature, The World and the Child, Hick-
Scorner, Everyman, Lusty Juventus,* etc. It is probable indeed that
the one allegorical figure Vice, in his Protean character of Infidel-
ity, Iniquity, Hypocrisy, Desire and the like, has played a more
conspicuous part upon the stage than any other single dramatic
personage.

Thus the familiar use of allegorical personages upon the stage
contributed to the popular taste for allegorical poems. The names
representing abstract qualities recalled so vividly the actual persons
seen upon the stage that the mere recitation of the qualities was
sufficient to body forth the form. The catalog of names in the
Assembly of Gods is tedious enough to the modern reader, but in an
age of objective dramatic presentation the names and persons were
intimately associated.

The *Assembly of Gods* finds its analogue then in the contempo-
rary Moral-plays. The poem may actually be divided into scenes

and the *personæ* speak in character. Some portions, as the assembly of the gods and the gathering of the different hosts, might take the form of a masque.[1] Poem and play differ only in the method of presenting the same form of thought.

The dramatic cast of the poem might well be expected in the case of Lydgate, who seemed as well able to direct a street pageant as to write verses in a cloistre. He devised pageants for the Mercers' and Goldsmiths' Companies in honor of Wm. Estfield, who was London's mayor in 1429 and 1437 (v. *Dict. Natl. Biog.*, XXXIV, p. 306). Stowe in his *Annals of England* (p. 385) witnesses that in 1445, at the reception in London of Queen Margaret, the wife of Henry VI., several pageants were exhibited at Paul's gate with verses written by Lydgate (v. *Hist. Eng. Pageants*, ed. Howes, p. 385; *Pur le Roy*, M. P.). According to Ritson (*Bibl. Poet*, p. 79) Lydgate wrote a Disguising or Mumming before the King at Eltham. Ritson also inserts in his list of Lydgate's works "a procession of pageants from the creation." This is exceedingly doubtful, for, as Halliwell says (M. P. p. 94), Ritson only copied from Tanner, whose conjecture it was that the Coventry Series of Miracle Plays was written by Lydgate. But the *Processioun of Corpus Christi* (title given by Shirley), attributed by Ritson to Lydgate and so printed by Halliwell, while not dramatic in form, contains an enumeration and description, as if in procession, of Patriarchs and Saints from Adam to Thomas Aquinas. The *Dance of Death* and the *Pilgrimage of the World* are essentially dramatic. The dramatic element of *Bycorne and Chichevache*, which was doubtless borrowed from a French mystery play,[2] is also worthy of note. Certainly not the least excellence of the *Assembly of Gods* is its dramatic picturesqueness. It was this characteristic which Collier noted that he remarked "the story is very dramatic, and far less dull than most pieces of the kind" (*An. of the St.* p. 31).

11. *The Allegory of the Vices and Virtues.*—In considering the central allegory of the *Assembly of the Gods* the reader is brought into relation with one of the great themes of literature, the almost universal subject of war, the war that proceeds within the soul—

---

[1] It seems to be well established that the English masque, and the pageants, derived their popularity and meaning from the allegorical poems and plays. Dunbar's Dance of the Sins is a masque in form. The Dance of Death was a graveyard processional.

[2] See Dodsley's *Old Plays*, XII. p. 302.

how man battles through trials and temptations to heaven's gate, how he falls oft but rises again, how he wins at length the victory over Sin and Death. This is in truth the dominant allegory of man. So universal, indeed, is the treatment in the literature of Christendom of the theme of man's salvation that the collected volumes of that literature may be said to constitute a veritable Epic of Penance. For note how often in great literatures, in the works of Dante, Langland, Chaucer, Spenser, Bunyan, Goethe, Tennyson and Browning, to name the greatest, the real content of life is described in the terms of pilgrimage and battle—the life that in the Middle Age was in very fact a Crusade and a Tournament, an ascent up the Mount of Purgatory, that was in Reformation times a Pilgrim's Progress and a Holy War, that is still a " War of Sense with Soul," where the obligation never ceases to " Fight on, fare ever." The literature of this struggle, wherein not only the soul of man is involved but also the spiritual powers beyond our world, where Earth and Heaven and Hell are mingled in contest, constitutes in its entirety the most stupendous epic which the genius of man has conceived.

In some form the subject is older than Christianity. War itself is a primitive theme. The heathen myths pictured the agents of nature as engaged in warfare, the healing and harmful forces, the Light and the Darkness, the Summer and the Winter, the sun-gods and the frost-giants. In one of the earliest of historic religions, Zoroasterism, the idea of antagonism in the moral life occurs, the contest between the Prince of Light and the Prince of Darkness being figured upon the earthly sphere. On the spiritual side Plato's myth of the contending steeds is again a record of the primitive soul. Thus the necessity has been laid on man from the first of "working out the beast" and "letting the ape and tiger die." It is true that Christianity brought into greater prominence the need of warfare. "*Estote fortes in bello et pugnato cum antiquo serpente*"—thus the Scriptures exhorted the Christian convert to the fearful battle against sin. Then when paganism came in contact with Christianity the terms of war and of military society were naturally applied to the new life and to the kingdom of Heaven. Christ was King. His apostles were thegns who went forth to the wars. With the spiritual conceptions of the new gospels was mingled the mythology which dealt with the warfare of Nature. The conflict between Day and Night was transferred to Christ and Satan, to Eternal Light and Eternal Darkness.

Chivalry, gathering from paganism all that was best in war, strength, prudence, courage, knightly honor, and from Christianity an ideal of spiritual perfection, now became the established principle of society, a society that received its personal ideal in the figure of King Arthur and its social ideal in the Order of the Round Table.

While society itself was thus being organized in accordance with the ideal of militant Christianity, the severest of spiritual battles were being fought out within the cloisters of the monks. A severer morality was naturally exacted from the monks than from the ordinary Christian. It was then within the monasteries of the third and fourth centuries that the "Olympian battle with Sin" began. By Ambrose (340–397) and his pupil Augustine (354–430) the Platonic virtues called "cardinal," Wisdom, Justice, Fortitude, and Temperance, were resolved into Christian graces. To these were added the triad of theological virtues, Faith, Hope and Love. Against these seven were arrayed for the trial of the saints seven deadly sins, Pride, Avarice, Anger, Gluttony, Lust, with two others selected from Envy, Vain-glory, Tristitia or Accidia. An intense and concentrated struggle against human weakness was thus set on foot. On the basis of these sins a penitential system was devised, some form of pilgrimage up the mount of Purgatory.

By the time that Dante wrote his *Comedia* the exactions of monastic virtue were enforced upon all the children of the Church and a penitential pilgrimage enjoined. In the *Inferno* a classification of the sins is given as found in the *Summa Theologica* of St. Thomas Aquinas, which is based upon the ethical principles of Aristotle as interpreted, probably, by Averrhoes. Sin, having been triumphant, is come to punishment in Hell according to what Dante calls the law of "contrapass" [retribution] (*Inferno* xxviii, 142.). But in Purgatory sin is not allowed to develop into act but appears as an inner incitement. It is shown, therefore, not as punishment but as recreation where struggle must enter, the will for holiness being victorious.

> "And I will sing that second realm instead,
> Wherein man's spirit frees itself from stain,
> And groweth worthy Heaven's high courts to tread."
> —*Purg.* ll. 4-6.

For this purpose Dante employed the popular penitential system of the Church which brought into prominence the necessity of discipline by struggle against sin in the pilgrimage of this world. Thus the various stairs of Penitence are named after the seven monastic moralities.

When Dante is resting on the fourth terrace of Purgatory, Virgil explains to him the nature and relation to each other of the seven mortal sins. He is explaining the teachings of St. Augustine and considers sin with respect to its causes. Love is the common ground. Love perverted by selfishness and erring in its object is pride, envy and anger. Love remiss, defective in vigor, is sloth. Love excessive is avarice, gluttony and lust. (So earlier Augustine defined virtue as *amor ordinatus*, vice as *amor non ordinatus* (*Civ. D.* XV. 221). Sin is mortal because it attacks the conditions of spiritual life, preventing in society the exercise of love. Pride is the most deadly, nearest therefore to the state of hell, because it strikes directly at love and hinders to the utmost the soul's higher life.

The current ethics of the church during the thirteenth and fourteenth centuries respecting the nature of the vices is also contained in a poem entitled *Septem Peccata Mortalia*, of doubtful authorship but ascribed by some (Witte, Krafft and others) to Dante.

> " In Pride the root of every sin doth lie :
>   Hence man himself doth hold in loftier fame
> Than others, and deserving lot more high.
>
> Envy is that which makes us blush for shame,
>   With grief beholding others' happiness,
> Like him, whom we the face of God proclaim.
>
> Wrath still more woe doth on the wrathful press,
>   For its fierce mood lights up hell's fiery heat ;
> Then ill deeds come, and loss of holiness.
>
> Sloth looks with hate on every action meet,
>   And to ill-doing ever turns the will,
> Is slow to work, and quick to make retreat.
>
> Then Avarice comes, through which the whole world still
>   Vexes its soul, and breaks through every law,
> And tempts with gain to every deed of ill.
>
> Both fool and wise foul Gluttony doth draw,
>   And he who pampers still his appetite,
> Shortens his life, to fill his greedy maw.
>
> And Lust that comes the seventh in order right,
>   The bonds of friendship breaks and brotherhood,
> At variance still with Truth and Reason's light."
>
> —Trans. by Plumptre, II., p. 324.

In tracing now in literature this allegory of life we are led back
to a favorite classic of the dark ages, the *Psychomachia* of Prudentius,
the work of a Christian poet who flourished during the early part of
the fifth century, who is best known to the modern world for his
Hymns, repeated editions of which were issued during the fifteenth,
sixteenth and seventeenth centuries.

The *Psychomachia*[1] (Migne, *Patrol.* Ser. L. Vol. 60), written in
hexameters in ecclesiastical Latin, represents allegorically the con-
flict between the vices and virtues for the soul of man. The poem
is an expansion of an earlier work by the same writer entitled
Hamartigenia (Migne, *Patrol.*, Vol. 59, p. 1007) which is theological
in character, an explanation of the origin of evil in refutation of
the heresies of the day, notably that of Marcion, the dualist. The
Psychomachia is an expansion of a portion of the *Hamartigenia*,
where Anger, Superstition, Sadness, Strife and Luxury, war against
the soul. The allegory in the later poem is carried out into great
detail, being intended to represent the successive stages of Christian
conflict amid the temptations of the world. A first struggle is neces-
sary to overcome the worship of the pagan gods and to become a Chris-
tian. The next conflicts occur between Chastity and Lust, and between
Patience and Wrath, resulting in victory for the virtues. Pride then
attacks Humility, Righteousness, Temperance, Fasting, Shame and
Simplicity. But a pit is dug for Pride by Treachery and by Hope
the vice is slain. Then comes the battle between Luxury, who is
driven in a chariot by Love scattering flowers, and Temperance who
bears the standard of the cross. These Desires having been
vanquished Avarice with her train appears and attacks the Christian
under the guise of Frugality, but Almsgiving rescues the soul.
The last battle is with Heresy, who is slain, and the soul is at
peace.

For the popular theological confirmation of such a warfare one
may turn to St. Augustine's *City of God*, the latter part of which was
contemporary with the *Psychomachia* and written perhaps with the
poem in mind. The 19th Book of the *City of God* reveals the dis-
cords between the heavenly and earthly cities and in the tenth
chapter announcement is made of the rewards prepared for the
saints: "There the virtues shall no longer be struggling against
any vice or evil but shall enjoy the reward of victory, the eternal
peace which no adversary shall disturb."

[1] Cf. *Hist. of Latin Lit.*, G. A. Simcox, II., p. 360.

The *Psychomachia*,[1] sanctioned by the usages and doctrines of the church, became the model for a series of poems, generally moral and didactic in motive, called variously Bataille, Debat, Tournoiement, Disputoison and Pélérinage (v. *Lit. Fr. au Moyen Age*, par Gaston Paris, pp. 158, 159, 169, 227, 228). Among the later works of this class are the *Anticlaudianus* (12th century) by Alanus; *Débat du corps et d l'âme* (12th century); *Tournoiement d' Antéchrist* (1235) by Huon de Méri, which contains the battle between the Vices and Virtues under the leadership of Antichrist and Christ respectively; *Pélérinage de la vie humaine* (1330-5), by Guil. De Deguilville, a favorite work in England and the prototype of Bunyan's *Pilgrim's Progress;* certain of the *Bestiares* which satirize the vices of the time, as the *Renart le Nouvel* (1288), by Jacquemart Giélée, the animals of which, attacking the holy castle Maupertius, fight like the seven deadly sins with which they are for the first time mixed; episodes also found in the love poems, that series of Ars d'Amour which ended with the *Roman de la Rose*, as the battle for the rose in the *Roman* (*Lit. Fr.* G. Paris, p. 169).

Typical of these mediæval works that deal with the war of the vices and virtues is the *Anticlaudianus, sive de Officio Viri Boni et Perfecti*,[2] one of the most important books of the period, and one familiar to Lydgate and his fellow monks. It was written by Alanus de Insulis, during the second half of the 12th century, to oppose an invective of Claudian against Rufinus, the prime minister of Theodosius the Great, who was represented as the embodiment of all that is vicious, having been perverted by all the passions of hell. The poem is well summarized by Mr. Steele in his edition of Lydgate's *Secrees* (note, p. 109) whose outline is here quoted.

"Nature, perceiving its failure in bringing about perfection, decides to join in one being all the virtues and excellences possible. She therefore summons all these allegorical personages, and lays

---

[1] The *De Consolatione Philosophiæ* by Boethius may be mentioned as one other source of the battle *motif.* A French version of a part of this work is found in a poem called *De Fortune et de Felicite* which is said by Warton (II, p. 216) to be the source of the *Tournoyement de l'Antichrist* (c. 1228) by Huon de Méri, which contains a combat of the Vices and Virtues; this latter work was employed by Langland for the battle scene of the Antichrist at the close of *Piers the Plowman* (Skeat). Gaston Paris, however, thinks that most of these scenes of moral warfare may be referred to the *Psychomachia.*

[2] v. Migne, *Patrol.* t. 210, or *Anglo-Lat. Satir. Poets.* Roll's Series, ed. Wright. Cf. Lounsbury's *Chaucer Studies*, II, p. 348.

before them her plan. Prudence (Phronesis) and Reason remark
that none of them can give to man the highest of all gifts—a soul,
and that they must ask it from God. This mission is imposed on
them; they at first refuse it, but Concord gets them to accept it. A
car is made for them by the seven liberal arts, to which five horses
representing the senses are yoked. Grammar lays the framework,
Logic makes the axles of the wheels, Rhetoric adorns the frame with
gems and flowers of silver, Arithmetic, Music, Geometry and
Astronomy make the wheels, and Reason drives the chariot.

"'They pass through the air, the clouds, the home of the evil
spirits of the air, the spheres of the planets, and arrive at the firma-
ment, when Reason faints and the senses become useless. Theology
appears, and on the condition that Reason and the senses—except
that of hearing—are abandoned, offers to guide Phronesis. The
firmament, the empyrean heavens, the dwellings of saints, angels,
and the Mother of God are next described. Here Prudence faints,
but Faith revives her, and explains the mysteries of human destiny,
grace, etc.

"God now orders Intelligence to frame a model of a soul such as
was asked for, and making it, it is sent to Nature, who makes a body
which Harmony, Music and Arithmetic fit for and join to the soul.
All the allegorical divinities add a gift—even Nobility and Fortune
bring theirs—which Wisdom checks and moderates.

"But Hell learning of this new creation resolves to destroy it,
and Allecto unites all the vices against it. After a long battle the
new man puts them all to flight, and inaugurates upon the earth the
reign of Justice and Happiness."

The English books of Penance are many in number. Among
the theological works in prose which treat in whole or in part the
subject of the vices and virtues there are to be mentioned especially
a Homily by Ælfric (Thorpe's ed. Ælfric Soc. II, p. 219), *Old
English Homilies* (E. E. T. ed. Morris), the *Ancren Riwle* (Morton's
ed. p. 198-204), Dan Michel's *Ayenbite of Inwyt* (Morris' ed. p. 16),
Vices and Virtues (E. E. T. ed. Holthausen), Dan John Gaytryge's
Sermon on Shrift and the *Mirrour of St. Edmund (Relig. P.* ed.
Perry, p. 1, 15), a sermon by Wyclif (Works ed. by Arnold III., p.
225) and Chaucer's *Persones Tale*. Among the religious pieces in
verse which treat the theme are Aldhelm's *De Octo Principalibus
Vitiis* (in Latin, Migne, *Patrol.* Ser. Lat. 89. p. 282), the book of
Penance added to the *Cursor Mundi* (E. E. T. pt. V., p. 1524

et seq.), verses in *Religious Pieces* and in *Political Religious and Love Poems* (E. E. T. ed. Furnivall, p. 215), the *Manuel of Sins*, translated from a work by Bishop Grosseteste by Robert Mannyng, tracts in the Vernon MS. (ed. Horstmann, E. E. T.) entitled *How to Live Perfectly* No. XXXII.) and *The Spur of Love* (No. XXXV.), being translations from the popular *Speculum* of Edmund Rich, in the same MS. the *Dispute Between a Good Man and the Devil* (No. XXXVII.), *The Mirrour of the Periods of Man's Life* in *Hymns to the Virgin and Christ* (E. E. T. ed. Furnivall, p. 58), and a poem by William de Shoreham entitled *De Septem Mortalibus Peccatis* (Percy Soc., Vol. 28, p. 102), etc.

These treatises set forth the common theory of ethics as taught by the Latin Church. In classification and definition of the principal vices and virtues the works generally accord. There is occasional difference in the number, in the order of mention of the cardinals and in the names and number of the "branches" which spring from the parent stems.

The English Benedictine monks, following the older continental system, enumerate eight principal vices and virtues. Ælfric (Hom. ed. Thorpe, Vol. II, p. 219) sets in opposition, on the one hand the vices gifernys (greediness), galnyss (lust), gitsung (covetousness), weamet (anger) unrotnys (discontent), asolcennys *odde* æmelnys (sloth or aversion), idel gylp (vain-glory), and modignys (pride); on the other hand the healing virtues gemetegung (moderation), clænnys (chastity), cystignys (bounty) gedyld (patience), gastlicer blis (ghostly joy), anrædnys (steadfastness), lufe (love) and eadmodnys (humility).

In the mediæval treatises the number of each class is regularly seven. The classification in the Parable of the Castle of Love in the *Cursor Mundi* (ll. 10040–10052) is the following : pride, envie, glotony, lust, gredines, wreth, hevynes, with the corresponding virtues, buxumnes, charite, abstinens, chastite, liberality, mekenes, and gostly gladnes. In the *Cursor Mundi's* Book of Penance the list is : pride, envy, wra*þ*, slau*þe*, couatyse, glotori and drunkenhede, lichery ; and mekeness, loue, thalmodenes, gastely ioy, lele of hert and fre of gyft, abstinence and sobirte, chastite.

The *Ayenbite of Inwyt* has in one place (p. 16 and 123) prede, envye, wre*þe*, sleau*þe*, icinge (avarice) couaytise, glotounye, lecherie ; and for virtues the Pauline triad of beleave, hope and charite, and the cardinals of the "yealde philosofes" sley*þe* (prudence) temperance, streng$\not{p}$e, and dom (justice); in another place (p. 159) prede, enuye, felhede (hate), slacnes, scarsnes, lecherie, glotounye and boysamnes (humility) loue, mildenes, proues, larges, chastete, sobrete.

In the *Mirrour of St. Edmund* occur pryde, envy, ire, slouth, couetyse, glotony, lechery; and wysdom, vndirstandynge, consaile, stalworthenes, cunnynge, pete, drede of Godde, four of which are said to be needful for the active life and three for the contemplative life. Dan Jon Gaytryge's sermon recounts the regular vices and for virtues, trouthe, hope and charyte, the theological virtues, and ryghtwysenes, sleghte (prudence), strenghe, and methe (temperance), the natural virtues. The Latin titles occur in *Gyf me Lysens to Lyve in Ease* (*Pol., Rel., and Love P. E. E. T.* ed. Furnivall p. 215) superbia, invidia, ira, avoryssia, accidia, gula, luxuria, with the corresponding umylitas, carytas, amor cum paciencia, vigilate et orate, elymosina, abstinaunce, chastite. In the tract *How to Live Perfectly* (Vernon MS. E. E. T. No. 32) the remedies for sin are the Seven Blessings of the Gospel and the medicine for the sins are Wisdom, Understanding, Strength, Counsel, Wit, Pity, Fear of God.

Chaucer's list in the *Persones Tale* is pride, envye, ire, accidie, avarice, glotenye, leccherie; and humilite, love, mansuetude and pacience, strengthe, misericorde and pite, abstinence, and chastite. Gower employs the same classification in his *Confessio Amantis.*

The most original treatise on the theme is perhaps Wyclif's tract on the *Seven Deadly Sins* (*Works*, ed. Arnold III, p. 119). The cardinals are the conventional ones but the condemnation of the practical sins of the clergy and people is from the Lollard point of view. The sins have this origin: "$\not{p}$e fende, and $\not{p}$o worlde, and monnis owne flesche, stiren hym to couyte ageynes God's wille. And so ich one takes at other, and $\not{p}$ese make seven. Pride, envye, and wrath ben synnes of $\not{p}$o fende; wrathe, slouthe, and avarice ben synnes of $\not{p}$e world; avarice, and glotenye, and $\not{p}$o synne of lechorye ben synnes of $\not{p}$o flesche" (p. 121). These are thus defined: "Pride is wicked liif of a monnis hyenesse;" "Envye is unordynel wille of mon to his neghtbore;" "Wrathe is unskillful wille of vengeaunce;" Slouthe is "slouthe in God's service;" "Covetise is "avarice of worldly godis;" "Glutonye falles $\not{p}$en to mon, when he takes mete or drink more $\not{p}$en profites to his soule;" "Lechorye stondis in $\not{p}$is $\not{p}$ing, $\not{p}$at mon mysusis lymes or powers of

his body, þat God haves ordeyned unto men for his kyndely gen-
drure" (p. 121 *et seq*).

In the more imaginative treatises various mystical and allegorical
features appear. Chaucer's Parson pictures the life of God's chosen
as a pathway filled with stumbling blocks. In the *Mirrour of the
Periods of Man's Life* a man is tempted from birth to age. In *Gyf
me Lysens to Lyve in Ease* the sins are as wounds to be healed by
medicines in the form of plasters and herbs, the remedial virtues.
In *Piers the Plowman* the sins are the muck with which Haukyn, the
active man, has soiled his coat (Pas. xiii). Often sin is described
as a tree with branches and twigs as in the *Ayenbite of Inwyt*. When
personified the sins may come as warriors in armor on horse or a
foot, as in the Parable of the Castle of Love in the *Cursor Mundi*, or
as in Lydgate's *Assembly of Gods*, Spenser's *Faery Queene*, Fletcher's
Purple Island and Bunyon's *Holy War*. In the moral play,
The World and the Child, the vices are exhibited as seven kings.
Chaucer in the "A B C" laments that he is chased by "theves
seven." Dunbar pictures the sins as dancers down in hell. Gower
assigns the vices to a lover. Langland describes the virtues as
"sisters," Pride alone among the vices being personified as a woman.
Dan Michel declares Pride to be the devil's own daughter. In the
Sawles Warde the cardinal virtues are the daughters of the lord of
the house. In the *Ancren Riwle* each sin is symbolized by an ani-
mal: Pride by a Lion, Envy by an Adder, Wrath by a Unicorn,
Lechery by a Scorpion, Avarice by a Fox, Gluttony by a Sow,
Sloth by a Bear. The *Ayenbite of Inwyt* presents most mystical
features: St. John in a vision saw a beast come out of the sea having
a leopard's body, a bear's feet, a lion's throat, and it had seven
heads and ten horns. This beast, explains Michel, betokeneth the
devil who cometh from the sea of hell; its guile is denoted by the
leopard's spots, his strength by the bear's feet, his cruelty by the
lion's throat. The seven heads are the seven deadly sins and the
ten horns the guilts of the commandments.

Without exception these writings accord in assigning to Pride
the first place among the sins. Pride, said Ælfric, is "ord and ende
ælces yfeles: se geworhte englas to deoflum and ælere synne anginn
is modignys." Pride in the *Cursor Mundi* is the chief sin that fights
against Love: it is said that Lucifer fell by pride, that it is fouler than
any devil in hell. *The Ayenbite of Inwyt* pictures Pride as the devil's
own daughter, the sin of Lucifer and the angels, the first to assail

our Lord and the last to abandon Him. In *Gyf me Lysens to Lyve in Ease*, Pride is the first wound "more bytter than ever was gall." By Wyclif Pride is considered to be the chief sin, being accorded to the Fiend. Said Gower "Pride is the heaved of all sinne" (I, p. 153). Barclay, at the beginning of the period of the Reformation, wrote of Pride that it is

> " A vyce so moche abhomynable
> That it surmountyth without any fable
> All other vyces in furour and vylenes
> And of all synne is it rote and maystres. "
>
> —*Ship of Fools*, II, p. 159.

So Pride leads the dance of the sins in hell in Dunbar's poem. It was the first to receive punishment in the *Shepheard's Kalendar*. It cast Satan and the rebel angels out from heaven in Milton's *Paradise Lost*. With Shakespeare it appears as ambition :

> " By that sin fell the angels." *Henry VIII*, III, 2, 441.

The consensus of mankind seems then to be written by Sir Thomas Browne that Pride is "the first and father sin, not only of man but of the devil ; a vice whose name is comprehended in a monosyllable, but in its nature not circumscribed with a world (Works, II, p. 435).

Turning from the theological treatises on the moralities, and taking up the works of real artistic value wherein the imagination of writers was truly kindled by a perception of the poetic capacities of the theme of battle and pilgrimage, we enter a most important field, perhaps to be called, when considering the actual epical and dramatic development of the theme, the most important field in early English literature. The many chivalric Romances would be included in the survey, perhaps also the earlier *Guthlac*. With a more specific treatment is the long series beginning with Bishop Grosseteste's *Chateau d'amour*, which received several translations at the hands of later writers, continuing in the parable of the Castle of Love in the *Cursor Mundi*, the English *Bestiares*, the Moral-plays, Langland's *Piers the Plowman*, Gower's *Confessio Amantis*, perhaps the *Romaunt of the Rose*, Lydgate's *Assembly of Gods*, Hawes's *Pastime of Pleasure*, Dunbar's *Dance of the Sins*, Barclay's *Ship of Fools* and *Mirrour of Good Manners*, the anonymous *Shepheard's Kalendar*, religious pieces of the type of the *Mirrour of the Periods of Man's Life*, Spenser's *Faery Queene*, John Day's *Peregrinatio Scholastica*, Bernard's *Isle of Man*, and, last of these stirring allegories, Fletcher's *Purple Island*

(1633), and Bunyan's *Pilgrim's Progress* (1678) and *Holy War* (1682).

In almost the earliest teaching on the subject of sin, in Ælfric's Homily on Midlent Sunday (ed. Thorpe, II, 212) the Christian life is described as a warfare. In the homilies the word commonly used for Virtues was *mihtan* (*Old-Eng. Hom.* I, p. 105), it being explained that by God's help, if fight were keen, the devilish sins would be overcome (p. 107).[1] The *Psychomachia* of Prudentius was known to the English monks as it is referred to by Beda in his *De Ratione Metrica* as the book "quem de virtutum vitiorumque pugna heroico carmine composuit." There is an echo of its triumph in *Guthlac* where the hero meets in deadly combat with Satan and his troops of sin-smiths that roar and rage like wild beasts. In the manner of the *Psychomachia* Aldhelm wrote in Latin his *De Octo Principalibus Vitiis* (Migne, *Patrol.* Lat. Ser., 89, p. 282) arraying the opposing forces in battle form.

For this warfare man was given the gift of Power. This is a Virtue described by Dan Michel (*Ayenbite of Inwyt*, p. 169) as a tree with seven boughs which betokened the seven battles that the Christian must wage. This Christian battle is again likened by Michel to the gladiatorial fights at Rome, wherein those who desired fame must overcome all who are sent against them by the master of the field ; the holy Christ is the master who suffers no one to be tried above his strength. Bishop Grosseteste, employing the chivalric idea, figures Love as a strong castle standing high on a polished rock. The castle is enclosed by four stone walls and a deep moat, and fortified with four towers and seven barbicans. A clear, all healing well springs from the central tower. Within the tower is a brilliant throne. Being interpreted, the castle is a shield to the human soul. The rock is Mary's heart. The four towers are the cardinal Virtues, Strength, Skill, Rightfulness, and Temperance. The seven barbicans are the seven virtues that receive the attacks of the deadly sins. The well is Mary's mercy. The throne is Christ. This figuration, so beautiful in its symbolism, caught the fancy of succeeding writers. The castle betokens refuge and strength and victory. As a symbol of the Virgin Mary it is employed in the *Cursor Mundi*, in the *Abbaye of Saynte Spirite* (*Relig. Pieces*, ed. Perry, E. E. T. p. 49) in a miracle play entitled *Originale de Sancta Maria Magdalena* (v. Collier, *Hist. Dr. P.* II, p. 153–6) and in Lydgate's *Life of St. Mary*.

[1] Virtue is also called *thewe* in Gaytryge's *Sermon*, p. 10.

In Langland's vision the tower on the toft, partly drawn from Grosseteste's *Chateau d'amour*, is the abode of Truth or God the Father (v. Prol. l. 14; Pass. v. ll. 594 *et seq*).   Grace is the doorward there and seven sisters the porters of the posterns, Abstenence, Humilite, . Charite, Chestite, Pacience, Pees, and Largenesse.   Mercy, or the Virgin Mary, mediates between the sinful ones at the gates and Christ and the Father.   The chief battle in Langland's poem is that waged against the church of Unity (Pass. xx) by Antichrist and seven giants.   Sloth and Avarice lead the assault.   Peace bars the gates.   But the virtues sleep and Conscience is forced to become a pilgrim over the world, seeking the Plowman.   In a 13th century homily, *Sawles Warde*, man is represented as a castle inhabited by Wit, his wife Will, five servants, the five senses, and four daughters, the cardinal virtues.

Among the Moral-plays the *Castle of Perseverance* well illustrates the prevailing conception.   The play was performed during the reign of Henry VI., but it is thought from its completeness that it must have had predecessors of the same kind (Collier, *Hist. Dr. P.*, II. p. 200 *et seq*.).   Humanum Genus has been conducted by Good Angels to the Castle of Perseverance, which is under the wardship of the Seven Virtues.   The Seven Deadly Sins attack the castle but are repulsed by the Virtues, being made "blak and blo" by the beating of roses which Charity and Patience fling from the walls. "Drery Death" alone has power over Humanum Genus whose soul is at last saved by the grace of Deity.

The later development of the theme needs only to be mentioned here.   The *Faery Queene* was a natural evolution of the mediæval chivalric idea.   Though the theological dogmatism is abandoned mankind is yet in the wilderness of this world, beset by sins on every side.   In Book II. there is set forth the struggle of the Soul against its enemies.   In Mammon's Cave the World is overcome. Arthur prevails against the Devil in the person of Maleger, the captain of the vices.   Guyon, in the bower of Acrasia, resists the temptations of the Flesh.   The ninth canto shadows forth the struggle of the Soul within the body.   Milton and Bunyan picture the redemptive system from the Protestant point of view.   For the first time in Milton's *Paradise Regained* the struggle is pictured as being withdrawn within the self — this is the beginning of the modern treatment of the theme.   But Bunyan writes directly in the manner of the "old fables" that dealt with "Mansoul's wars."

One of the last of these microcosmic encounters and the most ingenious and involved of all, is the *Purple Island*, published in 1633 by the poet Fletcher, who is called by Francis Quarles "the Spenser of this age." The Purple Island is Man. Its prince is Intellect. The Senses constitute a pentarchy. Cosmos captains the rout of Vices that attack the Island. The Virtues defend and conquer (v. cantos vii–viii, ix–x, xi–xii).

Considering the possibilities of Lydgate's theme it is to be regretted that he did not grapple with it more successfully. His work exhibits intelligence, some degree of imagination, but is devoid of passion and æsthetic apprehension. He marshaled numberless hosts, his design was so comprehensive as to include the upper firmament, the lowest hell, and the earth and man, yet the *Assembly of Gods* is almost the least of the poems attempting to portray the Holy War.

THE ASSEMBLY OF GODS.

By Don John Lydgate.

*Here foloweth the Interpretacion of the names of goddys & goddesses as ys rehersyd in þis tretyse folowyng as poetes wryte:

Phebus:	ys as moche to sey as þe Sonne.	Ceres:	Goddesse of Corne.
Apollo:	ys the same or ellys God of Lyght.	Cupido:	God of Loue.
		Othea:	Goddes of Wysdom.
Morpheus:	Shewer of Dremes.	Fortune:	þe variaunt Goddesse.
Pluto:	God of Hell.	Pan:	God of Shepardes.
Mynos:	Iuge of Hell.	Isys:	Goddesse of Frute.
Cerberus:	Porter of Hell.	Neptunus:	God of the See.
Eolus:	þe Wynde or God of þe Eyre.	Mynerue:	Goddesse of Batayll, or of
Diana:	Goddesse of Woode & Chace.		Haruest.
Phebe:	þe Mone or Goddes of Watyres.	Bachus:	God of Wyne.
Aurora:	Goddes of þe Morow or the Spryng of the Day.	Mercurius:	God of Langage.
		Venus:	Goddesse of Loue.
Mars:	God of Batayll.	Discorde:	Goddesse of Debate and
Iubyter:	God of Wysdom.		Stryfe.
Iuno:	Goddesse of Rychesse.	Attropos:	Dethe.
Saturne:	God of Colde.		

I

Whan Phebus in the Crabbe had nere hys cours ronne   1
  And toward the leon his iourne gan take,
To loke on Pictagoras speere I had begonne,
  Syttyng all solytary alone besyde a lake,   4
  Musyng on a maner how that I myght make
    Reason & Sensualyte in oon to acorde;
    But I cowde nat bryng about that monacorde.   7

When Phebus had nearly run his course in the Crab, alone beside a lake, I was musing how I might make Reason and Sensuality to accord.

* Omitted in B. C follows the Camb. MS., closing: Here endyth the Interpretacion of the names of Goddis and Goddesses as is rehercyd in thys treatyse folowynge.

2

For long er I myght, slepe me gan oppresse   8

In heaviness
I fell asleep.

So ponderously, I cowde make noon obstacle,

In myne heede was fall suche an heuynesse,

I was fayne to drawe to myn habytacle,   11

Morpheus
enters and
takes me by
the sleeve,

To rowne with a pylow me semyd best tryacle,

So leyde I me downe my dyssese to releue.

Anone came in Morpheus & toke me by the sleue. 14

3

And as I so lay half in a traunse,   15

Twene slepyng and wakyng he bad me aryse,

bidding me
arise and
attend the
Court of
Minos.

For he seyde I must yeue attendaunse

To the gret Court of Mynos, the iustyse.   18

Me nought auaylyd ayene hym to sylogyse:

For hit ys oft seyde by hem that yet lyues

He must nedys go that the deuell dryues.   21

4

When I sy no bettyr but I must go   22

I seyde I was redy at hys commaundment,

I obey and
go with him
towards the
parliament of
Pluto and
Minos.

Whedyr that he wold me leede to or fro.

So vp I aroose and forthe with hym went,   25

Tyll he had me brought to the parlyament,

Where Pluto sate and kept hys estate,

And with hym Mynos, the Iuge desperate.   28

5

But as we thedyrward went by the way,   29

I hym besought hys name me to tell.

On the way I
ask him his
name. He
replies,
"Morpheus."

"Morpheus," he seyde, "thow me call may."

"A syr." seyd I, "than where do ye dwell,   32

In heuen or in erthe outher elles in hell?"

"Where do you
dwell?" He
answers, "in
Fantasy."

"Nay." he seyde. "myñ abydyng most comonly

Ys in a lytyll corner callyd Fantasy."   35

6

And as sone as he these wordys had sayd,   36

Cerberus, the porter of hell, with hys cheyne

Having arrived
in Hell,
Cerberus, the
porter, brings
thither Eolus
in chains,
charged by
Neptune and
Diana with
traitorous
action.

Brought theder Eolus in raggys euyll arayd,

Agayn whom Neptunus and Diana dyd compleyne 39

Seying thus, "O Mynos, thow Iuge souereyne,

Yeue thy cruell iugement ageyn thys traytour soo

That we may haue cause to preyse thy lord Pluto." 42

7

Then was there made a proclamasion,   43
  In Plutoys name com*m*aundyd silence
Vppon the peyne of strayte correccion,
  That Diana and Neptun*us* myght haue audience   46
  To declare heȓ greefe of the gret offence
    To theym done by Eolus, wheron they compleynyd.
    And to begyñ Diana was constreynyd.   49

Silence is proclaimed by Pluto that Neptune and Diana may declare their grievance.

Diana, first, begins to speak,

8

Whyche thus began as ye shall here   50
  Seying in thys wyse, "O thow lord Pluto,
W*ith* thy Iuge Mynos, syttyng w*ith* the in fere,
  Execute youȓ fury vppon Eolus so   53
  Accordyng to the offence that he to me hath do,
    That I haue no cause forther to apele,
    Whiche yef I do shall nat be for youȓ wele.   56

demanding from Minos the execution of fury upon Eolus,

9

"Remembre furst howe I a goddesse pure   57
  Ouer all desertys, forestes and chases,
Haue take the guydyng and vndyr my cure.
  Thys trayto*ur* Eolus, hath many of my places   60
  Dystroyed w*ith* hys blastes and dayly me manaces.
    Where any wood ys he shall make hyt pleyn
    Yef he to hys lyberte may resorte ayeyñ.   63

the traitor, who had destroyed her forests,

10

"The grettest trees that any man may fynde   64
  In forest to shade the deere for her comfort,
He breketh hem asondre or rendeth hem roote & rynde
  Out of the erthe—thys ys hys dysport,   67
  So that the deere shall haue no resort
    W*ith*yn short tyme to no man*er* shade ;
    Wheȓ thorough the game ys lykly to fade.   70

breaking and uprooting the trees, wherefore the deer are without shelter.

11

"Whyche to my name a reproche syngler   71
  Shuld be for eu*er* whyle the world last,
And to all the godd*es* an hygh dyspleseȓ
  To see the game so dystroyed by hys blast ;   74
  Wherfore a remedy puruey in hast,
    And let hym be punysshyd aftyr hys offence.
    Consydeȓ the cryme and yeue youȓ sentence."   77

This brings reproach to Diana and displeasure to all the gods, and requires punishment.

12

And when thus Diana had made her compleynt   78
  To Mynos, the Iuge, in Plutoys presence,

Neptune next
rehearses his
complaint to
Minos.
Came forthe Neptunus, with vysage pale & feynt,
  Desyryng of fauour to haue audyence,   81
  Saying thus, " Pluto to thy magnyfycence
    I shall reherse what thys creature
    Eolus hath dooñ to me out of mesure.   84

13

"Thow knowest well that I haue the charge   85
  Ouer all the see, and therof god I am,
No shyp may sayle, keruell, boot ner barge,

For himself
he claims
jurisdiction
over the sea,
  Gret karyk, nor hulke with any lyuyng man,   88
  But yef he haue my safe condyte than.
    Who me offendeth wythyn my iurysdiccion
    Oweth to submyt hym to my correccion.   91

14

" But in as mekyll as hit ys now soo   92
  That ye hym here haue as your prysonere,
I shall yow shew my compleynt loo.
  Wherfore I pray yow that ye woll hit here,   95
  And let hym nat escape out of your daungere,
    Tyll he haue made full seethe and recompence
    For hurt of my name thorough thys gret offence. 98

15

" Furst, to begynne, thys Eolus hath oft   99
  Made me to retourne my course agayñ nature

but Eolus
causes him to
turn against
his course,
With hys gret blastys, when he hath be a loft,
  And chargyd me to labour ferre out of mesure,   102
  That hit was gret merueyle how I myght endure.
    The [foom] of my swet, wyll hit testyfy,
    That on the see bankes lythe betyn full hy.   105

16

" Secundly, where as my nature ys   106
  Bothe to ebbe and flowe and so my course to kepe,

and ebb and
flow out of his
season.
Oft of myñ entent hath he made me mys.
  Where as I shuld haue fyllyd dykes depe   109
  At a full watyr I might nat thedyr crepe
    Before my seson came to retorne ayeyne,
    And then went I fastyr than I wold certeyne.   112

17

"Thus he hath me dryuen ayen̄ myn entent   113   This Eolus had done to his dis-honour.
And contrary to my course naturall.
Where I shuld haue be he made me be absent
  To my gret dyshonouꝛ, & in especiall   116
  Oo thyng he vsyd that worst was of all,
    For where as I my sauegard grauntyd,
    Ay in that cost he comonly hauntyd.   119

18

"Of verrey pure malyce and of sylfe wyll,   120   Out of very mallice Eolus destroyed those to whom he had granted protec-tion,
  Theym to dystroy in dyspyte of me
To whom I promysyd, bothe in good and yll,
  To be heꝛ protectouꝛ in aduersyte,   123
  That to theym shuld fall opon the see,
    And euyn sodenly, er they coude beware,
    With a sodeyn pyry, he lappyd hem in care.   126

19

"And full oft sythe with hys boystous blast,   127   or else brought them to wreck; wherefore his name is held in dishonor.
  Er they myght be ware he drofe hym on the sande.
And other whyle he brak top seyle and mast,
  Whyche causyd theym to perysshe eꝛ they came to lande.
  Then cursyd they the tyme that euer they me fande.
    Thus among the pepyll lost ys my name
    And so by hys labouꝛ put I am to shame.   133

20

"Consydre thys mateꝛ and ponder my cause;   134   The great of-fense requires a grievous pun-ishment.
  Tendre my compleynt as rygouꝛ requyreth;
Shew forthe youꝛ sentence with a breef clause.
  I may nat long tary, the tyme fast expyreth,   137
  The offence ys gret, wherfore hyt desyreth
    The more greuous peyne and hasty iugement.
    For offence dooñ wylfully woll noon auysment." 140

21

And, when the god Pluto awhyle had hym bethought, 141   Pluto advises Minos to judge fairly between the parties.
He rownyd with Mynos to know what was to do.
Then he seyd opynly, "Loke thow fayle nought
  Thy sentence to yeue without favouꝛ so,   144
  Lyke as thow hast herde the causys meuyd the to;
    And so euenly dele twene these partyes tweyn,
    That nooñ of hem haue cause on the other compleyñ."

22

Minos asks for
further
charges,

Then seyd Mynos full indyfferently,   148
  To Dyane & Neptunus, " Ys ther any more
That ye wyll declare agayñ hym opynly ?"
    "Nay in dede," they seyde,"we kepe nooñ in store. 151
    We haue seyde ynough to punysshe hym sore.
      Yef ye in thys matyr be nat parciall,
      Remembre your name was wont to be egall."   154

23

and wishes to
hear what
Eolus can say
for himself.

"Well then," seyd Mynos, " now let vs here   155
  What thys boystous Eolus for hymself can sey,
For here, *prima facie*, to vs he doth apere
  That he hath offendyd—no man can sey nay.   158
  Wherfore thow Eolus, *with*out more delay,
    Shape vs an answer to thyne accusement.
    And ellys I most *pro*cede opon thy iugement." 161

24

A messenger
enters from
Apollo inviting
the gods to a
banquet and

And euyn as Eolus was onwarde to haue seyde   162
  For hys excuse, came yn a messynger
Fro god Apollo to Pluto, and hym prayde
  On hys behalfe that he *with*out daungere   165
  Wold to hym come & bryng *with* hym [in] feere
    Diane & Neptun*us* on to hys banket;
    And yef they dysdeynyd hym*s*ylf he wold hem fet. 168

25

requests the
suspension of
judgment upon
Eolus, if Diana
and Neptune
should be
therewith
content.

Moreou*er* he seyde to the god, Apollo   169
  Desyryd to haue respyte of the iugement
Of Eolus, bothe of Mynos & Pluto.
  So Dyane and Neptunus were ther*with* content, 172
  And yef they were dysposyd to assent
    That he myght come vnto hys pr*e*sence,
    He hit desyryd to know hys offence.   175

26

The Court is
therefore dis-
missed.

"What sey ye herto," seyd Pluto to hem tweyn,   176
  "Wyll ye bothe assent that hit shall be thus?"
" Ye," seyde the goddesse, " for my part certeyn."
  "And I also," seyde thys Neptunus.   179
  "I am well plesyd," quod thys Eolus.
    And when they had a whyle thus togedyr spoke,
    Pluto co*m*maundyd the court to be broke.   182

27

And then togedyᵣ went they in fere,
  Pluto & Neptunus ledyng the goddesse,
Whom folowyd Cerberus with hys prysonere.
  And alther last with gret heuynesse
  Came I & Morpheus to the forteresse
    Of the god Apollo vnto hys banket,
    Where many goddys & goddesses met.

183 Pluto, Neptune and Diana, Cerberus and Eolus, Morpheus and I,
186 come to the palace of Apollo, where many gods and goddesses are met.
189

28

When Apollo sye that they were come,
  He was ryght glad and prayed hem to syt.
"Nay," seyd Diane, "thys ys all and some.
  Ye shall me pardone, I shall nat syt yet.
  I shall fyrst know why Eolus abyte
    And what execucion shall on hym be do
    For hys offence." "Well," seyd Apollo,

190
Apollo welcomes them with gladness.
193 Diana refuses to sit until judgment is pronounced on Eolus.
196

29

"Madame, ye shall haue all your plesere,
  Syth that hit woll none other wyse be.
But furst I yow pray let me the mater here,
  Why he ys brought in thys perplexyte."
  "Well," seyde Pluto. "that shall ye sone se."
    And gan to declare euen by and by
    Bothe her compleyntes ordynatly.

197
200 Pluto recounts the complaints against Eolus,
203

30

And when Apollo had herd the report
  Of Pluto, in a maner smylyng he seyde,
"I see well, Eolus, thow hast small comfort
  Thy sylf to excuse; thow mayst be dysmayde
  To here so gret compleyntes ayene the layde.
    That natwithstandyng, yef thow can sey ought
    For thyne owne wele, sey and tary nought."

204
207 who is requested to give his excuses.
210

31

"Forsothe," seyd Eolus, "yef I had respyte,
  Her to an answere cowde I counterfete.
But to haue her grace more ys my delyte.
  Wherfore, I pray you all for me entrete,
  That I may, by your request, her good grace gete.
    And what pyne or greef ye for me prouyde,
    Without any grogyng I shall hit abyde."

211 Eolus speaks suing for the grace of Diana.
214
217

32

Apollo pleads
for Eolus that
the goddess
show pity, on
account of his
great sorrow,

"Lo, good Madame," seyd god Apollo.   218

"What may he do more but sew to *your* grace.

Beholde how the teares from hys eyen go.

Hit ys satysfaccion half for hys trespase.   221

Now gloryous goddesse shewe *your* pyteous face

To thys poore pryson*er* at my request.

All we for *your* honou*r* thynke thus ys best.   224

33

and assures
her if she for-
give Eolus and
he afterwards
rebel that for
every tree
destroyed a
hundred shall
grow

"And yef hit lyke yow to do in thys wyse,   225

And to foryeue hym clerely hys offense,

Oon thyng suerly I will yow promyse.

Yef he eft rebelle and make resystence   228

Or dysobey vnto *your* sentence,

For eu*er*y tree that he maketh fall.

Out of the erthe an hundred aryse shall.   231

34

for the pro-
tection of
game.

"So that *your* game shall nat dyscrese   232

For lak of shade, I dar vndyrtake."

"Well, sy*r* Apollo," seyde she than. "woll I cese

Of all my rancou*r* and mery *with* yow make."   235

And then god Neptun*us* of hys mater spake,

Diana grants
release.

Seying thus, "Apollo, though Diana hym relese,

Yet shall he su to me to haue hys pese."   238

35

"A," seyde Apollo, "ye wend I had foryete   239

Yow for my lady Diane, the goddesse.

For Neptune's
case Phebe is
accepted as
arbiter.

Nay. thynke nat so, for I woll yow entrete

As well as hyr *with*out long processe.   242

Wyll ye agre that Pheb[e] *your* mastresse

May haue the guydyng of *your* varyaunce?"

"I shall abyde," quod he, "her ordynaunce."   245

36

Apollo prays
the gods and
goddesses to
fall to the
banquet.

"Well then," quod Apollo. "I pray you godd*es* all.   246

And goddesses eke. that be heere pr*e*sent,

That ye compaygnably wyll aboorde fall."

Athena
requests that
due order be
preserved.

"Nay then," seyde Othea. "hit ys nat conuenyent. 249

A dew ordre in eu*er*y place ys expedyent

To be had. wherfore ye may nat let

To be *your* owne marchall at *your* owne banket." 252

37

And when Apollo sy hit wold nooñ other be,   253
    He callyd to hym Aurora, the goddesse,
And seyde, " Thowgh ye wepe yet shal ye before me
    Ay kepe youꝶ course & put youꝶ sylf in [presse]." 256
So he heꝶ set furst at hys owne messe,
    With heꝶ moyst clothes with teares all be spreynt.
The medewes in May shew therof heꝶ compleynt. 259

First, with Apollo, is set Aurora, wet with morning tears.

38

Next hyꝶ sate Mars, myghty god & strong,   260
    With a flame of fyre enuyround all about,
A crowne of yron on hys hede, a spere in hys hand.
Hyt semyd by hys chere as he wold haue fought.   263
And next vnto hym, as I perceue mought,
    Sate the goddese Diana, in a mantell fyne
    Of blak sylke, purfylyd with poudryd hermyne, 266

Next, Mars, environed with flame, an iron crown upon his head, a spear in his hand.

With him is Diana, in a mantle of silk and ermine.

39

Lyke as she had take the mantell & the ryng.   267
    And next vnto hyꝶ, arayed royally,
Sate the good Iupyter, in hys demenyng
    Full sad, and wyse he semyd sykerly.   270
    A crowñ of tynne stoode on hys hede.
       And that I recorde of all philosophres
       That lytyll store of coyne kepe in heꝶ cofres.   273

Jupiter sits next, sad and wise, wearing a crown of tin.

40

Ioynyd to hym in syttyng next ther was   274
    The goddesse Iuno, full rychely beseene
In a sercote that shone as bryght as glas,
    Of goldsmythes werke with spanglys wrought be-dene.
    Of royall rychesse wantyd she noone I wene.
       And next by her sate the god Saturne,
       That oft sythe causeth many ooñ to morne.   280

With him is Juno, dressed in royal richness.

Saturn next,

41

But he was clad me thought straungely,   281
    For of frost & snow was all his aray;
In hys hand he helde a fawchon all blody.
    Hyt semyd by hys chere as he wold make a fray.   284
    A bawdryk of isykles about hys nek gay
       He had, and aboue an hygh on hys hede,   [leede.
       Cowchyd with hayle stonys, he weryd a crowne of

arrayed in frost and snow, a bloody falchion in his hand, a ring of icicles about his neck, a crown of lead on high.

42

With him sits
Ceres in a gar-
ment of sack-
cloth embroid-
ered with
sheaves and
sickles.

And next in ordre was set by hys syde　　　　288
　　Ceres, the goddesse, in a garment
Of sak clothe made with sleues large & wyde,
　　Embrowderyd with sheues & sykelys bent.　　291
　　Of all maner greynes she sealyd the patent,
　　In token that she was the goddesse of corne.
　　Olde poetys sey she bereth the heruest horne.　294

43

Next Cupid,
dressed in
gallant array
with jewels, so
that the palace
shone. He
sits embracing
Ceres with one
arm.

Then was there set the god Cupido,　　　　295
　　All fresshe & galaunt & costlew in aray.
With ouches & rynges he was beset so
　　The paleys therof shone as though hit had be day.　298
　　A kerchyef of plesaunce stood ouer hys helme ay.
　　The goddesse Ceres he lookyd in the face
　　And with oon arme he hyr dyd enbrace.　　301

44

With him is
Athena, clad
in purple with
a pearly crown.

Next to Cupido in ordyr by and by,　　　　302
　　Of worldly wysdom, sate the forteresse
Callyd Othea, chyef grounde of polycy,
　　Rewler of knyghthode, of Prudence the goddese.　305
　　Clad all in purpur was she more & lesse,
　　Safe on her hede a crowne ther stood,
　　Cowchyd with perles, oryent, fyne and good.　　308

45

Pluto next,
environed in
mist and
clothed in a
smoky net,
smelling of
fire and sul
phur.

And next to her was god Pluto set,　　　　309
　　With a derke myst enuyrond all aboute,
Hys clothyng was made of a smoky net.
　　Hys colour was, bothe withyn & withoute,　　312
　　Foule, derke & dymme; hys eyen gret & stoute.
　　Of fyre and sulphure all hys odour wase :
　　That wo was me whyle I behelde hys fase.　　315

46

Fortune sits
with him; she
is dressed
gaudily in
green.

Fortune, the goddesse, with her party face　　316
　　Was vnto Pluto next in ordre set.
Varyaunt she was ; ay in short space
　　Hyr whele was redy to turne without let.　　319
　　Hyr gowne was of gawdy grene chamelet,
　　Chaungeable of sondry dynerse colowres,
　　To the condycyons accordyng of hyr shoures.　322

47

And by heᵹ sate though he vnworthy were,　　323
　The rewde god Pan, of sheperdys the gyde,
Clad in russet frese, & breched lyke a bere,
　With a gret tar box hangyng by hys syde.　326
　　A shepecrook in hys hand he sparyd for no pryde.
　　　And at hys feete lay a prykeryd curre.
　　　He ratelyd in the throte as he had the murre.　329

By her is god
Pan dressed
rudely, a tar-
box by his
side, a sheep-
crook in his
hand,

at his feet a
cur.

48

Ysys, the goddesse, bare hym company.　　330
　For at the table next she sat by hys syde,
In a close kyrtyll enbrowderyd curyously,
　With braunches & leues, brood, large & wyde,　333
　Grene as any gresse in the somertyde.
　　Of all maner frute she had the gouernaunce.
　　Of sauerys odoryferous was her sustynaunce.　336

Isys keeps him
company in a
dress embroid-
ered with
leaves and
branches.

49

Next hyr was then god Neptunus set.　　337
　He sauoryd lyke a fyssheᵹ—of hym I spake before.
Hyt semyd by hys clothes as they had be wet.　[score.
Aboute hym, in hys gyrdyll stede, hyng fysshes many a
Of hys straunge aray meruelyd I sore.
　A shyp with a toppe & scyle was hys crest.
　Me thought he was gayly dysgysyd at that fest. 343

Neptune sits
next.　Fishes
hang at his
girdle.　A ship
is his crest.

50

Then toke Mynerue, the goddesse, her sete　　344
　Joyntly to Neptunus, all in curas clad,
Gauntlettes on hyr handys, & sabatouns on hyr fete.
　She loked euer about as though she had be mad.　347
　An hamer and a sythe on her hede she had.
　　She weryd ii bokelers, ooñ by her syde,　[pryde.
　　That other ye wote where; thys was all her　350

With him sits
Minerva, clad
in armor, a
hammer and
scythe upon
her head.

51

Then came the good Bachus, and by heᵹ set hym downe,
　Holdyng in hys hande a cup full of wyne.
Of grene vyne leues he weryd a ioly crowne.
　He was clad in clustres of grapes good and fyne.　354
　A garland of yuy he chase for hys sygne;
　　On hys hede he had a thredebare kendall hood;
　　A gymlot and a fauset theᵹopon stood.　　357

Bacchus sits
by her, clad in
grape clusters,
a cup of wine
in his hand.
His sign is a
garland of
yew.

52

With him sits
pale Phebe,
boasting of her
rule.
Next hym sate Pheb[e], *with* hyſ colo*ur* pale.   358

 Fat she was of face but of complexyon feynt.

She seyde she rewlyd Neptun*us* and made hy*m* to avale,

And ones in the moneth w*ith* Phebus was she meynt.

Also ne were she Ceres were ateynt.

  Thus she sate & tolde the myght of hyſ nature.

 And on hyr hede she weryd a crowne of syluyr pure.

53

Mercury seats
himself next, a
god of golden
tongue. In
his hand he
has a box of
quicksilver.
Ioyntly to her M*er*curius tooke hys see   365

 As came to hys course — wytnesse the zodyak.

He had a gyldyn tong, as fyll for hys degree.

 In eloquence of langage he passyd all the pak,   368

For in hys talkyng no man cowde fynde lak.

 A box w*ith* quyksyluer he had in hys hand,

 Multyplyers know hit well in eu*er*y land.   371

54

His companion
is Venus,
bright of
chere, dressed
curiously, her
hair like gold
wire.
By him sate Dame Venus w*ith* colouſ crystallyne,   372

 Whoos long here shone as wyre of goold bryght.

Cryspe was her skyñ, heſ eyen colu*m*byne,

 Rauysshyd myñ hert her chere was so lyght.   375

Patronesse of plesaunce, be namyd well se myght.

 A smokke was her wede, garnysshyd curyously.

 But aboue all other she had a wanton ey.   378

55

On her hede she weryd a rede copyr crowne.   379

 A nosegay she had made full pleasauntly.

Between
Aurora and
Venus Apollo
sits him down.
He gives light
to the com-
pany. His
crown is of
gold.
Betwene her and Aurora, Apollo set hym downe.

 W*ith* hys beames bryght he shone so feruently   382

That he therw*ith* gladyd all the company.

 A crowne of pure gold was on hys hede set,

 In sygne that he was mastyr & lord of that banket.

56

Waiting at the
table are poets
and philoso-
phers:
Cicero, Aris-
totle, Ptolemy,
Dorothe,
Diogenes,
Plato, Mes-
sala, Socrates,
Thus was the table set rownde aboute   386

 With goddys & goddesses, as I haue yow tolde.

Awaytyng on the boorde was a gret route

 Of sage phylosophyrs & poetes many folde.   389

Ther was sad Sychero & Arystotyll olde,

 Tholome. Dorothe, w*ith* Dyogenes,

 Plato. Messehala, & wyse Socrates.   392

57

Sortes and Saphyrus wi*th* Hermes stood behynde.   393

Auycen and Aueroys with hem were in fere.

Galyen & Ipocras, that physyk haue in mynde,

Wi*th* helpe of Esculapion, toward hem drow nere.   396

Virgyle, Orace, Ouyde and Omere,

   Euclyde, and Albert yaue he*r* attendaunce,

      To do the goddys and goddesses plesaunce.   399

58

Whore berdyd Orpheus was there wi*th* hys harpe   400

And as a poet musykall made he melody.

Othyr mynstrall had they none, safe Pan gan to carpe

Of hys lewde bagpype, whyche causyd the company 403

To lawe. Yet many mo the*r* were, yef I shuld nat ly,

   Som yong, som olde, bothe bettyr and werse,

      But mo of her names can I not reherse.   406

59

Of all man*er* deyntees tne*r* was habundaunce,   407

Of metys & drynkes foyson plenteuous.

In came Dyscord to haue made varyaunce.

   But the*r*e was no rome to set hy*r* in that hous.   410

The goddys remembryd the scisme odyous

   Among the three goddesses that [s]he had wrought

   At the fest of Peleus, wherfor they thought   413

60

They wold nat wi*th* he*r* dele in auenture   414

Lest she theym brought to som inconuenyent.

She, seyng thys, was wrothe out of mesure

And in that gret wrethe out of the paleyce went,   417

Seying to hersylf that chere shuld *p*ey repent.

   And anone wi*th* Attropos happyd she to mete,

   As he had bene a goste came in wyndyng shete. 420

61

She toke hym by the hande & rownyd in hys eare   421

And told hym of the banket that was so delycate,

Howe she was resceuyd, what chere she had there,

   And howe eu*er*y god sate in hys estate.   [date!"

  "Ys hit thus!" quod Attropos, ",what in the deuyllys

   "Well," he seyde, "I see well howe the game gooth,

   Ones yet for you*r* sake shall I make hem wrooth." 427

62

who takes her
part, and
comes into the
palace.

And when she had hym all togedyr tolde,   428
From her he departyd and of hyr toke hys leue,
Seying that for hyr sake hys wey take he wolde
_ In to the paleyce hys matyrs to meue.   431
And eꝛ he thens went he trowyd hem to greue
Wi*th* suche tydyn*ges* as he shuld hem tell.
So forthe yn he went & spake wordys fell.   434

63

He looks like
a madman and
salutes the
company
rudely.

When he came in the presence of the godd*es* all,   435
As he had be woode he lookyd hym about.
His shete from his body dowñ he let fall,
And on a rewde mane*r* he salutyd all the rout,   438
Wi*th* a bold voyse, carpyng wordys stout.
But he spake all holow, as hit had be ooñ
Had spoke in another world ꝑ*at* had woo begooñ. 441

64

Atropos makes
his charge:

He stood forthe boldly wi*th* grym countenaunce,   442
Saying in thys wyse as ye shall here,
"All ye gret goddys yeue attendaunce

He reminds
the gods of his
office of death-
bringing

Vnto my wordys wi*th*out all daungere,   445
Remembre howe ye made me youꝛ offycere
All tho wi*th* my dart fynally to chastyse
That yow dysobeyed or wold your law dyspyse. 448

65

"And for the more sewerte ye seelyd my patent,   449
Yeuyng me full poweꝛ soo to occupy,
Wherto I haue enployed myñ entent
And that can Dame Nature well testyfy;   452
Yef she be examynyd she woll hit nat deny.
For when she forsaketh any creature,
I am ay redy to take hym to my cure.   455

66

unto every
man.

"Thus haue I dewly, wi*th* all my dilygence,   456
Executyd the offyce of olde antiquyte,
To me by yow grauntyd, by youꝛ comon sentence.
For I spared nooñ hygh nor low degre,   459
So that on my part no defaute hath be.
For as sone as any to me com*m*yttyd wase
I smete hym to the hert—he had nooñ other grase.

67

"Ector of Troy, for all hys chyualry,   463   All have
   Alexaunder, the grete & myghty conquero*ur*,   fallen:
Iulius Cesar, w*ith* all hys company,   Hector,
   Dauid, nor Iosue, nor worthy Artou*r*,   466   Alexander,
   Charles the noble, that was so gret of honou*r*,   Cæsar, David,
     Nor Iudas Machabee for all hys trew hert,   Joshua,
     Nor Godfrey of Boleyñ cowde me nat astert.   469   Arthur,
                         Charles,
                         Judas Macha-
                         beus, Godfrey,

68

"Nabugodonozor, for all hys gret pryde,   470   Nebuchad-
   Nor the King of Egypt, cruell Pharao,   nezzar,
Iason, ne Hercules, went they neue*r* so wyde,   Pharao,
   Cosdras, Hanyball, nor gentyll Sypio,   473   Jason, Her-
   Cirus, Achilles, nor many another mo,   cules, Cosdras
     For feyre or foule gat of me no grace.   Hannibal,
     But all be at the last I sesyd hem w*ith* my mace. 476   Scipio,
                         Cyrus and
                         Achilles.

69

"Thus hav I brought eue*ry* creature   477   All have been
   To an ende bothe man, fysshe, foule & beste,   brought to
And eue*ry* other thyng in whom Dame Nature   their end
Hath any iurysdiccion, owther most or leste,   480   except one.
Except oonly ooñ in whom yo*ur* beheste
     Ys to me broke ; for ye me promysyd
     That my myght of nooñ shuld haue be dyspysyd. 483

70

"Wherof the contrary, dar I well avowe,   484
   Ys trew; for ooñ there ys that wyll nat apply   This one the
Vnto my correccion nor in no wyse bowe   gods guard
   To the dynt of my dart for doole nor destyny. 487   contrary to
   What comfort he hath, nor the cause why   their agree-
     That he so rebelleth, I can nat thynke of ryght [dyght. ment.
     But yef ye haue hym grauntyd yo*ur* aldyrs saf con-

71

"And yef ye so haue, then do ye nat as goddys,   491
   For a godd*es* wrytyng may nat reue*r*syd be.   Therefore
Yef hit shuld I wold nat yeue II pesecoddys   justice is
   For graunt of you*r* patent of offyce ne*r* of fee. 494   demanded.
   Wherfore in thys mate*r* do me equyte
     Accordyng to my patent, for tyll thys be do
     Ye haue no more my se*r*uyce nor my good wyll lo."

72

And when all the godd*es* had Attropos herde,   498

The gods all
promise their
aid in destroy-
ing the man.

As they had be woode they brayde vp at oonys
And seyde they wold nat reste tyll he were conqueryd,
    Take*n* and dystroyed, boody, blood and boonys;   501
And that they swere gret othes for the noonys
    Her lawe to dyspyce, that was so malapert.
    They seyde he shuld be taught for to be so pert.   504

73

Apollo will
confound him
with his car.

"Well," seyde Apollo, "yef he on erthe bee,   505
    Wyth my brennyng chare I shall hym confound."

Neptune will
drown him.

"In feythe," quod Neptun*us*, "& yef he kepe the see.
    He may be full sure he shall sone be drownd."   508
"A syr," seyd Mars, "thys haue we well fownd
    That any dysobeyed owre godly pr*e*cept,
    We may well thynke we haue to long slept.   511

74

Mars will pur-
sue him with
thunder and
lightning,
Saturn will
freeze him,

"But neu*er*thelese where I may hym fynde   512
    W*ith* thundre and leyte about I shall hym chase."
"And I," quod Saturn*us*, "before and behynde
    W*ith* my bytter colde shall shew hy*m* hard grase." 515

Mercury will
deprive him of
speech.

"Well," seyd M*er*curius, "yef I may see hys fase,
    For euer of hys speche I shall hym depryue;
    So that hym were bettyr be dede than a lyue."   518

75

Athena sug-
gests that the
offender may
be in the air,
and without
help of Eolus
their anger is
in vain; there-
fore she coun-
sels that Nep-
tune forgive
his rancor.

"Ye," quod Othea, "yet may he well be   519
    In the eyre where he woll & ax yow no leue,
Wherfore, my counsell ys that all we
    May entrete Neptunus hys ranco*ur* to foryeue,   522
And then I dowte not Eolus wyll hym myscheue;
    So may ye be sewre he shall yow nat escape,
    And elles of all you*r* angre woll he make but a iape."

76

But I have
forgotten to
tell you how
Eolus came
into Pluto's
power.

But for to tell yow how Eolus was brought   526
    In daung*er* of Pluto yet had I foryete,
Wherfore o*n* thys mater ferther wyll I nought
    Procede, tyll I therof haue knowleche yow lete.   529

In wet
weather Eolus,
to revive his
spirits,

Hyt fell on a day the wedyr was wete
    And Eolus thought he wold on hys disport
    Go to reioyse hys spyryt*es* and comfort.   532

77

He thought he wold see what was in the grownd, 533   entered the earth by a crevice, which was com-
And in a krauers forthe he gan hym dresse.   pressed by the
A drowthe had the erthe late before fownd   water, shutting
That causyd hit to chyne & krany more and lesse. 536   Eolus in.
Sodeynly by weet constreynyd by duresse
    Was the ground to close hys superfyciall face
    So strayte that to scape Eolus had no space.   539

78

Thys seyng Eolus he styll with̄yn aboode,   540   He was reported to
Sekyng where he myght haue goon out fer or nere.   Pluto, who ordered Cer-
Anone he was aspyed and oon̄ to Pluto roode   berus to take charge of the
And told hym how Eolus was in hys daungere.   543   prisoner.
Then seyde he to Cerberus, " Fet me that prysonere
    Till I haue hym seene; let him nat go at large.
    As thow wylt answer̄ of hym I yeue þe charge." 546

79

Thus was thys Eolus take prysoner̄.   547   On that day the court of
Then happyd hit so that the same day   Minos sat, whither Eolus
Pluto had prefyxyd for a gret mater̄   was brought as I have told
Mynos to syt in his roob of ray.   550   you,
Wherfore Cerberus tooke the next way
    And led hym to the place where the court shalbe,
    Whedyr as I tolde yow Morpheus brought me. 553

80

So thedyr came Diana caryed in a carre,   554   and there Diana and
To make her compleynt as I told yow all.   Neptune made their com-
And so dyd Neptunus, that dothe bothe make & marre,   plaints as I said.
Walewyng with hys wawes & tomblyng as a ball. 557
    Her matyrs they meuyd fall what may befall.
    Ther was the furst syght that euer I theym sawe,
    And yet I neuer do efte I rekke nat a strawe. 560

81

Bot now to my matyr to returne ageyn̄   561   To return to my matter of
And to begynne newe where I left--   Atropos.
When all the goddes had done her̄ besy peyn̄
The wey to contryue how he shuld be reft   564
Of hys lyfe, that Attropos had no cause eft
    To compleyn̄, than Pheb[e] styrt vppon her̄ fete
    And seyd, " I pray yow let me speke a worde yete: 567   Phebe wishes to speak.

82

"Othea meneth well to sey on thys wyse,   568

She alone
dares to entreat
Neptune
But all to entrete Neptunus, I hope, shall nat nede.
Me semeth I alone durst take that entyrpryse
Ef I am begylyd, or elles I shall spede.   571
How say ye, Neptunus, shall I do thys dede?
Wyll ye youꝛ rancouꝛ sese at my request?"
"Madame," quod he, " reule me as ye lyketh best."574

83

"Gramercy," seyd she, "of your good wyll   575
to leave all old
rancor.
That hit pleseth yow to shew me that fauour,
Wherefore the goddes hygh plesure to fulfyll,
Performe my desyre & leeue all olde rancour,   578
For ouꝛ aldyrs wele & sauyng of our honour,
Ageyñ thys Eolus that ye long haue had."
Neptune
forgives.
"Hyt ys dooñ," quoth he, "forsoth then am I glad."

84

Seyde he, "Now then, Eolus, be thow to vs trew,   582
Kepe well the eyꝛ, and owre gret rebell
May we then soone euer to vs subdew."
Eolus agrees
to afflict the
offender with
his blasts.
"Yes and that," quod Eolus, "shall ye here tell   585
No where in the eyre shall he reste nor dwell.
Yef he do theꝛof, put me in defaute,
With my bytter blastys so shall I hym asaute."   588

85

Pluto asks
their enemy's
name.
"What," seyde the god Pluto, "what ys hys name   589
That thus presumeth ageyñ vs to rebell?"
Atropos
replies that it
is Virtue;
whereat Pluto
grants his
assistance
"Vertew," quod Attropos, "that haue he mykyll shame,
He ys neuer confoundyd, thus of hym here I tell."   592
"A," seyde thys Pluto, " in dede I know hym well,
He hathe be euer myn vtter enemy.
Wherfore thys mateꝛ ageyñ hym take wyll I.   595

86

"For all the baytys that ye for hym haue leyde,   596
Without myñ helpe, be nat worth a peere.
For though ye all the contrary had seyde,
Yet wolde he breede ryght nygh your althrys eere. 599
No maner of thyng can hym hurt nor dere
Saue oonly ooñ, a soñ of myñ bastard,
Whos name ys Vyce—he kepeth my vaward.   602

87

"Wherfore, yow Cerberus, now I the dyscharge 603 and sends Cerberus to bring Vice to make battle with Virtue.
Of Eolus, and wyll that thow hydyr sette
My dere son Vyce, & sey that I hym charge
  That he to me come wit*h*out any lette, 606
  Armyd at all poyntes, for a day ys sette,
    That he wit*h* Vertew for all the godd*es* sake,
    In our defense must on hym batayll take." 609

88

Forthe then went Cerberus wit*h* hys fyry cheyne 610 Cerberus leads forward Vice who comes riding on a winged serpent breathing fire.
And brought thedyr Vyce, as he co*m*maundyd was,
Ageyñ noble V*er*tew that batayll to dereygne.
  On a glydyng se*r*pent rydyng a gret pas, 613
  Formyd lyke a dragoñ, scalyd harde as glas,
    Whos mouth flamyd feere wit*h*out fayll.
    Wyngys had hit se*r*pentyne and a long tayll. 616

89

Armyd was Vyce all in cure boyle, 617
Hard as any horñ, blakker feř then soot. Following him is a host of captains, Pride on a lion, Envy on a wolf,
An vngoodly soort folowyd hym parde,
  Of vnhappy capteyns of myschyef croppe & roote. 620
  Pryde was the furst *p*at next hym roode, God woote,
    On a roryng lyoñ; next whom came Enuy,
    Syttyng on a wolfe—he had a scorñfull ey. 623

90

Wrethe bestrode a wylde bore, and next hem gan ryde. Wrath on a wild-boar,
  In hys hand he bare a blody nakyd swerde.
Next whom came Couetyse, that goth so feř and wyde, Covetousness on an elephant
  Rydyng on a olyfaunt, as he had beñ aferde. 627
  Aftyr whom rood Glotony, wit*h* hys fat berde. Gluttony on a bear,
    Syttyng on a bere, wit*h* hys gret bely.
    And next hym on a goot folowyd Lechery. 630 Lechery on a goat,

91

Slowthe was so slepy he came all behynde 631 Sloth on an ass.
On a dull asse, a full wery pase.
These were the capyteyns that Vyce cowde fynde
  B[e]st to set hys felde and folow on the chase. 634 Inferior captains are: Sacrilege, Simony, etc.
  As for pety capteyns many mo the[r] wase;
    As Sacrylege, Symony, & Dyssimulacion,
    Manslaught*er*, Mordre, Theft & Extorcion, 637

92

Arrogaunce, Presumpcion, w*ith* Contumacy,   638
   Contempcion, Contempt, & Inobedience,
Malyce, Frowardnes, Gret Ielacy,
   Woodnesse, Hate, Stryfe, and Impacience,   641
   Vnkyndnesse, Oppression, w*ith* Wofull Neglygence,
   Murmo*ur*, Myschyef, Falshood & Detraccion,
     Vsury, Per*iury*, Ly, and Adulacion,   644

93

Wrong, Rauyne, Sturdy Vyolence,   645
   False Iugement, w*ith* Obstynacy,
Dysseyte, Dronkenes, and Improuydence,
   Boldnes in Yll, w*ith* Foule Rybaudy,   648
   Fornycacion, Incest, and Anoutry,
     Vnshamefastnes, w*ith* Prodygalyte,
     Blaspheme, Veynglory, & Wordly Vanyte,   651

94

Ignoraunce, Diffydence, w*ith* Ipocrysy,   652
   Scysme, Ranco*ur*, Debate, & Offense,
Heresy, Erro*ur*, w*ith* Idolatry,
   New-Fangylnes, & sotyll False Pretense,   655
   Inordinat Desyre of Worldly Excellense,
     Feynyd Pouert, w*ith* Apostasy,
     Disclaundyr, Skorne, & Vnkynde Ielousy,   658

95

Hoordam̄, Bawdry, False Mayntenaunce,   659
   Treson, Abusion, & Pety Brybry;
Vsurpacion, w*ith* Horryble Vengeaunce,
   Came alther last of that company.   662
   All these pety capteyns folowyd by & by,
     Shewyng they*m*sylf in the palyse wyde,
     And seyde they were redy that batayll to abyde. 665

96

Idylnesse set the comons in aray   666
   W*ith*out the paleyse on a fayre felde.
But there was an oost for to make a fray!
   I trow suche another neu*er* man behelde!   669
   Many was the wepyn among he*m* þat þey welde!
     What pepyll they were that came to that dysport
     I shall yow declare of many a sondry sort.   672

97

Ther were bosters, braggars, & brybores,   673   boasters, braggers, etc.
  Praters, fasers, strechers, & wrythers,
Shamefull shakerles, soleyn shaueldores,
    Oppressours of pepyll, and myghty crakers,   676
    Meyntenours of querelles, horryble lyers,
      Theues, traytours, w*ith* false herytykes,
      Charmers, sorcerers, & many scismatykes,   679

98

Pryuy symonyak*es*, w*ith* false vsurers,   680
  Multyplyers, coyñ wasshers & clyppers,
Wrong vsurpers, w*ith* gret extorcioners,
    Bakbyters, glosers, & fayre flaterers,   683
    Malycious murmurers, w*ith* grete claterers,
      Tregetours, tryphelers, feyners of tales,
      Lastyuyous lurdeyns, & pykers of males,   686

99

Rowners, uagabound*es*, forgers of lesyng*es*,   687
  Robbers, reuers, rauenouse ryfelers,
Choppers of churches, fynders of tydyng*es*,
    Marrers of maters, & money makers,   690
    Stalkers by nyght, w*ith* euesdroppers,
      Fyghters, brawlers, brekers of lofedayes,
      Getters, chyders, causers of frayes,   693

100

Tytyuyllys, tyraunt*es*, w*ith* turmentoures,   694
  Cursyd apostat*es*, relygyous dyssymulers,
Closshers, carders, w*ith* comon hasardoures,
    Tyburne coloppys, and pursekytters,   697
    Pylary knyght*es*, double tollyng myllers,
      Gay ioly tapsters, w*ith* hostelers of the stewes,
      Hoores, and baudys — that many bale brewes, 700

101

Bolde blasphemers, w*ith* false ipocrytes,   701
  Brothelles, brokers, abhomynable swerers,
Dryuylles, dastard*es*, dyspysers of ryghtes,
    Homycydes, poyseners, & comon morderers, · 704
    Skoldes, caytyffys, comborouse clappers,
      Idolatres, enchauntours, w*ith* false renegates,
      Sotyll ambidextres, & sekers of debates,   707

102

Pseudo *prophetes*, false sodomytes,   708
 Quelmers of chyldren, *with* fornycatours,
Wetewold*es* that suffre syn in her syghtes.
 Auouterers, & abhominable auauntours   711
 Of syn, gret clappers, & makers of clamours :
  Vnthryftys, & vnlustes came also to that game,
  W*ith* luskes, & loselles that myght nat thryue for shame.

103

These were the comons came thedyr that day   715
 Redy bowne in batayll V*er*tew to abyde.
Apollo, theym beholdyng, began for to say

Apollo wishes
to send a
herald to warn
Virtue.
 To the godd*es* & goddesses beyng there that tyde.   718
 "Me seemeth conuenyent an herowde to ryde
  To V*er*tew, & byd hym to batayll make hym bone,
  Hymsylf to defende, for sowght he shalbe sone.   721

104

"And let hym nat be sodenly take   722
 All dyspurueyde or then he beware,
For then shuld ou*r* dyshono*ur* awake

Vice protests.
 Yef he were cowardly take in a snare."   725
 "Ee," quod Vyce, "for that haue I no care.
  I will auauntage take where I may."
  That heryng, Morpheus pryuyly stale away,   728

105

But Morpheus
steals away to
prepare Virtue
for the battle.
And went to warne V*er*tew of all thys afray,   729
 And bade hym awake & make hymsylf strong.
For he was lyke to endure that day
 A gret mortall shoure, e*r* hit were euesong.   732
 W*ith* Vyce, wherfore he bade him nat long
  Tary to sende aftyr more socou*r* ·
  Yef he dede, hit shuld turne hym to dolou*r*.   735

106

And brefely the matyr to hym he declaryd,   736
 Lyke as ye haue herde begynnyng & ende.
"Well," quoth V*er*tu, "he shall nat be sparyd.
 To the felde I wyll wende how hit wende.   739
 But gram*er*cy, Morpheus, my*n* owne dere frende,
  Of you*r* trew hert & feythefull entent
  That ye in thys mate*r* to me ward haue ment."   742

107

Thys doon, Morpheous departyd away   743
  Fro Vertu to the palyce retornyng ageyñ.

Virtue makes ready, sending out his messenger, Imagination, to bid his people to come in to his help.

Nooñ hym aspyed, that I dar well say.
  In whyche tyme Vertew dyd hys besy peyñ   746
Pepyll to reyse hys quarell to menteyñ.
    Ymaginacion was hys messyngere—
    He went to warne pepyll bothe fer & nere.   749

108

And bade hem come in all the haste they myght   750
  For to streyngthe Vertu, for, without fayll,
He seyde he shuld haue, long or hit were nyght,
  With Vyce to do a myghty strong batayll;   753
Of vngracious gastes he bryngeth a long tayll.
  "Wherfore hit behoueth to helpe at thys nede
  And aftyr thys shall Vertu rewarde yowre mede."   756

109

When Imaginacion had gooñ hys cyrcute   757
  To Vertews frendys thus all aboute,

Virtue's host assembles.

Withyn short tyme many men of myght
  Gaderyd to Vertew in all that they mowte.   760
They hym comfortyd & bad hym put no dowte
  Hys vttyr enemy Vyce to ouerthrow,
  Though he with hym brought neuer so gret arow.

110

And when Vertew sy the substaunce of hys oost,   764
  He prayed all the comons to the felde hem hy,

They are led towards the field.

With her pety capteynys both lest & moost,
  And he with hys capteynys shuld folow redyly.   767
For he seyde he knew well that Vyce was full ny.
  And who myght furst of the felde recouer the centre
  Wold kepe out that other he shuld nat esyly entre. 770

111

Then sent he forthe Baptyiñ to the felde before, 771

Baptism is sent to spy out the ground.

  And prayed hym hertyly hit to ouerse,
That no maner trayne nor caltrop theryn wore
  To noy nor hurt hym nor hys meyne.   774
And wheñ he thedyr came he began to see
  How Vyce hys purseuaunte, Cryme Oryginall,

Original Sin had entered before him

  Was entryd before and had sesyd vp all.   777

112

but fled at
Baptism's
approach.

But as sone as heᵭof Baptym had a syght,   778
   He fled fast awey and left the felde alone.
And anone Babtyñ entred *with* hys myght,
   Serchyng all about where thys Cryme had gone.   781
   But the felde was clene defaute; fonde he none.
     Then cam Vertew aftyr *with* hys gret oost,

Virtue and his
host follow.

     And hys myghty capytayns, bothe leste & moost. 784

113

But to enforme yow howe he thedyᵭ came.   785
   And what maner capyteyns he to the felde brought —

Virtue leads,
sitting in a car
adorned with
gold and
stones, and
crowned with
laurel.

Hymsylfe, sekerly, was the furst man
   Of all hys gret hoost that thedyrward sought,   788
   Syttyng in a chare that rychely was wrought,
     With golde & peerles & gemmes *pre*cious,
     Crownyd *with* laureᭉ as lord vyctoryous.   791

114

Four knights
guide the car.
Righteousness,
Prudence,
Strength and
Temperance.

Foure dowty knyghtys about the chare went   792
   At *eue*ry corner on hit for to gyde,
And convey accordyng to Vertew hys entent.
   At the furst corner was Ryghtwysnes that tyde,   795
   Prudence at the second was set to abyde,
     At the thryd Streyngth, the fourth kept Tempe*raunce.
     These the chare gydyd to Vertew hys plesaunce. 798

115

Following
Virtue come
seven captains
each with an
appropriate
crest, Humility
on a lamb,

Next to the chare, seuen capteyns theᭉ roode,   799
   Ychone aftyr other in ordre by and by.
Humylyte was the furst ; a lambe he bestroode,
   With countenaunce demure he roode full soburly. 802
     A fawcon gentyll stood on hys helme on hy.

Charity on a
tiger,

     And next aftyr hym came there Charyte
     Rydyng on a tygre, as fyll to hys degre.   805

116

Roody as a roose ay he kept hys chere.   806
   On hys helme on hygh a pellycan he bare.

Patience on a
camel,

Next whom came Pacyence, *þ*at nowhere hath no pere,
   On a camell rydyng, as voyde of all care.   809
     A fenyx on hys helme stood.   So forthe gan he fare.

Liberality on a
dromedary,

     Who next hym folowyd but Lyberalyte,
     Syttyng on a dromedary, *þ*at was bothe good & free.

117

On hys helme for hys crest he bare an ospray.   813
  And next aftyr hym folowyd Abstynence,
Rydyng on an hert, hys trapure was gay,
    He semyd a lorde of ryght gret excellence.   816
    A popyniay was hys crest; he was of gret dyffence.
      Next hym folowyd Chastyte on an unycorñ,
      Arymd at all poyntes behynde and beforñ.   819

(margin: Abstinence on a hart,)
(margin: Chastity on a unicorn,)

118

A turtyldoue he bare an hygh for hys crest.   820
  Then came Good Besynesse, last of the seuyn,
Rydyng on a panteř, a sondry colouryd best,
    Gloryously beseene as he had come from heuyn.   823
    A crane on hys hede stood, hys crest for to steuyn.
      All these seuyn capteynes had standardes of pryce,
      Eche of hem acordyng aftyr hys deuyse.   826

(margin: Good Business on a vari-coloured beast.)
(margin: Each captain bears a standard with a device.)

119

Many pety capteyns aftyr these went,   827
  As Trew Feythe, & Hoope, Mercy, Peese, & Pyte,
Ryght, Trowthe, Mekenesse, with Good Entent,
    Goodness, Concorde, & Parfyte Vnyte,   830
    Honest Trew Loue, with Symplycyte,
      Prayer, Fastyng, Preuy Almysdede,
      Ioynyd with the Artycles of the Crede,   833

(margin: Many minor captains come next, True Faith, Hope, etc.)

120

Confession, Contrycion, and Satysfaccion,   834
  With Sorow for Synne, & Gret Repentaunce,
Foryeuenes of Trespas, with Good Dysposicion,
    Resystence of Wrong, Performyng of Penaunce,   837
    Hooly Deuocion, with Good Contynuaunce,
      Preesthood theym folowyd with the Sacramentes,
      And Sadnesse also with the Commaundementes, 840

121

Sufferaunce in Trowble, with Innocency,   841
  Clennesse, Continence. and Virginite,
Kyndnesse, Reuerence. with Curtesy,
    Content & Plesyd with Pyteous Pouerte,   844
    Entendyng Well, Mynystryng Equyte
      Twene ryght & wrong. Hoole Indyfferency,
      And Laboryng the Seruyce of God to Multyply, 847

122

Refuse of Rychesse & Worldly Veynglory,   848
Perfeccion, *with* Parfyte Contemplacion,
Relygyoñ, Profession well kept in Memory.
   Verrey Drede of God, *with* Holy Predycacion,   851
   Celestiall Sapience, *with* Goostly Inspiracion ;
   Grace was the guyde of all thys gret meyny.
   Whom folowyd Konnyng *with* hys genalogy— 854

123

That ys to sey, Gramer, and Sophystry,   855
Philosophy Naturall, Logyk, & Rethoryk,
Arsmetry, Geometry *with* Astronomy,
   Canon & Cyuyle, melodyous Musyk,   858
   Nobyll Theology, and Corporall Physyk,
   Moralizacion of Holy Scripture,
   Profounde Poetry and Drawyng of Picture—   861

124

These folowyd Konnyng & thedyr *with* hym came,   862
With many ooñ moo offryng her seruyce
To Vertew at that nede; but natw*ith*standyng than

Virtue refuses
some captains,
Nigromancy,
etc.
   Som he refusyd and seyde in nowyse   865
   They shuld *with* hym go, and, as I coude auyse,
   These were her names: fyrst, Nygromansy,
   Geomansy, Magyk, and Glotony,   868

125

Adryomancy, Ornomancy, *with* Pyromancy,   869
Fysenamy also, and Pawmestry,
And all her sequelys, yef I shult nat ly.
   Yet Konnyng prayed Vertu he wold nat deny   872
   Theym for to know nor dysdeyne *with* hys ey
   Oñ hem to loke, wherto Vertew grauntyd.
   How [be] hit in hys werres he wold nat þey hauntyd. 875

126

who then
choose Vice as
their master
   So had they Connyng lyghtly to depart   876
   From Vertew hys felde, and they seyng thys
By comon assent hyryd theym a cart
   And made hem be caryed toward Vyce y-wys.   879
   Fro thensforth to serue hym they wold nat mys.
   Full lothe they were to be mastyrles;
   In stede of the bettyr the worse theï they ches. 882

127

But foorth to relese all the remenaunt   883
  Of pety capteyns that *with* V*er*tu were,
Moderat Dyete, & Wysdom auenaunt,
   Euyn Wyght & Mesure, Ware of Contagious Geere, 886
   Lothe to Offende, and Louyng ay to Lere,
     Worshyp, & Profyt, w*ith* Myrthe in Manere,
     These pety capteyns w*ith* V*er*tew were in fere. 889

Other minor captains with Virtue are Moderate Diet, etc.

128

Comones hem folowyd a gret multitude.   890
  But in [comparyson] to that other syde
I trow ther was nat, brefely to conclude,
  The x^(th) man that batayll to abyde.   893
  Yet neu*er*thelese, I shall nat fro yow hyde
    What man*er* pepyll they were & of what secte,
    As neere as my wyt therto wyll me dyrecte. 896

A great multitude of commons follows, yet numbering no one-tenth of Vice's host.

129

The*i* were notable and famous doctours,   897
  Example yeuers of lyuyng gracyous,
P*er*petuell prestes and dyscrete confessours,
   Of Holy Scriptu*r* declares fructuous,   900
   Rebukers of synne & myschef*es* odyous,
     Fysshers of fowles, & lovers of clennes,
     Dyspysers of veyñ & worldly ryches,   903

There are famous doctors etc.

130

Pesyble p*re*lates, iustyciall gou*er*nours,   904
  Founders of churches, w*ith* m*er*cyfull peeres,
Reformers of wrong of her progenitours
   On peynfull poore pyteous compassioners,   907
   Well menyng m*er*chaunt*es*, w*ith* trew artyfyceres,
     Vyrgyns pure, and also innocent*es*,
     Hooly matronys, w*ith* chaste contynent*es*,   910

131

Pylgryms, & palmers, w*ith* trew laborers,   911
  Hooly heremytes, godd*es* solycitours,
Monasteriall monkes, & well dysposyd freres,
   Chanons, & nonnes, feythfull professoures,   914
   Of worldly peple trew coniugatoures,
     Louers of Cryst, confounders of yll,
     And all that to godward yeue he*r* good wyll, 917

132

Mayntenours of ryght, verrey penytent*es*,   918
Distroyers of errou*r*, causers of Vnyte,
Trew actyf lyuers that set her entent*es*
  The dedes to p*er*forme of m*er*cy and pyte,   921
  Contemplatyf peple that desyre to be
    Solytary s*er*uaunt*es* vnto God alone,
    Rather then to haboundc in rychesse eu*er*ychone.   924

133

These, w*ith* many mo then I reherse can,   925
  Were come thedyr redy that batayll to abyde,
And take such part as fyll to V*er*tew than.
  Vyce to ou*er*come they hopyd for all hys pryde,   928
  All though that he had more pepyll on hys syde,
    For the men that V*er*tu had were full sewre
    To trust on at Nede & Konnyng in armure.   931

134

Macrocosme was the name of the felde   932
  Where thys gret batayle was set for to be.
In the myddes therof stood Conscience, & behelde
  Whyche of hem shuld be brought to captyuyte.   935
  Of that nobyll tryu*m*phe iuge wold he be.
    Synderesys sate hy*m* w*ith*yn closyd as in a parke.
    W*ith* hys tables in hys hand her dedys to marke.   938

135

To come in to the felde were hygh weyes fyue,   939
  Free to bothe partyes, large, broode and wyde.
Vertu wold nat tary, but hyghyd hym thydyr blyue,
  Lest he were by Vyce deceuyd at that tyde.   942
  Long out of the felde lothe he was to abyde,
    In auentu*r* that he out of hyt were nat kept,
    For then wolde he haue thought he had to long slept.

136

In thys mene tyme whyle V*er*tu thus preuydyd   946
  For hym and hys pepyll the feld for to wynne,
He chargyd eu*er*y man by Grace to be guydyd,
  And all that eu*er* myght the felde to entre ynne.   949
  In all that seso*n* went Orygynall Synne
    To lete Vyce know how Baptyi*n*, w*ith* hys oost,
    Had entryd Macrocosme & serchyd eu*er*y coost.   952

Marginal notes:

The name of the field is Microcosm.

In the midst is Conscience, the judge of the combat.

Five highways lead to the field.

Thither Virtue hastens.

Meanwhile Original Sin had reported to Vice.

137

"A," seyde Vyce, " than I se well hit ys tyme   953
   Baners to dysplay & standardys to auaunce.
Allmost to long haddyst thow taryed, Cryme,
   To let vs haue knowlege of thys puruyaunce.   956
    Yet I trow I shall lerne hem a new daunce.
     Wherfore I commaunde yow all without delay
     Toward the felde drawe, in all the haste ye may." 959

138

Then seyde the god Pluto that all men myght here, 960
   "Vyce, I the charge, as thow wylt eschew
Our heynous indignacion, thow draw nat arere
   But put the forthe boldly to ouerthrow Vertew."   963
   "In feythe," quoth Attropos, "and I shall aftyr sew
    For yef he escape your handys thys day,
    I tell yow my seruyce haue ye lost for ay."   966

139

Forthe then rode Vyce with all hys hoole streyngth, 967
   On hys steede serpentyñ, as I tolde yow before.
The oost that hym folowyd was of a gret leyngth.
   Among whom were penowns & guytornes many a score.
   But as he went thederward—I shall tell yow more
    Of hys pety capteyns—he made many a knyght,
    For they shuld nat fle but manly with hyñ fyght. 973

140

He dubbyd Falshood, with Dyssymulacion,   974
   Symony, Vsure, Wrong, and Rebawdy,
Malyce, Deceyte, Ly, with Extorcion,
   Periury, Diffidence, and Apostasy,   977
   With Boldnesse in Yll to bere hem company—
    These xiiii knyghtes made Vyce that day ;
    To wynne theyr spores they seyde they wold asay.

141

In lyke wyse, Vertew dubbyd on hys syde   981
   Of hys pety capteynes other fourtene,
Whyche made her avowe with hym to abyde.
   Her spores wold they wynne þat day, hit shuld be sene
   These were her names, yef hit be as I wene :
    Feythe, Hope and Mercy, Trouthe, & also Ryght,
    With Resystence of Wrong, a full hardy wyght, 987

142

Confession. Contricion, with Satisfaccion,　　　　988
　　Verrey Drede of God, Performyng of Penaunce,
Perfeccyon, Konnyng, and Good Dysposicion.
　　　And all knyt to Vertu they were by allyaunce.　　991
　　　Wherfore to hym they made assewraunce,
　　　　That felde to kepe as long as they myght
　　　And in hys quarell ageyñ Vyce to fyght.　　994

143

The Lord of Macrocosme and rewler of that fee　　995
　　Was callyd Frewyll, chaungeř of the chaunse,
To whom Vertew sent embassatours three,
　　　Reson, Discresion, & Good Remembraunse,　　998
　　　And prayed hym be fauorable hys honour to enhaunse.
　　　For but he had hys fauour at that poynt of nede
　　　He stoode in gret doute he coude nat lyghtly spede.

144

In lyke wyse, Vyce embassatours thre,　　　1002
　　'For hys party, vnto Frewyll sent,
Temptacion, Foly, & Sensualyte,
　　　Praying hym of fauour that he wold assent　　1005
　　　To hym, as he wolde at hys commaundment
　　　Haue hym, eftsones, when he lyst to call
　　　Oñ hym for any thyng þat aftyrward myght fall. 1008

145

Answere yaue he nooñ to neyther party,　　　1009
　　Saue oonly he seyde the batayle wold he se.
To wete whyche of hem shuld haue the victory,
　　　Hit hyng in hys balaunce the ambyguyte.　　1012
　　　He seyde he wold nat restrayne hys lyberte.
　　　When he come where sorow shuld awake.
　　　Then hit shuld be know what part he woll take. 1015

146

Whan Vertew and Vyce, be heř embassatours,　　1016
　　Knew of thys answere, they stood in gret doute.
Neuerthelese, they seyde they wold endure tho shoures
　　And make an ende shortly of that they went aboute.
　　　So forthe came Vyce with all hys gret route.
　　　Eř he came at the felde he sent yet pryuyly
　　　Sensualyte before, in maner of a spy,　　　1022

147

Whyche sewe the felde w*ith* hys vnkynde seede   1023

  That causyd Vertu aftyr mykyll woo to feele.

For the*r*of grew nought but all oonly weede,

  Whyche made the grounde as slepyr as an yele.   1026

  He went ayene to Vyce and told hym eue*r*y dele

    How he had done, and bade hym com away   [day.

    For he had so purueyde that Vyce shuld haue the

who sows the field with wicked seed of weeds.

148

Soo, as hit happyd, at the felde they mete,   1030

  Freewyll, Ve*r*tew & Vyce, as trypartyte,

Safe Ve*r*tew a lytell before the felde had gete,

  And elles hys auauntage forsothe had he full lyght

  Nat for then encombryd so was neu*er* wyght

    As Ve*r*tew and hys men were w*ith* the ranke wede

    That in the felde grew of Sensualytees sede.   1036

Virtue's men are encumbered by Sensuality's weeds.

149

But as sone as Vyce of Vertu had a syght,   1037

  He gan swage gonnes as he had be woode.

That heryng, Ve*r*tew co*m*maundyd eue*r*y wyght

  To pauyse hym vndyr the sygne of the roode,   1040

  And bad hem nat drede but kepe styll whe*r* they stoode.

    Hyt was but a shoure shuld soone confound. [grou*n*d.

    Wherfore he co*m*maundyd they*m* stand & kepe he*r*

Virtue commands every man to pause under the sign of the cross.

150

And when Vyce came nere*r* to the felde,   1044

  He ca!lyd soore for bowes and bade hem shote faste.

But Ve*r*tew and hys meyny bare of w*ith* the shelde

  Of the blessyd Trynyte ay tyll shot was paste.   1047

  And when shot was dooñ, Vyce came forthe at laste,

    Purposyng the felde w*ith* assawte to wyn.   [theryn.

    But Ve*r*tew kept hit long — he myght nat enty*r*

They ward off the shots of Vice by the shield of the Holy Trinity.

Vice proposes to make assault.

151

All that tyme Frewyll & hy*m* bethought   1051

  To whyche he myght leue & what part he wold take.

At last Sensualyte had hym so fer brought

  That he seyde pleynly he Vertu wold forsake,   1054

  And in Vyce hys quarell all hys power make.

    "Y-wis," quoth Reason, "that ys nat for the beste."

    "No forse," seyde Frewyll, "I wyll do as my lyste."

Freewill inclines to the side of Vice.

¹⁵²

Vertu was full heuy, when he sy Frewyll   1058
  Take part with Vyce, but yet neuerthelesse

He dyd that he myght the felde to kepe styll.
    Tyll Vyce, with Frewyll, so sore gan hym oppresse
    That he was constreynyd clerely by duresse
      A lytyll tyne abak to make abew retret.
      All thyng consyderyd hit was the best feet.   1064

¹⁵³

Furst to remembre how Vyces part was   1065
  Ten ayene oon strengor by lyklynes.
And than how Frewyll was with hym allas,
    Whoo cowde deme Vertew but in henynes;   1068
    Moreouer to thynke how that slyper gres,
      That of Sensualyte hys vnkynde seede grew
      Vndyr foote in standyng encombryd Vertew.   1071

¹⁵⁴

Yet natwithstandyng, Vertew hys men all   1072
  Nobully theym bare and faught myghtyly.
Howe be hyt, the slepyr grasse made many of hem fall,
    And from thense in maner depart sodeynly.   1075
    That seyng, Vyce hys oost began to showt and cry
      And seyde, "On in Pluto name! On! & all ys owre!
      For thys day shall Vyce be made a conquerour!"

¹⁵⁵

Thus Vertew was by myght of Vyce & Frewyll   1079
  Dreuen out of the felde—hit was the more pyte.

Howe be hit, yet Baptym kept hys ground styll,
    And with hym aboode Feythe, Hoope and Unyte, 1082
    And Kunnyng also, with comons a gret meyne,
      Confessyon, Contricion were redy at her hande,
      And Satysfaccion, Vyce to wythstande.   1085

¹⁵⁶

But all the tyme whyle Vertew was away   1086
  A myghty conflycte kept they with Vyce his rowte,
And yet neuerthelese for all that gret affray
    Hoope stood vpryght & Feythe wold neuer lowte; 1089
    And euermore seyd Baptym, "Syres put no dowte
      Vertu shall retorne & haue hys entente.
      Thys felde shalbe our & elles let me be shent."

157

And whyle these pety-capteynes susteynyd thus the feelde,
   With Vertew hys rerewarde came Good Perseueraunce,
An hogy myghty hoost, & when he beholde
   How Vertew hym withdrew he toke dysplesaunce, 1096
And when he to hym came he seyde, "Ye shall your chaunce
   Take as hit falleth, wheffore returne ye must.
Yet oonys for your sake with Vyce shall I iust. 1099

Virtue is reinforced by Perseverance who chides him for his retreat.

158

"Allas that euer ye shuld leese thus your honour, 1100
   And therwith also, the hygh perpetuell crowne,
Whyche ys for yow kept in the celestiall tour.
   Wherfore be ye callyd Cristes Champyoñ? 1103
How ys hit that ye haue no compassyon
   On Baptyiñ, Feythe, & Hoope, Konnyng, & Vnyte,
   That stant so harde be stadde & fyght as ye may see?

159

"All the tresour erthely vndyr the fyrmament, 1107
   That euer was made of goddes creacion
To rewarde theym euynly, were nat equyualent
   For her noble labour in hys afflyccion. 1110
Wherfore take vppon yow your iurysdyccion.
   Rescu yondyr knyghtes & recontynu fyght.
   And elles adew your crowne for all your gret meryt."

160

With these & suche wordys, as I haue yow tolde, 1114
   By good Perseueraunce vttryd in thys wyse,
Vertu hym remembryd & gan to wex bolde
   And seyd, "Yeue trew knyghtes to rescu I auyse. 1117
Let vs no lengor tary from thys entrepryse."
   Agayñ to the felde so Vertew retornyd,
   That causyd hem be merypat long afore had mornyd.

Virtue returns to the struggle

161

"Avaunt baner," queth he, "in the name of Ihesu." 1121
   And with that hys pepyll set vp a gret showte
And cryed with a lowde voyce, "A Vertew! A Vertew!"
   Then began Vyce hys hooste for to loke abowte, 1124
But I trowe Perseueraunce was nat long withowte
   He bathyd hys swerde in hys foes blood.
   The boldyst of hem all nat oonys hym withstood.

in the name of Jesus.

162

They are victorious.

Constaunce hym folowyd & brought hym hys spere. 1128
But when Perseueraunce saw Vyce oñ hys stede,
No man cowde hym let tyll he came there.
  For to byd hym ryde, I trow hit was no nede. 1131
  All Vertew hys ost prayde for hys good spede.
    Agayñ Vyce he roode with hys gret shaft
    And hym ouerthrew for all hys sotyll craft. 1134

163

Freewill comes to Conscience to repent and asks counsel;

That seyng, Frewyll came to Conscience. 1135
  And gan hym to repent that he with hym had bee,
Praying hym of counsell for hys gret offence

Conscience sends him to Humility,

That he agayñ Vertew had made hys armee. 1138
  What was best to do. "To Humylyte," [sent
    Quoth Conscience, "must þou go." So he hym thedyr
    Disguysyd that he were nat knowen as he went. 1141

164

Humility to Confession;

And when he thedyr came, Humylyte hym took 1142
  A token, & bad hym go to Confessyon.

thence to Contrition,

And shew hym hys mater with a peteous look.
  Whyche dooñ he hym sent to Contrycion, 1145
  And fro thensforth to Satysfaccion.

Satisfaction, and lastly to Penance.

    Thus fro poost to pylour was he made to daunce.
    And at the last he went forthe to Penaunce. 1148

165

But now for to tell yow—when Vyce was ouerthrow 1149
  A gret parte of his oost about hym gan resorte.
But he was so febyll that he cowde no man know.

Vice is carried from the field, meeting Despair who fetches his reward.

  And when they sy þat they knew no comforte, 1152
  But caryed hym awey be a pryuy porte.
    And as they hym caryed Dyspeyre with hym met;
    With Vyce hys reward he came theym for to fet. 1155

166

Alpha and Omega despatch from the heavens two goodly ladies; one named Prescience to chastise Vice and his host;

Then came ther downe goodly ladyes tweyne, 1156
  From the hygh heuyn aboue the firmament,
And seyde the gret Alpha & Oo. most souereyne,
  For that nobyll tryumphe, had hem thedyr sent; 1159
  Ooñ of hem to dryue Vyce to gret torment
    With a fyry scourge that she bare in her hande.
    And so he dede dyspeyre and all his hoole bande.

167

The name of thys lady was callyd Prescience.   1163
  She neuer left Vyce, ne nooñ that wold hym folow,
Tyll they weƀ commyttyd by the diuine sentence
  All to peyne perpetuell and infynyte sorow.   1166
  Ryghtwysnes went to see that no man shuld hem borow.
    Thus all entretyd sharpely were they, tyll Cerberus
    Had hem beshut withyn hys gates tenebrus.   1169

she pursues them through the gate of Hell.

168

And all the whyle that Prescience with heƀ scorge smert
  To rewarde Vyce gan hyr thus occupy,
With all hys hoole bende, aftyƀ heƀ desert,
  That other gloryous lady that came fro heuyn on hy, 1173
  Hauyng in heƀ hande the palme of vyctory,
    Came downe to Vertu and toke hym to that present,
    Seying thus that Alpha & Oo haue hym sent.   1176

The other lady bears to Virtue the palm of victory.

169

And as ferre as I aryght cowde vndyrstand   1177
  That ladyes name was Predestinacion.
Vertu & hys hoost she blessyd with her hand
  And in heuen grauntyd hem habitacion,   1180
  Where to eche of hem reseruyd was a crowñ,
    She seyde, in token that they enherytours
    Of the glory were and gracious conquerours.   1183

Her name is Predestination; she grants them a heavenly habitation.

170

Whyche dooñ, thoo ladyes ayene togedyr met   1184
  And toward heuyn vp they gan to [fly],
Embrasyd in armes as they had be knet
  Togedyr with a gyrdyll; but so sodenly   1187
  As they were vanysshyd saw I neuer thyng with ey.
    And anon Vertew with all hys company
    Knelyd dowñ and thankyd God of that vyctory. 1190

Which done, the ladies depart suddenly.

Virtue and his host thank God for the victory.

171

Yet had I foryete when Vyce was ouerthrow   1191
  To haue tolde yow how many of Vyce hys oost
Gan to seek Peese, and darkyd downe full low,
  And besought Mercy, what so euer hys cost,   1194
  To be her mene to Vertew, elles they were but lost.
    And som in lyke wyse to Feythe & Hoope sought
    What to do, for peese they seyde they ne rought. 1197

Some of Vice's host seek Peace, beseeching mercy to plead to Virtue, or Faith, or Hope,

172

Som also to Baptyñ sewyd to be heꝛ mene ;   1198
  Som to ooñ, som to other, as they hem gete myght.
But all to Confession went to make hem clene.   [lyght,

And as they came by Conscience he theym bad goo
Eꝛ than olde Attropos of hem had a syght.
  For yef he so theym tooke lost they were for euer.
  He seyde Vyce to forsake ys bettyr late then neuer.

173

Som eke for socouꝛ drew to Circumcysion,   1205
  But by hym cowde they gete but small fauour,
For he in that company was had but in derysion.
  Neuerthelese to Feythe he bade hem go labour,   1208
  Praying theym for olde acqueyntance theym socour.
    "Well," quoth Feythe, "for hys sake, I shall do that I
  But furst for the best wey Baptyñ go ye to. [may do

174

"For by hym sonnest shull ye recouer grace,   1212
  Whyche shall to Vertu bryng yow by processe ;
Wherfore in any wyse looke ye make good face,
  And let no man know of youꝛ heuynes."   1215
  So they were by Baptym brought out of dystres —

Turnyd all to Vertew ; & when thys was dooñ,
  Vertu commaundyd Frewyll before hym coñ.   1218

175

To whom thus he seyde, "I haue gret meruayll   1219
  Ye durst be so bolde Vyces part to take.
Who bade yow do so & yaue yow that counsayll ?
  Iustly vnto that ye shall me pryuy make."   1222
  Then seyde Frewyll & swemfully spake,
    Knelyng on hys kne with a chere benygne,
  "I pray yow, syꝛ, let pyte your eares to me enclyne

176

"And I shall yow tell the verrey sothe of all,   1226
  Howe hit was, & who made me that wey drawe,
For sothe, Sensualite, hys propre name they call."
  "A," seyde Reason, "then I know well that felawe.
  Wylde he ys & wanton, of me stant hym noon awe."
    "Ys he soo ?" quod Vertu, "well he shalbe taught
    As a pleyeꝛ shuld to drawe another draught." 1232

177

And w*i*t*h* that came Sadnesse w*i*t*h* hys sobre chere, 1233   Sadness brings
  Bryngyng Sensualyte, beyng full of thought,   Sensuality prisoner to Virtue.
And seyde that he had take hym prysonere.   [sought.
  "A welcome!" seyde V*er*tew, "now haue I that I
  Blessyd be that good lord as thow wolde ys hit nought."
    "Why art thow so wantoun & wylde," he seyde, "for shame!
    Er thow go at large thow shalt be made more tame.

178

"But stande apart awhyle tyll I haue spoke a woorde 1240
  W*i*t*h* Frewyll a lytell, & then shalt thow know
What shalbe thy finaunce;" & then he seyde in boorde
  Vnto Frewyll, "The bende of you*r* bowe   1243   Virtue requires
  Begynneth to slake, but suche as ye haue sowe
    Must ye nedes recpe — the*r* ys nooñ other way.
    Natw*i*t*h*standyng that let see what ye can say.   1246

179

"What ys yo*u*r habylyte me to recompense   1247
  For the gret harme that ye to me haue do?"   recompense from Freewill.
"Forsothe," seyd Frewyll in opyn audyense,
  "But oonly Macrocosme more haue I nat lo.   1250   Freewill agrees to deliver Microcosm
  Take that, yef hit plese yow, I wyll that hit be so.
    Yef I may vndyrstand, ye be my good lorde."
    "In dede," seyde V*er*tu, "to that wyll I acorde." 1253

180

Then made Vertu Reson hys lyeftenaunt,   1254   which is given again to the charge of Reason and Freewill.
  And yaue hym a gret charge Macrocosme to kepe.
That dooñ, Sensualyte yelde hym recreaunt,
  And began for to angre byttyrly to wepe.   1257
  For he demyd sewerly hys sorow shuld nat slepe.
    Then made Vertu Frewyll bayll[e] vndy*r* Reson,
    The felde for to occupy to hys behoue that seson. 1260

181

And then seyde Vertu to Sensualyte,   1261   Virtue orders Sensuality to forsake his fragility and be guided by Sadness.
  "Thow shalt be rewardyd for thy besynesse.
Vndyr thys fourme all fragylyte
  Shalt thow forsake, bothe more & lesse,   1264
  And vnder the guydyng shalt thow be of Sadnesse.
    All though hit somewhat be ageyñ thy hert,
    Thy iugement ys yeuyn — thow shalt hit nat astert."

182

With that
Nature enters,
protesting that
Sensuality,
her servant,
should be
given liberty.

And euen w*ith* that came in Dame Nature,   1268

   Saying thus to V*er*tew, "Syr ye do me wrong

By duresse & constreynt to put thys creature,

   Gentyll Sensualyte, that hath me s*er*uyd long,   1271

   Cleerly from hys liberte, & set hy*m* among

      They*m* that loue hym nat, to be her vnderlowte,

      As hit were a castaway or a shoo clowte.   1274

183

   "And, parde, ye know well a rewle haue I must   1275

Virtue grants
Sensuality
freedom within
Microcosm
under the
restraint of
Sadness.

   Withyn Macrocosme; forsoth, I sey nat nay."

Quoth V*er*tu, " But Sensualyte shall nat p*er*forme y*our* lust

   Lyke as he hath do before thys, yef I may.   1278

   Therfro hym restrayñ Sadnesse shall assay.

      Howe be hit, ye shall haue y*our* hoole lyberte

      Wi*th*yn Macrocosme, as ye haue had, fre."   1281

184

And when V*er*tu had to Nature seyd thus,   1282

   A lytyll tyne hys ey castyng hym besyde,

This done,
Virtue sees
Morpheus
standing by,

He sy in a corn*er* standyng. Morpheus,

   That hy*m* before warnyd of the verryly tyde.   1285

   "A syres," seyd V*er*tu, "yet we must abyde.

      Here ys a frende of owre may nat be foryete.

      Aftyr hys desert we shall hym entrete."   1288

185

and thanks
him for his
troth and labor,

   "Morpheus," seyd V*er*tu, "I thanke yow hertyly   1289

   For yo*ur* trew hert & yo*ur* gret labo*ur*,

That ye lyst to come to me soo redyly,

   When ye undyrstood the co*m*myng of that shou*r*. 1292

   I thanke God & yow of sauyng of myñ hono*ur*.

      Wherfore thys pryuylege now to you I graunt,

      That wi*th*yn Macrocosme ye shall haue yo*ur* haunt.

186

He is given
care of the five
gates.

   "And of fyue posternes the keyes shall ye kepe,   1296

   Lettyng in and out at hem whom ye lyst,

As long as in Macrocosme yo*ur* fadyr woll crepe.

   Blere whos ey ye woll hardyly wi*th* y*our* myst, 1299

   And kepe yo*ur* werkes close there as in a chyst.

      Safe I wold desyre yow spare Pollucion.   [cioñ."

      For nothyng may me plese that sowneth to corrup-

187

And when he had thus seyde, þe keyes he hym tooke, 1303
 And toward hys castell wi*th* hys pepyll went,
Byddyng Reasoñ take good heede & about looke,
 That Sensualyte by Nature were nat shent. 1306
  "Kepe hym short," he seyde, "tyll hys lust be spent.
  For bettyr were a chylde to be vnbore,
 Then let hyt haue the wyll & for eu*er* be lore." 1309

Virtue and his people leave for the castle.

188

And when olde Attropos had seeñ & herde all thys, 1310
 How V*er*tew had opteynyd, astonyed as he stood,
He seyd to hymsylf, "Somwhat theꝝ ys amys,
 I trow well my patent be nat all good," 1313
And ran to the palyse as he had be wood,
  Seying to the godd*es*, "I see ye do but iape,
  Aftyr a worthy whew haue ye made me gape. 1316

Atropos again complains to the gods.

189

"Howe a deuyll way shuld I Vertu ou*er*throw, 1317
 When he dredyth nat all youꝝ hoole rowte!
How can ye make good youꝝ patent, wold I know.
 Hyt ys to impossybyll to bryng that abowte ; 1320
For stryke hym may I nat — that ys out of dowte."
  "A, good Attropos," seyd god Apollo,
  "An answeꝝ conuenyent shalt thow haue herto. 1323

Apollo answers:

190

"The wordys of thy patent, daꝝ I well say, 1324
 Streche to no fertheꝝ but where dame Nature
Hath iurisdiccion ; there to haue thy way,
 And largesse to stryke as longeth to thy cure. 1327
  And as for Vertu he ys no creature
  Vnder the p*re*dicament conteynyd of quantyte.
 Wherfore hys destruccion longeth nat to the." 1330

His patent is legal only within the jurisdiction of Nature. The destruction of Virtue is therefore no for him.

191

"A haa !" seyd Attropos, " then I se well 1331
 That all ye godd*es* be but counterfete.
For oo God theꝝ ys that can eu*er*y dell
 Turne as hym lyst, bothe dry & whete, 1334
 In to whos s*er*uyce I shall assay to gete.
  And yef I may ones to hys s*er*uyce come
  Youꝝ names shalbe put to oblyuyone." 1337

Atropos departs in wrath.

192

Thus went Attropos fro the paleyce wrooth.   1338

But in the mene tyme, whyle that he there was,

Glydyng by the palyce, Resydynacion gooth

Toward Macrocosme, with a peyntyd fase.   1341

Clad lyke a pylgryṁ, walkyng a gret pase,

In the forme as he had bene a man of Ynde.

He wende haue made Reson & Sadnesse boþe blynde.

Meanwhile Residivacion, disguised like a pilgrim, makes his way to Microcosm.

193

With Sensualyte was he soone aqueyntyd.   1345

To whoṁ he declaryd hys matyr pryuyly.

Yet he was espyed for all hys face peyntyd.

Then Reson hym commaundyd pyke hym thens lyghtly.

"For hys ease," quoth Sadnes, "so counseyll hym wyll I."

So was Sensualyte ay kept vndyr foote.

That to Resydyuacion myght he doo no boote. 1351

He becomes acquainted with Sensuality but is ordered by Reason to depart.

194

Then went he to Nature & askyd hyꝑ auyse,   1352

Hys entent to opteygne what was best to do.

She seyde: " Euer syth Vertew of Vyce wan the pryse,

Reson with Sadnes hath rewlyd the fylde so.   1355

That I and Sensualyte may lytyll for the do.

For I may no more but oonly kepe my cours.

And yet ys Sensualyte strengor kept & wours." 1358

No help is found in Nature.

195

Thus heryng, Residiuacion fro thens he went ageyṅ, 1359

Full of thought & sorow þat he myght nat spede.

Then Reson & Sadnesse toke wede hokẽs tweyṅ.

And all wylde wantones out of the fylde gan wede, 1362

With all the slyper grasse that grew of the sede

That Sensualyte before theꝛyn sew ;

And for thens forthe kept hit clene for Vertew. 1365

Residivacion leaves full of sorrow.

Then Reason and Sadness clear the ground of the seeds of Sensuality.

196

Then began new gresse in the fylde to spryng,   1366

All vnlyke that other, of colouꝛ fayre & bryght.

But then I aspyed a meruelous thyng.

For the grounde of the felde gan wex hoore & whyte.

I cowde nat conceyue how that be myght,

Tyll I was enformyd & taught hit to know.

But where Vertew occupyeth must nedys well grow.

New grass springs up in a marvelous manner.

197

Yet in the mene tyme, whyle the fylde thus grew,　1373
　And Reson with Sadnesse therof had gouernaunce,
Many a pryuy messynger thedyr sent Vertew,
　To know yef hit were guydyd to hys plesaunce;　1376
　Now Prayer, efte Fastyng, & oftyn tyme Penaunce,
　　And when he myght goo pryuyly, Almesdede,
　　And bade hym to hys power helpe wher he sy nede.

Virtue sends secret messengers to Microcosm.

198

Whyle that fylde thus rewlyd Reson with Sadnes.　1380
　Mawgre Dame Nature for all her carnall myght,
Came thedyr Attropos, voyde of all gladnes,
　Wrappyd in hys shete, & axyd yef any wyght　1383
　Cowde wysshe hym the wey to the Lorde of Lyght,
　　Or ellys where men myght fynd Ryghtwysnesse.
　　"Forsothe," seyde Reason, "I trow, as I gesse,　1386

Atropos draws near and asks Reason the way to the Lord of Light.

199

"At Vertu hys castell ye may soone hym fynde,　1387
　Yef ye lyst þe labour thedyr to take,
And there shall ye know, yef ye be nat blynde,
　The next wey to the Lorde of Lyght, I vndyrtake."　1390
So thedyr went Attropos, peticion to make
　To Ryghtwysnes, praying that he myght
　　Be take in to the seruyce of the Lord of Lyght.　1393

He is directed to Virtue's castle.

Atropos seeks from Righteousness to serve the Lord of Light.

200

"What," seyde Ryghtwysnes, "thow olde dotyng foole,
　Whome hast thow seruyd syth the world began
But oonly hym? Where hast thow go to scoole?
　Whether art thow double, or elles the same man　1397
　That thow were furst?" "A syr," seyde he than,
　　"I pray yow hertly holde me excusyd.
　　I am olde & febyll; my wittes ar dysvsyd."　1400

He is assured by Righteousness that the Lord is his master.

201

"Well," seyde Ryghtwysnes, "for as moche as thow　1401
　Knowest nat thy mastyr, thy name shall I chaunge.
Dethe shalt thow be callyd, from hens forward now,
　Among all the pepyll thow shalt be had straunge.　1404
　But when thow begynnest to make thy chalaunge,
　　Dredde shalt thow be, wher so thow become,
　　And to no creature shalt thow be welcome.　1407

His name is changed to DEATH, and to no creature shall he be welcome.

202

Those whom
he formerly
served shall be
put to oblivion.

"And as for theym whom thow dedyst serue,   1408
  For as moche as they presume on hem to take
That hygh name of God, they shall as they deserue
  Therfore be rewardyd. I daŕ vndyrtake,   1411
    With peyñ perpetuell, among fendes blake,
    And heŕ names shall be put to oblyuyoñ
    Among men, but hit be in derysyon."   1414

203

"A ha!" seyde Attropos, "now begyñ I wex gladde 1415
  That I shall thus avengyd of hem be,
Syth they so long tyme haue made me so madde."
  "Yee," quoth Ryghtwysnes, "here what I sey to the:
  The Lord of Lyght sent the worde by me

Death is given
a place in
Microcosm.

    That in Macrocosme sesyne shalt thow take;
    Wherfore thy darte redy loke thow make."   1421

204

And as sone as Vertu that vndyrstood,   1422

Virtue then
despatches
Priesthood to
the field with
the sacraments.

  He seyde he was plesyd that hit shuld so be.
And euyñ forthewith he commaundyd Presthood
  To make hym redy the felde for to se.   1425
    Soo thedyr went Presthood with benygnyte,
    Conueying thedyr the blessyd sacrament
    Of Eukaryst.   But furst were theder sent   1428

205

Previously had
come thither
Confession,
etc.

Confession, Contricion, and Satisfaccion,   1429
  Sorow for Synne, & gret Repentaunce,
Holy Deuocion, with Good Dysposicion—
  All these thedyr came & also Penaunce,   1432
    As her dewte was to make puruyaunce
    Ageyñ the commyng of that blessyd Lorde.
    Feythe, Hoope, & Charyte therto were acorde. 1435

206

The field is
cleansed
within and
without, and
the Lord of
Light is
received with
fitness.

Reason with Sadnes dyd hys dylygence   1436
  To clense the fylde withyn & without.
And when they sy the bodyly presence
  Of that hooly Eukaryst, lowly gan they lowte.   1439
    So was that Lord receuyd, out of dowte,
    With all humble chere, debonayŕ & benygne,
    Lykly to hys plesure—hit was a gret sygne.   1442

207

Then came to the fylde the mynystre fynall,   1443
  Called Holy Vnccion, with a crysmatory.
The v hygh weyes in especiall

    Therof he anoyntyd & made hit sanctuary.   1446
    Whom folowyd Dethe, whych wold nat tary
      Hys feruent power there to put in vre,
      As he was commaundyd, grauntyng Dame Nature.

208

He toke hys darte, callyd hys mortall launce,   1450
  And bent hys stroke toward the feldys herte.
That seyng, Presthoode bade Good Remembraunce
  Toward the felde turne hym & aduerte.   1453
  For except hym all vertues thense must sterte.

    And euyn with that, Dethe there sesyne took;
    And then all the company clerely hit forsook. 1456

209

And as sone as Dethe thus had sesyñ take,   1457
  The colour of the felde was chaungyd sodenly,
The grasse theryn, seere as though hit had be bake.
  And the fyue hygh weyes were muryd opon hy, 1460
  That fro thensforward nooñ entre shuld therby.

    The posternes also were without lette,
    Bothe inward & outward, fyn fast shette.   1463

210

Whyche dooñ, sodenly Dethe vanysshyd away,   1464
  And Vertu exaltyd was aboue the firmament,
Where he toke the crowne of glory that ys ay

    Preparate by Alpha & Oo omnipoten[t].   1467
    The swete Frute of Macrocosme þedyr with hym went.
    And on all thys mater as I stood musyng thus,
    Agayn fro the felde to me came Morpheus,   1470

211

Seying thus, "What chere! howe lyketh the thys syght?
  Hast thow sene ynowgh, or wyll thow se more?"
"Nay syr," I seyde," my trouthe I þow plyght,
  Thys ys suffysyent, yef I knew wherfore   1474

    Thys was to me shewyd, for therof the lore
    Coueyte I to haue, yef I gete myght."
    "Folow me," quod he, "and haue thy delyght." 1477

212

So I hym folowyd, tyll he had me brought   1478
  To a fouresquare herber wallyd round about.
"Loo," quoth Morpheus, "here mayst thow *þat þow* sought
  Fynde, yef thow wyll, I put the out of dout."   1481
A lytyll whyle we stood styll there wi*th*out,
  Tyll Wytte, chyef porte*r* of that herber gate,

  Requyryd by stody, let vs in the*r* ate.   1484

213

But when I came in I me*r*uelyd gretly   1485
  Of that I behelde & herde there reporte.
For furst, in a chayar, apparaylyd royally,

  There sate Dame Doctryne, her chyldren to exorte.
And about her was many a sondry sorte ;
  Som wyllyng to lerne dyu*er*se seyence,
  And som for to have p*er*fyte intellygence.   1491

214

Crownyd she was lyke an Emp*er*esse,   1492

  Wi*th* iii crownes standyng on her hede on hy.
All thyng about hy*r* an infynyte processe
  Were to declare, I tell yow certeynly.   1495
Neu*er*thelese som in mynde therof haue I.
  Whyche I shall to yow, as God wyll yeue me grace,
  As I sawe & herde, tell in short space.   1498

215

Fast by Doctryne on that ooñ syde,   1499
  As I remembre, sate Holy Texte,
That openyd hys mouthe to the pepyll wyde,
  But nat in comp*a*rysoñ to Glose that sate next. 1502
Moralyzacion wi*th* a cloke context

  Sate ; & Scrypture was scrybe to they*m* all.
  He sate ay wrytyng of that that shuld fall.   1505

216

These were tho that I there knew—   1506
  By no man*er* wey of olde aqueyntaunce,
But as I before saw theym wi*th* V*er*tew
  Company in felde & hauyng dalyaunce.   1509
And as I thus stood half in a traunce,
  Whyle they were occupyed in her besynesse,

  Abowte the walles myn ey gan I dresse.   1512

217

Where I behelde the meruelous story   1513

That euer I yet saw in any pycture,

For on tho walles was made memory

    Singlerly of euery creature   1510

    That there had byñ, bothe forme and stature;

      Whos names reherse I wyll, as I can

      Bryng theym to mynde in ordre — euery man   1519

218

Furst, to begyñ, there was in portrature   1520

    Adam; & Eue holdyng an appyll round;

Noe in a shyp; & Abraham hauyng sure

    A flynt stone in hys hand; & Isaac lay bound   1523

    On an hygh mount; Iacob slepyng sound,

      And a long laddyr stood hym besyde;

      Ioseph in a cysterne was also there that tyde.   1526

219

Next whom stood Moyses, with hys tables two;   1527

    Aaron & Vrre, hys armes supportyng;

Ely in a brennyng chare was there also.

    And Elyze stood, clad in an hermytes clothyng;   1530

    Dauid with an harpe & a stooñ slyng.

      Isaye, Ieremy, and Ezechiell;

      And closyd with lyons, holy Danyell;   1533

220

Abacuc, Mychee, with Malachy;   1534

    And Ionas out of a whales body commyng;

Samuell in a temple; & holy Zakary

    Besyde an awter all blody standyng;   1537

    Osee with Iudyth stoode there conspyryng

      The dethe of Oloferne; and Sal[a]mon also,

      A chylde with hys swerde dyuydyng in two.   1540

221

Many moo prophetys certeynly there were,   1541

    Whos names now come nat to my mynde.

Melchisedech also aspyed I there,

    Bred & wyne offryng as fyll to hys kynde.   1544

    Ioachym and Anne stood all behynde,

      Embrasyd in armes to the gyldyn gate.

      And holy Iohñ Baptyst in a desert sate.   1547

where is portrayed a marvelous story.

First on one wall in portraiture is the story of Adam and Eve, Noah, etc. (Old Testament).

222

And now co*m*myth to my remembraunce   1548
  I am avysyd I saw Sodechy,
And Amos also, w*it*h sobre countenaunce,
  Standyng w*it*h her faces toward Sophony.   1551
  Neemy & Esdras bare hem company.
    The holy man Ioob as an impotent,
    Then folowyd in pycture w*it*h Thoby pacyent. 1554

223

These, w*it*h many mo, on that oon syde   1555
  Of that grene herber portrayed were.
"A," seyde Morpheous, "a lytyll tyme abyde.
  Turne thy face where thy bak was ere   1558
  And beholde well what thou seest there."
    Than I me turnyd as he me bade.

Upon the opposite wall I see Peter, Paul, etc. (New Testament and Church Fathers).

    W*it*h hert stedefast & countenaunce sade   1561

224

Where I saw Petyr, with hys keyes, stande;   1562
  Poule w*it*h a swerde; Iames also
W*it*h a scalop; & Thomas holdyng in hys hande
  A spere; & Phylyp aprochyd hym too.   1565
  Iames, the lesse, next hem in pycture loo
    Stood, w*it*h Bartylmew, whyche was all flayñ.
    Symon & Thadee shewyd how they were slayñ. 1568

225

Mathy and Barnabe, drawyng lottys, stood.   1569
  Next whom was Marke, a lyon hym by
Hys booke holdyng; & Mathew, in hys mood,
  Resemblyd an Aungell w*it*h wyng*es* gloryosly.   1572
  Luke had a calfe to holde hys booke on hy.
    And Iohñ w*it*h a cupp & palme in hys hande;
    An Egle bare hys booke—thus saw I hem stande.

226

Gregory and Ierome, Austyn and Ambrose,   1576
  W*it*h pylyons on her hedys, stood lyke doctours.
Bernard w*it*h Anselme, and, as I suppose,
  Thomas of Alquyñ, & Domynyk, confessours,   1579
  Benet, & Hew, relygyous gou*er*nours,
    Martyne, & Iohñ, w*it*h bysshops tweyne,
    Were there also, & Crysostoñ certeyne.   1582

227

Behynde all these was worshipfull Beede.   1583
  All behynde & next him stood Orygene,
Hydyng hys face, as he of hys deede
  Had hem ashamyd — ye woot what I mene ;   1586
  For of errour was he nat all clene.
    And on that syde stood there, last of all,
    The nobyll prophetyssa, Sybyll men hyr call.   1589

228

Let me remembre me, now I yow pray,   1590
  My brayne ys so thynne, I deme in myñ hert
Som of the felyshyp that I there say,
  In all thys whyle, have I ouerstert.   1593
  A benedycyte nooñ ere cowde I aduert
    To thynke on Andrew the Apostyll with hys crosse,
    Whom to forgete were a gret losse.   1596

229

Many ooñ moo were peyntyd on that wall,   1597
  Whos names now come nat to my remembraunce.
But these I markyd in especiall.

In the midst of the harbor sits Doctrine richly appareled.

  And moo cowde I tell, in contynuaunce   1600
  Of tyme, but forthe to shewe yow the substaunce
    Of thys matyr, in the myddes of that herbere,
    Sate Doctryne, coloryd as any crystall clere.   1603

230

Crownyd as I tolde yow late here before,   1604
  Whos apparayll was worthe tresour infynyte —
All erthely rychesse count I no more
  To that in comparyson valewyng then a myte.   1607
  Ouer her heede houyd a culuer fayre & whyte,
    Oute of whos byll procedyd a gret leme   Over her head hovers a culver.
    Downward to Doctryne, lyke a son beme.   1610

231

The wordys of Doctryne yaue gret redolence,   1611 Her words savor sweet.
  In swetness of sauour, to her dysciples all.
Hyt ferre excedyd myrre and frankensence
  Or any other tre spyce or ellys gall.   1614

She bids me come near.

  And when she me aspyed, anon she gan me call.
    And commaundyd Morpheus that he shuld bryng me neere ;
    For she wolde me shew the effecte of my desyre. 1617

232

Doctrine
interprets the
vision.

She seyde, "I know the cause of thy commyng   1618
Ys to vndyrstand, be myñ enformacion,
Sensybly, the mateŕ of Morpheus hys shewyng
As he hath the ledde aboute in vysyon.   1621
Wheŕfore now I apply thy naturall resoñ
Vnto my wordys, &, eŕ thow hens wende,
Thow shalt hit know, begynnyng & ende.   1624

233

Imprisonment
of Eolus
signifies that
unbridled
wealth
increaseth
misrule.

" Furst, where Eolus to Pluto was brought,   1625
By hys owne neglygence takyñ prysonere
Withyn the erthe : for he to ferre sought —
Sygnyfyed ys nomore be that matere   1628
But oonly to shew the howe hit dothe apere
That welthe, vnbrydelyd dayly at thyne ey,
Encreseth mysrewle & oft causyth foly.   1631

234

" For lyke as Eolus, beyng at hys large,   1632
Streytyd hym sylf thorow his owne lewdenesse —
For he wold deele where he had no charge —
Ryght so wantons, by her wyldenesse,   1635
Oft sythe bryng hem sylf in dystresse,
Because they somtyme to largely deele.
What may worse be suffryd than ouer mykyll weele

235

Minos judges
every man
according to
his wicked-
ness.

" By Mynos, the iuge of hell desperate,   1639
May he vndyrstand Goddes ryghtwysnes,
That to euery wyght hys peyne deputate
Assygneth, acordyng to hys wykydnes.   1642
Wheŕfore he ys callyd Iuge of crewelnes.
And as for Diana & Neptunus compleynt,
Fyguryd may be fooles reson feynte.   1645

The complaint
of Diana and
Neptune
against Eolus
signifies the
folly of fools
in attempting
the impossible.

236

" For lyke as they made heŕ suggestion   1646
To haue me Eolus from course of hys kynde
Whyche was impossible to bryng to correccion,
For euermore hys liberte haue wyll the wynde.   1649
In lyke wyse, fooles otherwhyle be blynde,
Wenyng to subdew, with her ooñ hande,
That ys ouer mekyll for all an hoole lande.   1652

237

"But what foloweth therof that shall thow heere: 1653
  When they were come to the banket,
The gret Apollo, with hys sad chere,
  So fayre & curteysly gan theym entrete,   1656
  That he made heř beerdys on the new gete.
    Loo, what wysdom̃ dothe to a foole —
    Wherfore ar chyldren put to scoole.   1659

Apollo at his banquet causes their complaint to be forgotten.

238

"Oft ys hit seene, with sobre contenaunce,   1660
  That wyse men fooles ouercome ay,
Turnyng as hem lyst and all her varyaunce,
  Chaunge from ernest in to mery play.   1663
  What were they bothe amendyd that day?
    When they were dreuyn to her wyttes ende,
    Were they nat fayne to graunt to be hys frende?   1666

239

"Ryght so fooles, when they haue dooñ   1667
  All that they can, than be they fayne
Yeue vp her mater to oblyuyoñ.
  Without rewarde they haue no more brayne.   1670
  And yet full oft hath hit be seyne,
    When they hit haue foryete and set at nought,
    That they full deere haue aftyrward hit bought.   1673

So fools give up their matter to oblivion.

240

"And as for all tho that repr esent   1674
  To be callyd goddys at that banket,
Resemble false ydollys; but to thys entent
  Was Morpheous commaundyd thedyr the to fet,   1677
  That thow shuldest know the maner & the get
    Of the paynym lawe and of her beleue,
    How false idolatry ledeth hem by the sleue.   1680

The Gods resemble false idols.

241

"For soone vppon the worldys creacion,   1681
  When Adam & Eue had broke the precept —
Whyche clerkes call the Tyme of Deuyacion,
  The worldly pepyll in paynym law slept,   . 1684
  Tyll Moyses vndyr God the tables of stone kept.
    In whyche tyme poetys feynyd many a fable
    To dyscrete reson ryght acceptable.   1687

In the beginning people slept in pagan law.

The poets feigned many fables

242

"And to the entent that they should sownde   1688
To the cares of hem the more plesauntly

which were
given ground
and names and
called gods.
That they shuld reede or here, þey yaue theym a grounde
And addyd names vnto theym naturally :   1691
Of whom they spake & callyd hem goddes hy,
Som for the streyngthe & myght of her nature,
And som for her sotyll wytty coniecture.   1694

243

"By nature thus as the seuyn planettys   1695
Haue her propre names by astronomers,
But goddys were they called by oold poetys,
For her gret feruency of wyrkyng in her speres —   1698
Experyence preueth thys at all yeres.
And for as other that goddes callyd be
For sotyll wytte, that shall I teche the.   1701

244

"How they by that hygh name of god came.   1702
In thys seyd tyme, the pepyll was so rude
That what maner creature, man or woman,
Cowde any nouelte contryue & conclude   1705
For the comon wele, all the multitude
Of the comon peple a god shuld hym call,
Or a goddesse, aftyr hit was fall   1708

245

Thus Ceres
was thought to
increase the
product of
corn and was
therefore
called Goddess
of Corn.
"Of the same thyng that was so new founde —   1709
As Ceres, for she the craft of tylthe founde,
Wherby more plenteuosly corne dyd habounde,
The pepyll her callyd thorout euery londe   1712
Goddesse of Corne, wenyng in her honde
Had leyn all power of cornys habundaunce.
Thus wer the paynemes deceyuyd by ignoraunce.

246

So Isis, Pan,
etc.
"In lyke maner, Isys was callyd the Goddesse   1716
Of Frute, for she fyrst made hit multyply
By the meane of gryffyng : and so by processe
The name of Pan gan to deyfy.   1719
For he furst founde the mene shepe to guy.
Som tooke hit also by her condicioñ
As Pluto, Fortune, & suche other doñ.   1722

247

"Thus all that poetys put vndyr couerture 1723
Of fable the rurall pepyll hit took
Propyrly as acte, refusyng the fygure;
   Which errour som of hem neuer forsook. 1726
   Oft a false myrrour deceyueth a mannys look,
     As thow mayst dayly proue at thyne ey.
     Thus were the paynyms deseuyd generally. 1729

248

"That seyng, the dedely enemy of mankynde, 1730
   By hys power permyssyue, entryd the ymages
Withyn the temples to make the pepyll blynde
   In her idolatry, standyng on hygh stages; 1733
   In so moche, whoo vsyd daungerous passages,
     Any maner wey by watyr or be londe,
     When hyd hys sacryfyce, hys answere redy founde.

249

"Thus duryng the Tyme of Deuyacion. 1737
   From Adam to Moyses, was idolatry
Thorow the world vsyd in comon opynyoñ.
   These were the goddys that thow there sy. 1740
   And as for the awayters that stood hem by
     They polytyk philosophyrs & poetes were,
     Whyche feynyd the fables that I speke of here. 1743

The gods at the banquet are the idols, the waiters are the poets and philosophers who feigned the fables.

250

"Then sesyd the Tyme of Deuyacion, 1744
   When Moyses receuyd that tables of stone,
Entryng the Tyme of Reuocacion.
   On the Mount of Synay, stondyng alone, 1747
   God yaue hym myght ayene all hys fone.
     And then began the Olde Testament
     Whyche to the pepyll by Moyses was sent. 1750

The three times. Deviation, Revocation,

251

"And that tyme duryd to the incarnacion 1751
   Of Cryst, & then began hit to sese.
For then came the Tyme of Reconsylvacion
   Of man to God—I tell the doutlese— 1754
   When the Soñ of Man put hym in prese,
     Wylfully to suffre dethe for mankynde.
     In holy scrypture thys mayst thow fynde. 1757

Reconciliation,

252

"Thys Reconsylyacion was the Tyme of Grace,   1758
When foundyd was the churche vppoñ the feyr stooñ,
And to holy Petyr the key delyueryd was
   Of heuyn ; then helle dyspoyled was anooñ.   1761
   Thus was mankynde delyueryd from hys fooñ.
   And then began the New Testament
     That the Crystyñ pepyll beleue in present.   1764

253

"Whyche iii tymes, a sondry deuydyd,   1765

are portrayed
upon the walls.
   Mayst thow here see, yef thow lyst beholde.
The furst behynde the yn pycture ys prouydyd.
   The second of the lyft hande shewe prophetes olde. 1768
   The iii^de on the ryght hande here hit ys to the tolde.
   Thus hast thow in vysyon the verrey fygure
     Of these iii tymes here shewyd in purtrayture.   1771

254

"That ys to sey, furst, of Deuyacion   1772
From Adam to Moyses, recordyng Scripture ;
Secund, fro Moyses to the incarnacion
   Of Cryst kepeth Reuocacions cure.   1775
   And as for the thryd, thow mayst be verrey sure,
   Wyll dure from thens to the worldes ende.
     But now the iiii^th must thow haue in mynde,   1778

255

The time of
Pilgrimage or
of War is
figured upon
the fourth wall.
"Whyche ys callyd propurly, the Tyme of Pylgremage 1779
   Aftyr som ; & som name hit otherwyse
And call hyt the Tyme of Daungerous Passage ;
   And som Tyme of Werre, that fully hyt dyspyse.   1782
   But what so hit be namyd, I woll the auyse —
   Remembre hit well and prynte hit in thy mynde,
     Wherof the fygure mayst thow me behynde.   1785

256

"And elles remembre thysylf in thyñ hert,   1786

This is
signified by
the battle
between Vice
and Virtue.
   Howe Vyce & Vertu dayly theym occupy,
In maner, ooñ of hem hym to peruert.
   Another, to bryng hym to endeles glory.   1789
   Thus they contynu fyght for the victory.
   Hyt ys no nede herof to tell the moore,
     For in thys short vysyoñ thow hast seen hit before.

257

"And as for Attropos greuous compleynt   1793
  Vnto the goddes betokeneth nomore
But oonly to shewe the how frendely constreynt
  On a stedfast hert weyeth full soore.   1796
   Good wyll requyreth good wyll ayene therfore.
    Dyscorde to Dethe hathe ay byñ a frende,
    For Dyscorde bryngeth many to her ende.   1799

258

"Wherfore Dethe thought he wolde avengyd be   1800
  Oñ hys frendes quarell yef that he myght,
For heř gret vnkyndnes, in so moche as she
  Was among hem all had so in despyte   1803
  And at that banket made of so lyte;
    Whyche causyd hym among hem to cast in a booñ,
    That found theym gnawyng ynough euerychooñ. 1806

259

"Thus oft ys seeñ oo frende for a notheř   1807
  Wyll say & do & somtyme matyrs feyne;
And also kynnysmen, a cosyñ, or a brotheř,
  Woll for hys aly, eř he haue cause, compleyne.   1810
   And where that he loueth do hys besy peyne,
    Hys frendes matyř as hys owne to take,
    Whyche oft sythe causeth mochyll sorow awake. 1813

260

"Be hyt ryght or wrong, he changeth nat a myte— 1814
  As toward that poynt he taketh lytell heede.
So that he may haue hys froward appetyte
  Performyd, he careth nat howe hys soule speede, 1817
  Of God or deuyll haue suche lytyll dreede.
    Howe be hyt, ooñ theř ys þat Lorde ys of all,
    Whyche to euery wyght at last rewarde shall.   1820

261

"And as for the batayll betwene Vyce & Vertew holde,
  So pleynly appereth to the inwardly,
To make exposicioñ theřof, new or olde,
  Were but superfluyte—therfore refuse hit I.   1824
  In man shall thow fynde that werre kept dayly,
    Lyke as thow hast seeñ hit fowtyñ before thy face;
    The pyctuř me behynde shewyth hit in lytyll space.

262

<table>
<tr><td>Microcosm is
the world of
man.</td><td>"And as for Macrocosme, hit ys no more to say
But the lesse worlde, to the comon entent</td><td>1828</td></tr>
</table>

Microcosm is
the world of
man.

"And as for Macrocosme, hit ys no more to say   1828
But the lesse worlde, to the comon entent
Whyche applyed ys to mañ both nyght and day —
So ys man the felde to whyche all were sent   1831
Oñ both partyes; & they that thedyr went
Sygnyfy nomore but aftyr the condicioñ
Of euery mans opynyoñ.   1834

263

Perseverance
betokens the
continuance of
virtuous
living.

"And as for the nobyll knyght *Perseueraunce*,   1835
Whyche gate the felde when hit was almost gooñ,
Betokeneth nomore but the contynuaunce
Of vertuous lyuyng tyll dethe hath ouergooñ.   1838

Whoso
perseveres is
rewarded with
a crown.

Who so wyll doo, rewardyd ys anoñ,
As Vertu was with the crowne on hy,
Whyche ys nomore but euerlastyng glory.   1841

264

Prescience and
Predestination
are the
rewarders of
vice and
virtue.

"And as for Prescience and Predestinacion,   1842
That eche of hem rewardyd aftyr hys desert,
Is to vndyrstond nomore but dampnacion
To vycyous pepyll ys the verrey scourge smert   1845
Rewarde; for they fro Vertu wolde peruert.
And endelese ioy ys to hem that be electe
Rewardyd & to all that folow the same secte.   1848

265

The five keys
are man's five
wits.

"And as for the keyes of the posterns fyue,   1849
Whyche were to Morpheus rewardyd for hys labour,
Sygnyfy nat ellys but whyle man ys on lyue
Hys v inwarde wyttes shalbe euery houre   1852
In hys slepe occupyed, in hele and in langoure,
With fantasyes, tryfyls, illusions & dremes,
Whyche poetys call Morpheus stremes.   1855

266

Residivacion
signifies the
return of man
to sin.

"And as for Resydiuacion ys nomore to sey   1856
But aftyr confessioñ turnyng ayene to syn,
Whyche to euery man retorneth sauns deley
To vycyous lyuyng ageyñ hym to wyn.   1859
Whyle any man lyueth wyll hit neuer blyn,

Reason and
Sadness
prevent such
conclusion.

That cursyd conclusion for to bryng abowte,
But Resoñ with Sadnes kepe hit styll owte.   1862

267

"Here hast thow propurly the verrey sentence   1863
Herde now declaryd of thys vysyoñ.
The pycture also yeueth clere intellygence,
  Therof beholdyn with good discresyoñ.   1866
  Loke well aboute & take consyderasioñ,
    As I haue declaryd, whether hit so be."
      "A syr," quoth Morpheus, "what tolde I the! 1869

268

"Hast thow nat now thyne hertes desyre?   1870
  Loke on yoñ wall yonder before."
And all that tyme stood I in a wyre
  Whyche way furst myñ hert wold yeue more   1873
  To looke; in a stody stood I therfore.
    Neuerthelese at last, as Morpheus me badde,
    I lokyd forward with countenaunce sadde,   1876

269

Where I behelde in portrayture   1877
  The maner of the felde, euyñ as hit was
Shewyd me before; & euery creature
  Oñ boothe sydes beyng drawyn in small space   1880
  So curyously, in so lytell a compace,
    In all thys world was neuer thyng wrought;
    It were impossyble in erthe to be thought.   1883

All things as described are portrayed upon the wall.

270

And when I had long beholde that pycture—   1884
  "What," quoth Morpheous, "how long shalt thow looke,
Daryng as a dastard, oñ yoñ portrayture?
  Come of for shame; thy wytte stant a crooke."   1887
  I heryng that myñ hert to me tooke,
    Towarde the iiii^th wall turnyng my vysage,
    Where I sawe poetys & phylosophyrs sage,   1890

I look to the fourth wall, where are poets and philosophers.

271

Many ooñ mo then at the banket   1891
  Seruyd the goddes, as I seyde before.
Soiñ were made standyng, & som in chayeres set,
  Som lookyng oñ bookes, as they had stodyed sore, 1894
  Soin drawyng almenakes, & in her handes bore
    Astyrlabes, takyng the altytude of the sonne—
    Among whoiñ Dyogenes sate in a tonne.   1897

272

And as I was lokyng on that fourthe wall,   1898
  Of Dyogenes beholdyng the ymage,
Sodeynly Doctryne began me to call,
  And bad me turne toward hyr my vysage.   1901
  And so then I dyd with humble corage.   [thentent
    "What thynkest thow," she sayde, "hast thow nat
    Yet of these foure wallys —what they represent? 1904

273

Doctrine
explains the
pictures of the
Times.
"The pycture on the fyrst, that standeth at my bake, 1905
  Sheweth the the present Tyme of Pylgremage,
Of whyche before I vnto the spake,
  Whyche ys the Tyme of Daungerus Passage.   1908
  The secund, dyrectly ageyñ my vysage,
    The Tyme expresseth of Deuyacion,
    Whyle paynyñ lawe had the domynacion.   1911

274

"The thryd wall, standyng on my lyft hande,   1912
  The Tyme represententeth of Reuocacion.
And the fourth, standyng on my ryght hande,
  Determyneth the Tyme of Reconsylyacion.   1915
  Thys ys the effect of thy vysion.
    Wherfore the nedyth nomore theron to muse—
    Hit were but veyñ thy wittes to dysvse.   1918

275

Spend well the
Time of
Reconcilia-
tion.
"But duryng the Tyme of Reconsiliacion   1919
  Thy Tyme of Pylgremage looke well thow spende
And then woll gracious Predestinacion
  Bryng the to glory at thy last ende."   1922
  And euyn with that cam to my mynde
This reminds
me of my
former doubt.
  My furst conclusion that I was abowte
    To haue drevyñ, er slepe made me to lowte— 1925

276

I pray
Doctrine to
reconcile
Reason and
Sensuality.
That ys to sey, howe Sensualyte   1926
  With Reason to acorde myght be brought aboute.
Whyche causyd me to knele downe on my kne
  And beseke Doctryne determyne that doute.   1929
  "Oo Lord God!" seyde Doctryne, "canst thow nat with
    Me that conclusioñ bryng to an ende?   [oute
    Ferre ys fro the wytte & ferther good mende." 1932

277

And euen w*ith* that Dethe gan appere,   1933   Death enters;
   Shewyng hymsylf as though that he wolde
Hys darte haue occupyed w*ith*yn that herbere.
   But the*r* was nooñ for hym, yong nor olde,   1936
   Saue oonly I, Doctryne hym tolde,
     And when I herde hyr w*ith* hy*m* comon thus,
     I me w*ith*drew behynde Morpheus,   1939

278

Dredyng full soore lest he w*ith* hys dart,   1940   of whom I am afraid.
   Thorow Doctrynes word*es*, any entresse
In me wolde haue had or claymed any part —
   Whyche shuld haue causyd me gret heuynesse.   1943
   W*ith*yn whyche tyme & short processe,
     Came theder Reason & Sensualyte.   Reason and Sensuality come thither.
     "A," quoth Doctryne, "ryght welcome be ye.   1946

279

"Hyt ys nat long syth we of yow spake.   1947
   Ye must, er ye go, det*er*myne a dowte."
And euyñ w*ith* that she the mate*r* brake
   To they*m* and tolde hit eu*er*y where abowte.   1950
   I wold haue be thens, yef I had mowte.
     For feere I lookyd as blak as a coole.   I am more afraid.
     I wold haue cropyn in a mouse hoole.   1953

280

"What!" quoth Doctryne, "where ys he now,   1954
   That meuyd thys mater straunge & diffuse?
He ys a coward — I make myñ avow.
   He hydeth hys hede, hys mocion to refuse."   1957
     "Blame hym nat," quoth Reson, "alwey that to vse   Reason excuses my fear, since Death is to be shunned.
     When he seeth Dethe so neere at hys hande.
     Yet ys hys part hym to wythstande.   1960

281

"Or, at the leste way, ellys fro hym flee   1961   With which sentiment Sensuality accords.
   As long as he may — who dothe otherwyse
As an ydiote." Quoth Sensualyte,
   'Who dredyth nat Dethe wyse men hym dyspyse."
   "What!" seyde Doctryne, "how long hathe thys gyse
     Beholdyn & vsyd thus atwyx yow tweyne?
     Yee were nat wont to acorde certeyne."   1967

282

"Yes," quoth Reson, "in thys poynt, alway   1968
 To euery man haue we yeuen our counsayll
Dethe for to flee as long as they may.
  All though we otherwyse haue done our trauayll 1971
  Yche other to represse, yet withoute fayll
   In that poynt oonly dyscordyd we neuer.
   Thus condescendyd theryñ be we for euer." 1974

283

"A! A!" seyde Doctryne, "then ys the conclusion 1975
 Clerely determynyd of the gret dowte

That here was meuyd" — & halfe in derysion
  She me then callyd & bade me loke owte. 1978
  "Come forthe," she seyde, "and feere nat thys rowte."

   And euen with that, Reson and Sensualyte
   And Dethe fro thens were vanysshyd all thre. 1981

284

Then lokyd I forthe as Doctryne me badde. 1982
 When Dethe was gooñ, me thought I was bolde
To shew my sylf, but yet was I sadde.
  Me thought my dowte was nat as I wolde, 1985

  Clerely and opynly declaryd & tolde.
   Hit sownyd to me as a parable,
   Derke as a myste, or a feynyd fable. 1988

285

And Doctryne my conceyte gan espy.   1989
 "Wherfore," seyde she, "standyst thow so styll?
Whereyn ys thy thought? Art thow in stody
  Of thy question? Hast thow nat thy fyll 1992
  To the declaryd? Tell me thy wyll.
   Herdest thow nat Reson & Sensualyte
   Declare thy dowte here before the?" 1995

286

"Forsothe," quoth I, "I herde what they seyde. 1996
 But neuerthelese my wyt ys so thynne,
And also of Dethe I was so afrayed,
  That hit ys oute where hyt went ynne. 1999
  And so that matyr can I nat wynne
   Without your helpe & benyuolence
   Therof to expresse the verray sentence." 2002

287

"Well," quoth Doctryne "then ycue attendaunce 2003 Doctrine interprets my vision.
Vnto my wordes, & thow shalt here
Opynly declaryd the concordaunce
  Atwene Sensualyte & Reson in fere. 2006
  Ycf thow take hede, hit clerely dothe apere
    How they were knette in ooñ opynyon.
    Bothe agayñ Dethe helde contradyccyon. 2009

288

"Whyche concordaunce nomore sygnyfyeth 2010
  To pleyne vndyrstandyng, but in euery mane In one point Reason and Sensuality
Bothe Sensualyte & Reson applyeth   accord—in the
  Rather Dethe to fle then with hit to be tane. 2013 fear of Death.
  Loo in that poynt accorde they holly thane.
    And in all other they clerely dyscorde.
    Thus ys trewly set thy doutfull monacorde." 2016

289

I, heryng that, knelyd on my kne 2017
  An thankyd her lowly for hyr dyscyplyne,
That she vouchesafe, of hyr benygnyte,
  Of tho gret dowtys me to enlumyne. 2020
  Well was she worthy to be called Doctryne,
    Ycf hit had be nomore but for the solucion
    Of my demaunde and of thys straunge vysyon. 2023

290

And as I with myne heede began for to bow, 2024
  As me well ought to do hyr reuerence, Doctrine suddenly vanishes.
She thens departyd — I cannat tell how.
  But withyn a moment gooñ was she thens. 2027
  Then seyde Morpheus, "Let vs go hens.
    What shuld we heere tary lengere?
    Hast thow nat herde a generall answere 2030

291

To all thy matyrs that thow lyst to meue? 2031
  My tyme draweth nere that I must rest."
And euyn therwith he tooke me by the sleue
  And seyde, "Goo we hens, for that hold I best. 2034
  As good ys ynowgh as a gret feste. Morpheus leads me back
    Thow hast seeñ ynowgh; hold the content."
    And euyn with that forthe with hym I went, 2037

292

to my bed
Tyll he hade me brought agene to my bedde,   2038
  Where he me founde, and then pryuyly
He stale awey. I cowde nat vndyrstande

and secretly
steals away.
Where he became, but sodenly   2041
  As he came, he went — I tell yow veryly.

Then I awake
Whyche doon, fro slepe I gan to awake.
  My body all in swet began for to shake   2044

293

in great dread.
For drede of the syght that I had seene,   2045
  Wenyng to me all had be trew
Actuelly doon where I had beene,
  The batayll holde twene Vyce & Vertew.   2048
But when I sy hit, hit was but a whew,
  A dreme, a fantasy, & a thyng of nought.

It is all a
dream.
To study theron I had nomore thought.   2051

294

Tyll at the last I gan me bethynke   2052
  For what cause shewyd was thys vysyon.
I knew nat; wherfore I toke pen & ynke
  And paper to make therof mencion   2055

Lest fault be
found in me,
I write down
what I have
seen.
In wrytyng, takyng consideracion
  That no defaute were founde in me,
Wheron accusyd I ought for to be   2058

295

For slowthe, that I had left hit vntolde —   2059
  Nowthyr by mowthe nor in remembraunce
Put hit in wrytyng; wher thorow manyfolde
  Weyes of accusacion myght turne me to greuaunce. 2062
All thys I saw as I lay in a traunce,
  But whedyr hit was with myne ey bodyly
Or nat in certayn, God knoweth and nat I.   2065

296

That to dyscerne I purpose nat to dele.   2066
  So large by my wyll hit longeth nat to me.
Were hit dreme or vysion, for your own wele,
  All that shall hit rede, here rad, or se,   2069
Take therof the best & let the worst be —

Take from my
writing the
best and leave
the chaff.
  Try out the corne clene from the chaff
And then may ye say ye have a sure staff   2072

297

To stande by at nede, yef ye woll hit holde   2073
   And walke by the way of Ver̃tu hys loore.
But alwey beware, be ye yong or olde,
     That your̃ frewyll ay to Ver̃tu moore   2076   Walk the way of Virtue.
      Apply than to Vyce, the eysyer̃ may be boore
       The burdyn of the fylde, that ye dayly fyght
       Agayñ your̃ iii enemyes, for all her gret myght. 2079   Fight against your enemies,

298

That ys to sey, the Deuyll & the Flesshe   2080   the Devil, the Flesh, and
   And also the Worlde, wit*h* hys glosyng chere,   the World.
Whyche oñ yow looketh euer̃ newe & fresshe —
   But he ys nat as he doth apere.   2083
    Lok ye kepe yow ay out of hys daungere.
     And so the vyctory shall ye obteyne,
     Vyce fro yow exylyd & Ver̃tew in yow reyne.   2086   Let Virtue in you reign.

299

And then shall ye haue the triu*m*phall guerdouñ   2087   Thine be the glory and the
   That God reser̃ueth to euer̃y creature   celestial mansion.
Aboue in hys celestiall mansiouñ,
   Joy and blys infinite, eternally to endure.   2090
   Wher̃of we say we wold fayñ be sure.
     But the wey thedyr̃ward to holde be we lothe,
     That oft sythe causeth the good Lorde to be wrothe.

300

And by oure desert oure ha*b*itacion chaungeth   2094
   Fro ioy to peyne & woo per̃petuelly,
From hys gloryous syght thus he vs estraungeth,
For our̃ vycyous lyuyng, thorough owre owne foly. 2097
Wherfore let vs pray to that Lord of Glory,
     Whyle we in erthe bee, that he wyll yeue vs grace,   Let us pray the Lord of Glory to give
     So vs here to guyde that we may haue a place, 2100   us grace.

301

Accordyng to oure regeneracion,   2101
   Wit*h* heuynly spyryt*es*, hys name to magnyfy   Let us magnify
Whyche downe descendyd for our̃ redempcion,   His name.
   Offryng hym sylf on the crosse to hys fadyr on hy. 2104
   Now benygne Ihesu, that borñ was of Mary,
     All that to thys vysion haue yovyn her audyence,   Jesus, grant eternal joy to
     Graunt eternall ioy aftyr thy last sentence.   2107   the readers of my book.
       Amen.

NOTES.

In the notes and introduction references are made to the following editions :

Lydgate's Minor Poems, including Pur le Roy, Chorle and Bird, and Testament, Halliwell, Percy Soc.

Æsop, Sauerstein (Anglia, IX).

Temple of Glas, Schick, E. E. T. Soc.

Dance of Macabre, MS. Bodl. 686.

Falls of Princes, Pynson's print, Brit. Mus.

Story of Thebes, Speght's Chaucer, Lond. 1598.

Secrees of Old Philisoffres, Steele, E. E. T. Soc.

Chaucer's Works, Skeat, one vol. (Macmillan) ; also the Aldine.

Langland's Piers the Plowman, Skeat, E. E. T. Soc. Text B.

Gower's Confessio Amantis, Pauli, 3 vols.

Mapes's Latin Works, Wright, Camden Soc.

Michel's Ayenbite of Inwyt, Morris.

Rolle of Hampole's Pricke of Conscience, Morris.

Ancren Riwle, Morton.

Wyclif's Works, Arnold, 3 vols.

Chronicle of Robert of Brunne (Anglia, IX).

Hawes's Pastime of Pleasure, Percy Soc.

Douglas's Works, Small, 4 vols.

Dunbar's Works, Small, Scot. Text. Soc.

Lyndesay's Works, E. E. T. Soc.

King James's Quair, Skeat, Scot. T. Soc.

Skelton's Works, Dyce.

Barclay's Ship of Fools, Jamieson, 2 vols.

Spenser's Works, Morris, one vol. (Macmillan).

Other works, as specially indicated.

P. 1, l. 1. The time is near the middle of July. Lydgate has a similar opening in *A Poem against Self-Love* (M. P., p. 156):

> " Toward the eende of froosty Ianuarye,
> Whan watry Phebus had his purpoose take
> For a sesoun to soiourne in Aquarye
> And Capricorn hadde uttirly forsake,
> Toward Aurora a-morwe as I gan wake. . . . ."

Cf. the imitation by Hawes in the *Pastime of Pleasure* :

> " When Phebus entred was in Geminy,
> Shynyng above in his fayre golden spere,
> And horned Dyane then but one degree
> In the Crabbe had entred fayre and cleare ;
> When that Aurora did well appeare
> In the depured ayre and cruddy firmament,
> Forth then I walked without impediment."

The prototype is found in Mapes' poem "*Apocalypsis Goliae Episcopi*," which contains also a reference to Pythagoras as the teacher to the Greeks of the seven Arts of the Schools. P. is there represented as having the signs of

62

the Arts on different portions of the body. Astrology, the highest form of knowledge, is marked prominently on the forehead. (Works, Camden Soc., ed., Wright.)

Hawes, in his *Past. of Pleas.*, p. 105, affirms that

"Thus God hym selfe is chief astronomyer."

l. 2. *gan.* This usage is maintained to the present. See Browning's *Easter Day:*

"Which gan suspire."

Used as auxiliary in l. 624.

l. 3. *Pictagoras speere.* The spelling "Pictagoras" occurs in the *Rom. of the Rose* (l. 5649) for the French "Pythagoras" (l. 5007). Chaucer has "Pictagoras" in the *Bk. of the Duch.* (l. 1167). Lydgate uses "Pictagoras" in Min. P. (p. 84, 87). The philosopher was known in England for his science of number. Cf. Lydgate's *Pur le Roy* (M. P., p. 11):

"And Arsmetryk, be castyng of nombrary,

Chees Pyktegoras for her parte."

Chaucer notes he "the firste finder was of the art (of music)"—*Bk. of the Duch*, l. 1168.

The sphere is according to his mathematics the most perfect figure; it is the circle of the heavens. It was used to symbolize the Soul, the Microcosm, implying final harmony in "the Diapason closing full in man." Other figures were the triangle, the least perfect figure, symbolizing the body, and the quadrate, in the perfect proportion of 7 to 9, embracing all the powers of man. Cf. Spenser, *Faery Queene*, Bk. II., c. 9, st. 22 :

"The frame thereof seemd partly circulare,

And part triangulare, O worke divine, ...

And twixt them both a quadrate was the base,

Proportiond equally by seven and nine ;

Nine was the circle set in heavens place ;

All which compacted made a goodly Diapase."

The ninth or cosmological sphere represented harmony, to which end, according to the philosophy, opposing elements were united. The Pythagorean sphere thus taught the poet the lesson he was seeking of concord.

P. 2, l. 9. *obstacle, habytacle, tryacle.* Other sets of rimes occur thus : obstacle, spectacle, myracle, tryacle (*Test.*, Min. P. p. 236); triacle, obstacle (*Æsop*, Fab. 4, ll. 148-50); obstacle, myracle (*Secr.*, ll. 120-22); obstacle, oracle (*Secr.*, ll. 624-26); obstacle, myracle (Chau. *Fr. Tale*, ll. 571-72); miracle, triacle (Chau. *Man of L. Tale*, ll. 379-81), etc.

l. 11. *habytacle.* Cf. Chau. *Ho. of Fame*, l. 1194 :

"Weren sondry habitacles ;"

Lydgate, *Min. P.* p. 140 :

"Whan th'olygoost made his habitacle ;"

Hawes, *Past. of Pleas.*, p. 218 :

"First God made heaven is propre habitacle," etc.

l. 12. *rowne.* Commonly in M. E. a distinction is made between rowne (to mutter) and whisper. Here=to commune.

l. 12. *tryacle.* Theriaca was the name given to a medicine compounded by a Roman physician Andromachus. For the history of the word see Morley, *Lib. of Engl. Lit.*, p. 21. Lydgate uses the term frequently; thus "Gostly tryacle", Min. P. p. 98 ;

"Ther is no venome so parlious in sharpnes

Os whan it hathe of treacle a lyknes—" *Ch. and Bd.*, Min. P. p. 186 ;

"Ageyne verray poyson ordeyned is triacle—" *Æsop*, Fab. 4, l. 148 ;

"The name of Ihesu ! sweltest of namys alle !

Geyn goostly venvms, holsomest tryacle—"*Test.*, M. P. p. 236.

It is found in Chaucer, *Man of L. Tale*, l. 381 :

"Crist, which that is to every harm triacle ;"

and in *Piers Pl.* Pas. 2, l. 146:
> "Love is triacle of hevene."

Cf. Beau. and Fl., *Sea Voyage* (Dyce, viii., p. 360):
> "This may be treacle
> Sent to preserve me after a long fast."

The figurative use is very common.

l. 14. *Morpheus.* These dreamers almost invariably have guides. Boethius was directed by Philosophy, Dante by Virgil and Beatrice, Mapes by Pythagoras, King James by Good Hope, etc.; Morpheus as a shewer of fancies appears again in Higgin's *Mirrour for Magistrates* (1576).

l. 18. *Mynos the iustyse.* Minos is first seen as Judge of the lower world in the Odyssey. Virgil followed Homer (*Aen.* 6, 431). Dante selected him as the typical judge in the Inferno (c. v.) in the second circle of which he abides and examines sins at the entrance.

l. 19. *sylogyse.* A general term. Cf. Hawes, *Past. of Pleas*, p. 32:
> "Agaynst your fables wyll often solisgyse."

l. 21. *he must nedys go, etc.* The proverb occurs again in Skelton's *Garl. of Laur.*, l. 1434:
> "Nedes must he rin that the dèvyll dryvith."

Greene uses it in *The Carde of Fancie*, ed. Grosart, p. 79, l. 4. Hazlitt in his *Proverbs* quotes an instance from *Triall of Treasure* (1567).

l. 34. *abydyng.* Used as a noun. Cf. *Æsop*, Fab. 6, ll. 122–23:
> "Yonder on that other side
> Is myn abidyng."

Cf. guydyng, l. 59.

l. 35. *Fantasy.* For the dwelling place of Morpheus see Chaucer's *Ho. of Fame*, Invoc.; *Bk. of the Duch.*, l. 153; Spenser, *Faery Queene*, Bk. I., c. 1, st. 39; Ariosto, *Orl. Fur.*, xiv., 92; Ovid, *Met.*, xi., 592. Gower describes the Cave of Sleep in *Confes. Am.*, II., pp. 102–3. Cf. "The House of Sleep," Cook, Mod. L. Notes, V., p. 10.

l. 37. *Cerberus.* The constable is a somewhat new role for Cerberus, whom Dante describes as a demon, a cruel and monstrous beast tearing and flaying and rending the spirits in Hell (*Infer.*, c. 6). As opposing Christ he appears in Lydgate's *Test*, p. 236:
> "Ihesu
> Took out of helle soulys many a peyre,
> Mawgre Cerberus and al his cruelte."

He is called "chief porter of hell" in *Story of Thebes*, fol. 375. He was known to Bunyan as the Porter of Hell, serving also as one of the captains of Diabolus in the *Holy War*.

P. 3, l. 45. *strayte correccion.* Cf. *Æsop*, Fab., 4, l. 36:
> "Straitly requyreng the iuge in this matiere;"

Scerees, ll. 762–3:
> "Twen moche and lyte a mene to devise
> Of to mekyl and streight coveitise;"

idem, l. 799:
> "But he that is streyght in his kepyng."

l. 52. *in fere* = in company, together; O. E. *ge-fera*, a companion; M. E. *in fera* is a corruption of *yfera* which is restored in Spenser; and cf. Tennyson, *Conf. of Sens. Mind*:
> "And in the flocks
> The lamb rejoiceth in the year,
> And raceth freely with his fere."

Chaucer has *yfere* in *Leg. of G. W.*, Pr., l. 263. Douglas uses *yfeir*.

l. 58. *chases.* Technically a chase is a private open hunting ground to which game resorts, differing from a "forest" in being open and private. Cf. Cheviot Chase or Chevy Chase.

l. 59. *cure.* Cf. Chaucer, *Ho. of Fame*, l. 464:
> "For Iupiter took of him cure."

l. 65. *comfort.* This word has a variety of meanings in M. E. Cf. Glossary.

l. 66. *roote and rynde*=wholly. Cf. l. 620, "croppe and roote." See Gower, *Conf. Aman.* I, p. 152:
> "Of flour and gras and roote and rinde."

l. 69. *maner.* For this use of maner see Chaucer, *Compleynte unto Pite*, l. 24:
> "What maner man dar now holde up his heed?"

The Compl. of Mars, l. 116:
> "For she ne fond ne saw no maner wight."

See l. 5:
> "Musyng on a maner,"

l. 1735:
> "Any maner wey."

Cf. *Secrees*, l. 7:
> "To euery maneer wyght;"

idem, l. 741:
> "In no maner wyse."

l. 71. *syngler.* Cf. *Secrees*, l. 332:
> "For my moost vertuous and singuleer counfort;"

idem, l. 1128:
> "To his noblesse and his singuler glorye."

P. 4, l. 87. *kervell.* Cf. Kersey's Dict.: "Caravel or carvel, a kind of light round ship with a square Poop, rigg'd and fitted out like a Galley, holding about six score or seven score Tun." Columbus's ships were called "caravels." The vessel which Douglas saw in his vision (*Pal. of H.*) that was driven upon the sands was called the "Carwell of the State of Grace."

l. 88. *karyk*=cark, a large ship. Cf. Chaucer, *Som. Tale*, Pr., l. 24:
> "Brodder than of a carrik is the sayl" (the first use of word in Engl.).

The "Universal Ship" that carried Barclay's fools is called a "carake"; and see *Ship of Fools*, II., p. 220:
> "That all the shyppes ne galeys vnto Spayne
> Nor myghty carakes cannot them well contayne."

Cf. Beaumont and Fletcher, *Two Nob. Kins:*
> " Then would I make
> A carrack of a cockle-shell."

l. 90. *who.* Note the use of who as relative. See l. 769.

l. 96. *daungere.* The M. L. *damnum* signified (1) a fine (2) the territory over which a lord ruled (3) the enclosed field of a proprietor (4) power to exact a penalty. In M. E. danger meant in general simply power or jurisdiction. Cf. *Æsop*, Fab. 5, l. 39:
> "Thow were in my daungere."

See l. 543=territory or jurisdiction. It had also the modern meaning of danger as in the *Secrees*, l. 1103:
> "Avoydyng al daungeer."

See Wedgwood for the history of the word.

l. 97. *seethe* = satisfaction. Cf. *Digby Myst.*, N. Shak. Soc., p. 143, l. 121-3:
> "Wysdom that was god and man right,
> Made a full seth to the fader of hevyn
> By the dredfull deth to hym was dight."

l. 101. *a loft.* Cf. *Temp. of Glas*, l. 41:
> "Now lowe and eft aloft;"

idem, l. 645:
> "I am set on loft;"

Secrees, l. 1244:
> "Planetys a-lofte."

l. 104. *foom.* This was often used of sweat as in Chaucer, *Ch. Yeo. Tale*, Pr., l. 12:
> "He was of fome (from sweat) al flekked as a pye."

l. 105. *betyn.* Cf. Lydgate, Min. P., p. 168:
> "Abydithe so longe til he be betyn doune."

P. 5, l. 116. *in especiall.* A very common phrase in Lydgate. Cf. *Secrees*, ll. 536, 653, 1041, 1088, etc. I find a modern use of the phrase in Poe's *Phil. of Composition:*
> "It is this latter, in especial, etc."

l. 110. *cost.* Frequently used for neighboring country. Cf. *Piers Plow.*, Pas. ii., l. 85 (B):
> "The counte of coueitise and alle the costes aboute."

l. 126. *pyry.* Cf. Ir. piorra, a blast of wind. This is an earlier instance than that given in the Cent. Dict. Cf. Hawes, *Past. of Pleas.* p. 53:
> "In the stormy pery."

lappyd = wrapped. Cf. Rob. of B. *Chron*. l. 1149:
> "And bylapped hem on ylk a side;"

Ode by Rich. Barnfield, l. 24:
> "All thy friends are lapt in lead;"

Breton, *Arb. of Am. Delights* (1593):
> "Sing lullaby and lap it warm."

Browning uses it in *Strafford*, Act V, 2, l. 332:
> "lapped round with horror."

l. 127. *boystous.* This is the form of the word in Chaucer. Cf. *Mann. Tale*, l. 107:
> "I am a boistous man;"

Morte Arthure, Th. MS., l. 615:
> "Thos bustous churlles."

The *Story of Thebes* has "boistouslie" (fol. 370).
Boisterous is found by Shakespeare's time.

l. 140. *auysment.* Cf. Chaucer, *Parl. of F.*, ll. 554-55:
> "The water-foules han her hedes leyd
> Togeder, and of short avysement;"

Troy. and Cris., II, l. 343:
> "Avysement is good bifore the nede."

P. 6, l. 154. *egall* = equall. Cf. Lydgate, *Secrees*, l. 386:
> "Ye wer of lyff egal with hooly seyntes;"

Min. P. p. 210:
> "So egally ther doomys to avaunce."

Paregall occurs often in Skelton. Unperegall is found in Marston, *Dutch Courtezan*, IV, v.

l. 157. *prima facie.* The date of the first instance of the Engl. usage of this phrase given in the Stanford Dict. (Latin in Engl.) is 1646. Cf. Chaucer in *Troil. and Cris.* III, l. 918:
> "This accident so pitous was to here
> And eek so lyk a sooth, at pryme face."

l. 162. *onwarde.* Skeat says this did not appear before Sir Th. More! (Dict.).

l. 163. *messynger.* Formed from the Fr. *message.* When was the *n* introduced?
Gower has messagere in *Conf. Am.*, III, p. 249. Lydgate in *Story of Thebes* uses messengers (fol. 372) and messagere (fol. 380, 386), Chaucer has both messager and messanger (see Glossary of Ch.).

l. 167. *banket.* In the fourteenth century the cloth or cushion covering a bank or bench on which dessert was served was called a "banker"; a feast came to be called a "banket" (*Mem. of Lond.*, ed. Riley, I, p. 179 and p. 44).

P. 7, l. 191. *ryght glad.* Right used in this manner is generally considered to be an Americanism (Southern) but this usage, like the American "I guess," is good Middle English.

l. 192. *all and some* = the long and short of it (Skeat). This is one of the most common phrases in L. M. E. Cf. Chaucer, *Fr. Tale*, l. 878 :
"This al and som, there is no more to seyn;"
Parl. of F., l. 650 :
"This al and som, that I wolde speke and seye," etc., etc.
Rom. of the Rose, l. 740 :
"So faire they weren alle and some;"
Gower, *Conf. Am.*, II, p. 379 :
"There ben the lordes all and some;"
Lydgate, *Temp. of Glas,* l. 1037 :
"This is al and some, the fine of my request," etc.
Cf. Spenser, *Faerie Queen*, III, xii, 30.
I remember to have seen the phrase used by Swinburne. Browning has in *Ring and Book* :
"So do I see, pronounce on all and some."

l. 202. *by and by* = one after the other, separately. See l. 302. Chaucer has in *Rv. Tale*, l. 223 :
"Right in the same chambre, by and by;"
Rom. of the Rose, l. 4581 :
"These were his wordis by and by."

l. 217. *grogyng.* The most common word of its class in Lydgate's vocabulary, commonly spelled grucchyng.
Min. P. p. 67 :
"Nat grucchyng, but mery like thi degre;"
idem, p. 83 :
"List thank God voyde al grucchyng;"
Æsop, Fab. 2, l. 161 :
"Nor grucche in pouerte."
Often in *Temp. of Glas* (see ll. 187, 424, 853, 879, 1266) and *Secrees* (ll. 113, 775, 778, 780).
Piers the Plow., Pr., l. 153 :
"And gif we grucche of his gamen."
In Chaucer's *Pers. Tale* grucching is declared a species of Envy.
Cf. Mary Wilkin's *Pembroke*, Ch. 12 :
"I don't begrutch it to her."

P. 8, l. 232. *dyscrese.* From L.L. *discrescere.* Gower has discreseth (*Conf. Am.* II, p. 189).

l. 233. *I dar vndyrtake.* A common formula; Chaucer has it in the *Ml. Tale,* l. 355. Cf. Prol. l. 288 :
"And he nas nat right fat, I undertake."

l. 243. Neptune's *mastresse.* Cf. Chaucer, *Fr. Tale*, ll. 319-20 :
"Though Neptunus have deite in the see,
Yet emperesse aboven him is she (Lucina)."

l. 249. *Othea.* I have retained the spelling in the text, though I am confident that Athena is the right reading.

l. 252. *marchall.* It was the office of the marshal of a feast to set the guests in order of rank.

P. 9, l. 253. The Gods. The delineation of the pagan deities in the manner of pictorial art is perhaps the best thing done in the poem. For models of these images he had, perchance, the work of Albricus Philosophus, entitled *De Deorum Imaginibus,* containing sketches of the heathen gods (Van Stavernes *Auctores Mythog. Lat.*); also, of course, the work of Fulgentius (Introd. p. xl) ; or for that he would not need to go much farther than Gower's *Conf. Aman.* Bk. IV. In l. 294 he refers to "olde poetys " for his authority. There is a minor assembly of gods in Lydgate's *Æsop* where judgment is given concerning the marriage of Phebus. See also The Assembly in Dunbar's *Golden Targe.*

l. 256. *presse.* The MS. preef is changed to presse because of the riming word messe.

l. 258. *be spreynt.* Cf. Chaucer, *Compl.,* l. 10 :
"To Pite ran I, al bespreynt with teres : "
" dew-besprent " occurs in *Comus,* l. 541. Browne notes that besprent is Spenserian.

l. 260. *Mars myghty god and strong.* A translation of the more common epithet of Mars, "armypotent "— borrowed from Virgil (*Æn.* IX, 717). Cf. Boccaccio, *Teseide,* VII. 32.

l. 262. *yron* and the other metals. The association of the different metals with the planets is attributed to Geber (see Thomson, *Hist. of Chem.,* I, 117). The temple of Mars built by Theseus (*Knight's Tale*) was all of steel. In Chaucer's *Ho. of Fame* (ll.1446-8) it is said that " Yren Martes metal is : "
" And the leed, withouten faile,
Is, lo, the metal of Saturne."
The Chanouns Yeman explains the seven "bodies" (*Ch. Y. Tale,* ll. 273-6):
" Sol gold is, and Luna silver we threpe ;
Mars yren, Mercurie quicksilver we clepe ;
Saturnus leed, and Iubiter is tin,
And Venus coper, by my fader kin."
Gower gives the complete list in *Conf. Am.,* Bk. 4, II, p. 84 :
" The gold is titled to the sonne ;
The mone of silver hath his part ;
And iron, that stond upon Mart ;
The leed after Satorne groweth ;
And Iupiter the brass bestoweth ;
The copper set is to Venus,
And to his part Mercurius
Hath the quick-silver."
Note the description by Hawes of the monster of the seven metals whose head and face were gold, the neck silver, the breast and heart steel, the forelegs brass, the back copper, the hindlegs tin, the tail lead (*Past. of Pleas.* p. 192).

l. 266. *poudryd.* A term in heraldry for sprinkled.

l. 267. *take the mantell and the ryng.* This saying refers to the assumption by a widow of a ring and a " widow's mantel," probably of black silk, as evidence of a vow of perpetual widowhood. See Lydgate, *Dance of Mac.:*
" Chastely receyved the mantel and the rynge : "
Min. P., p. 34 :
" She wol perhappous maken hir avowe
That she wol take the mantle and the ryng."

P. 9, l. 269. *demenyng.* Cf. the *Secrees,* l. 1082:
> "Sad of his cheer, in his demenyng stable;"

Temp. of Glas, l. 750:
> "Hir sad demening."

l. 270. Words like sad, wise and end are dissyllabic in Chaucer, sad | de, wys | e, end | e.

l. 272. *philosophres: cofres.* A stock rime from Chaucer; cf. *Cant. Tales* Pr. l. 297-8:
> "And albe that he was a philosophre
> Yet hadde he but litel gold in cofre;"

see also *Man of L. Tale,* ll. 25-6; *Fr. Tale,* ll. 843-4; *Ch. Y. Tale,* ll. 283-4; *Dr. of Ph. Tale,* Pr. l. 5-6; *Leg. of G. W.,* Pr. ll. 380-1; Gower uses it in *Conf. Am.,* II., p. 197 and III., p. 163; Lydgate employs it again in *Æsop,* ll. 1-3, in *Secrees,* ll. 34-5, 435-7, 540-2. Chaucer rimes philosophre again with profre (*Sec. N. Tale,* ll. 489-90; *Ch. Y. Tale,* ll. 111-12).

l. 275. *rychely beseene.* Cf. Skelton, *Garl. of Laur.,* ll. 482-3:
> "Wherein was set of Fame the noble Quene,
> All other transcendynge, most rychely besene;"

Temp. of Glas, l. 1167:
> "Ai fressh and welbesein."

l. 280. *morne: Saturne.* Cf. *Temp. of Glas,* ll. 480-1, *mourne: turne,* 858-9, *mourne: refourme.*

P. 10, l. 296. *fresshe*=gorgeous, gay. Cf. Skelton, *Garl. of Lau.,* l. 39:
> "Garnysshed fresshe after my fantasy."

l. 306. *purpur.* The M. E. spelling. Cf. Chaucer, *Leg. of G. W.,* I., l. 75:
> "With al her purpre sayle."

i. 308. *perles oryent.* Cf. Chaucer, *Leg. of G. W.,* Pr., l. 221:
> "For of oo perle, fyne, oriental;"

see the *Flow. and Leaf,* line 148:
> "As greate pearles, round and oriente;"

Skelton, *Garl. of Lau.,* l. 485:
> "Fret all with orient perlys of garnete;"

Lydgate's *Æsop.,* l. 26:
> "Perlis white, cliere, and oriental;"

John Day's Works (ed. Bullen, p. 37): "And as jewels, so the stones be orient, artfully cut and orderlie sett."

l. 314. *sulphure.* Cf. Chaucer, *Ho. of Fame,* ll. 1507-11:
> "And next him on a piler stood,
> Of sulfre . . . .
> Dan Claudian . . . .
> That bar up al the fame of helle,
> Of Pluto, and of Proserpyne."

l. 316. *Fortune the goddesse.* This is that Fortune that was known to the Middle Ages. Boethius gave her form and figure in the second book of *De Cons. Phil.* Dante places her in the Fourth Circle of Hell (c. vii), saying that for the splendors of the world there was ordained a general mistress and guide who should ever and anon transfer the vain goods from race to race, and from one blood to another beyond the resistance of human wit (Norton). This is the import of Cavalcante's fine Song of Fortune, beginning,
> "Lo! I am she who makes the wheel to turn;
> Lo! I am she who gives and takes away."

She is shewn in full form with her wheel in the *Roman de la Rose* (2d part, ll. 4863-8492). The English *Romaunt* speaks of "The froward Fortune and contraire" (l. 5414). Chaucer describes her as going upright and yet halting, as looking fair and yet foul (*Bk. of the Duch.,* ll. 642-5):

> 'She is th' envyous charite
> That is ay fals, and semeth wele
> So turneth she her false whele
> Aboute, for it is no-thing stable."

Lydgate says in the Min. P., p. 122 :

> "Fortune shewithe ay, by chaungyng hir see,
> How this world is a thurghefare ful of woo."

For a later description of Fortune and her wheel see King James' *Quair*, st. 158–172. Fluellen said to Pistol (*K. Hen. V.*, Act III., Sc. 6): "Fortune is painted blind with a muffler afore her eyes, to signify to you that Fortune is blind; and she is painted also with a wheel, to signify to you, which is the moral of it, that she is turning and inconstant, and mutability, and variation; and her foot, look you, is fixed upon a spherical stone, which rolls and rolls." Note the painting of Fortune and her wheel by E. Burne-Jones. The mediæval Fortune was pictured by Raphael on the walls of the Vatican.

l. 316. *party face.* Cf. *Court of Love*, ll. 1191–2 :

> "Dissemble stode not ferre from hym in trouth,
> With party mantill, party hode and hose."

The *Temp. of Glas*, l. 1155, has the formula "in parti or in al."

l. 320. *gawdy grene chamelet.* Chamelet was a cloth made of camel's hair and silk. Cf. Chaucer, *Knights Tale*, l. 1221 :

> "In gaude greene hir statue clothed was (Diana)."

l. 322. *shoures.* Figuratively=distribution, bestowment. See another usage in l. 732=assault of battle.

P. 11, l. 325. *russet.* Russet was a name given to a coarse woolen cloth, reddish brown in color and commonly worn by shepherds ; "clad in russet" was proverbial for homeliness. See Skeat's note in *Piers Plow.*, p. 208. The color is taken from the cloth. Cf. Shaks. *Hamlet*, Act I., i. 166 :

> "The morn in russet mantle clad."

Frese=frieze, a coarse woolen cloth.

l. 326. *tar box.* Every shepherd carried a box containing tar, which was used to annoint the sores in sheep. Cf. *Chest. Pl.*, p. 120 :

> "Heare is tarre in a potte
> To heale from the rotte."

Skeat cites a carol in a Balliol MS., 354 (notes to *Piers Plow.*, p. 195) :

> "The sheperd upon a hille he satt,
> he had on hym his tabard and his hat,
> hys tarbox, hys pype, and hys flagat."

See Percy's *Reliq.*, II., p. 256 :

> "And least his tarbox should offend, he left it at the folde."

l. 329. *the murre*=a cold with hoarseness. Cf. Skelton, *Magnyf.*, l. 2287 :

> "And I gyve hym the cowghe, the murre, and the pose" (pose=rheum in the head).

l. 330. *Isys the goddesse.* Lydgate, in his *Fall of Princes*, describes again a number of the Divinities. Of Isis he says :

> "She was right wise above other creatures,
> Secrete of cunnynge, wele experte in science,
> She taught first letters and figures
> To Egipciens by pleyn experience,
> Yave theym cunnynge and intelligence
> To till the londe, taught the labourerys
> To sowe their greyne and multiplie by yeres."

l. 340. *in hys gyrdyll stede* =in place of his girdle. But cf. Stubbes' *Anat. of Abuses* where gyrdlestead, used as a noun, signifies waist (I., p. 60).

l. 343. *dysgysyd* = decked out in strange guise. Cf. Lang., *Piers Plow.*, Pr., l. 24 :
> "And some putten hem to pruyde . . . . comen *disgised.*"

Cf. *Secrees*, l. 1170:
> "As the sonne shewith in his guyse."

l. 344. *Mynerue.* Minerva as Pallas appears in Lydgate's *Temp. of Glas,* "with her cristal sheld" (see Schick's notes, p. 87).

l. 350. *that other ye wote where,* i. e., on her breast.

l. 356. *kendall.* Probably the "Kendal Green," formerly manufactured by the Flemish weavers who had established themselves in Kendall in the 14th century.

P. 12, l. 361. *meynt* = joined, p.p. of mingen. Cf. *Temp. of Glas,* l. 276:
> "That Rose and lileis togedir were so meint ; "

Spenser, *F. Q.* III. xi. 36 :
> "When she with Mars was meynt in joyfulnesse."

l. 362. *ne wer she.* A common M. E. idiom. Cf. *Piers Plow.*, Pr., l. 199 :
> "Nere (ne were) that cat of that courte that can yow ouerlepe ; "

idem, Pas iii., l. 134 :
> "Shireues of shires were shent gif she nere ; "

idem, Pr., l. 82 :
> "Gif thei nere ; "

Chaucer, *Man of L. Tale,* l. 34 :
> "Nere (ne were) that a marchaunt, goon is many a yere ; "

Lydgate in *Daunce of Poules:*
> "Also ne were it myn entent."

See Glossary of Chaucer's Works under "nere."

l. 365. *Mercurius.* Mercury, as god of eloquence, appears in *Temp. of Glas,* ll. 130–32, and in Hawes' *Past. of Pleas.,* p. 34. Lydgate speaks of him in *Falls of Princes* as "Right fresshe, ryght lusty and full of hardyness." See Schick's notes, pp. 80–1. Cf. *Secrees,* l. 1207 :
> "In Rethoryk helpith Mercuryvs."

l. 365. *see* = seat. Cf. O. F. *se;* used in the sense of seat or throne in *Faery Queene,* iv., 10, 30.

l. 368. *passyd* = surpassed, excelled. Cf. *Flow. and Leaf,* l. 168 :
> "That of beautie she past hem everichone."

l. 371. *multyplyers.* For the "cursed craft" of multiplying, its materials and processes, see the Prolog to the Chanouns Yeman's Tale and Gower's *Conf. Am.,* II., p. 84. The "spirits" employed were quicksilver, armoniac, sulphur and arsenic. The multipliers, along with coin washers and clippers, are classed among the vices (l. 681).

l. 373. *whoos long here shone as wyre of goold bryght,* i. e., as the fine glittering threads of goldsmiths' work. A favorite and tell-tale simile of Lydgate's. See Schick, *Temp. of Glas,* notes, p. 88–90; Kölbing, *Sir B. of Hamtoun,* notes, pp. 244–5 ; also the introduction to this text, p. lvi.

l. 374. *cryspe* = fresh or firm. Most often crisp meant curled, as when describing hair (cf. Chaucer, *Knights Tale,* l. 1307) or rippled, as Milton's "crisped shades" (*Comus,* l. 984). Leigh Hunt has the present use in " It (laurel) has been plucked nine months, and yet looks as hale and crisp as if it would last ninety years." Cf. Browning, *Ring and Book:*
> " The first crisp youth that tempts a jaded taste."

l. 374. *columbyne* = either dove-like or in color like the columbine. In Lydgate's *Pur le Roy* (Min. P., p. 8) the word is used in the first sense :
> "Most columbyne of chere and of lokyng."

Chaucer (in *March. Tale*, l. 897) has,
"Come forth now with thin eyghen columbine."
Venus is always, of course, associated with doves and roses. Cf. the
Knights Tale, ll. 1102-4 :
"And on her heed, ful semely for to see,
A rose garland ful swete and wel smellyng,
And aboven hire heed dowves flikeryng."
Cf. any mediæval or modern painting of Venus when represented as the
"patronesse of plesaunce."

l. 383. *gladyd* made glad. For this transitive use of glad cf. Chaucer,
Bk. of the Duch, l. 702 :
"May gladde me of my distresse ; "
Ho. of Fame, l. 962 :
"And gladded me ay more and more ; "
Piers Plow., l'as. vi., l. 121 :
"Shal no greyne that groweth glade yow at nede ; "
Temp. of Glas, l. 1211 :
"Hertes to glade itroubled with derkness ; "
Browning, *Ring and Book*, p. 57 :
"What else shall glad our gaze."
Cf. Wyclif *Magnificat*: "My spiryt hath gladed in God myn helthe."
Lydgate also uses, l. 532, "reioyse" (= make glad) which came to take the
place of glad in this sense.

l. 389. *phylosophyrs and poetes.* Lydgate follows Dante in placing the
pagan philosophers and poets in Hell. See *Inferno*, c. iv. Dante men-
tions among the ancient teachers Socrates, Plato, Democritus, Diogenes,
Anaxagoras, Thales, Empedocles, Heraclitus, Zeno, Dioscorides, Orpheus,
Tully, Linus, Seneca, Euclid, Ptolemy, Hippocrates, Avicenna, Galen, and
Averrhoes, and of course, Virgil, Homer, Horace, Ovid and Lucan. These
were in the First Circle, which contained the spirits of those who lived vir-
tuously but without Christianity. This is such a list as Hawes gives of
those who have achieved fame, and also Douglas of those who inhabit the
Palace of Honor.

P. 13, l. 397. *Orace, Ouyde and Omere.* This is the common spelling of these
names. Cf. Chaucer, *Ho. of Fame* ll. 1466, 1477, 1487. Omerus is found
in *Secrees* l. 378, etc. Euclyte occurs in Min. P. p. 88.

l. 400. *Orpheus.* He is mentioned also in *Temp. of Glas* (l. 1308), playing
upon a harp.

l. 402. *carpe.* Commonly meaning to talk, the term is sometimes found
applied to music, as here. Often in Lydgate in the sense of talk. Cf.
Chorl and Bird, Min. P., p. 191 :
"It ware but foly withe the more to carpe ";
Secrees, l. 708 :
"To whoos counsayl in Arrabye folk carpe," etc.
See *carpyng*, l. 439.

l. 404. *to lawe.* Cf. Chaucer, *Cant. Tales*, Pr. l. 474, "lawghe ;" *Piers Plow.*,
iv, l. 153, "lawghyng ;" and *Secrees*, l. 2535 :
"Man which lawheth with wyl and herte."

l. 408. *foyson.* Cf. Chaucer, *Ml. Tale*, Pr., l. 57 :
"So that he fynde Goddes foyson there ";
Lydgate, *Chorl and Bird*, Min. P., p. 184 :
"And of alle deyntes plente and foisoun ; "
Secrees, l. 1644 :
"Or drynk old wyn in greet foysoun."
It is used in *The Tempest*, II. 1.

l. 413. *the fest of Peleus.* The story is that Discord (Eris), being excluded from the feast of Peleus and Thetis, threw among the company a golden apple inscribed "To the fairest." Then arose the dispute between Here, Aphrodite and Athena, wherein Paris was involved as judge of the fairest. The prize fell to Aphrodite, who gave to Paris Helen, whence rose the Trojan war. This was one of the most famous of the mediæval tales of romance. The strife of the goddesses is recorded in Gower's *Conf. Am.* Bk. V. The story is referred to in *Temp. of Glas,* ll. 461–67. Robert of Bruune gives a full account of the rape of Helen and the causes thereto in his *Chron.* ll. 459 *et seq.*

l. 425. *what in the deuylls date.* The meaning of this exclamation is indicated by a passage in Skelton's *Speke, Parrot,* ll. 437–38:
> "Ryn God, rynne Devyll! yet the date of ower Lord
> And the date of the Devyll dothe shrewlye accord."

The Marriage charter of Lady Mede in *Piers Plow.* (Pass. ii) is sealed "in the date of the devil," as other documents are written in the date of the Lord. Cf Skelton, *Bowge of Court,* ll. 375 and 455:
> "Lete theym go, lowse theym, in the deuylles date";

Magnificence ll. 2198 and 954:
> "What neded that, in the dyuyls date !"

l. 426. *howe the game gooth.* Cf. *Rom. of the Rose,* l. 5030:
> "But how that evere the game go."

P. 14, l. 441. *woo begoon.* The opposite phrase is "well begon" as in *Roman of the Rose,* l. 693.

l. 447. *my dart.* In mediæval imagery Death is most often represented as a skeleton figure hurling against all men a spear or a dart. Cf. *Mirrour of the Per. of Man's Life:*
> "Now schaketh he his spere to smite me";

Court of Love, l. 294:
> "Though Deth therefore me thirlith with his spere";

Occleve, *De Reg. Prin.* (ed. Wright, p. 76):
> "Death might have stayed his dart for a time."

See text l. 1935.
The identification of Atropos (here a male figure) with Death is one of the curious features of the poem. Cf *Temp. of Glas,* l. 782–3:
> "Right so shall I, til Antropos me sleithe
> For wele or wo, hir faithful man be found."

Atropos is one of the fates in *Story of Thebes,* fol. 374.
Cf. Bullein, *A Dialogue against the Fev. Pest.* (E. E. T, p. 114):
"Me thinke I doe see the fearful horseman lighted in the valley with a marvelous fearful saying, *En adsum vobis mors vltima linia rerum, etc.* Oh, where shall we hide vs from him ? He casteth forthe his III dartes, and taketh them vp again . . . . . it is merciless Death most fearful," etc.

ll. 449 *et. seq. Death's patent.* It was one of the favorite subjects of contemplation how death brought every man to an end, however exalted his estate. It was customary to refer to the "Nine Worthies"[1] by way of illustration; these were Joshua, Gideon, Samson, David, Judas Maccabaeus, Alexander, Julius Cæsar, Charles the Great, and Godfrey of Boulogne. When it was desirous to prove that the world was false and vain, the question would be asked, Where now is Solomon, Samson, Absalom, Jonathan, Cæsar, Dives,

---

[1] The Nine Worthies furnished stock illustrations to a late date. They are constantly referred to by the dramatists as by Beaumont and Fletcher in *Thierry* and *Theodoret* (Dyce ed. l, p. 143), *Laws of Candy* (V, p. 331), *The Double Marriage* (VI, p. 387), *The Prophetess* (VIII, p. 266). They appear on the stage in character in Middleton's *The World Lost at Tennis* (Bullen ed. VII, p. 165), where they are described by Pallas as they dance in the masque. They were favorite subjects for tapestry (Weber) as appears in Beau. and Fl. *Doub. Mar.* (Dyce ed. VI, p. 387):
> "Thou woven Worthy in a piece of arras,
> Fit only to enjoy a wall."

Tully, or Aristotle (see *Hymns to the Virgin*, E. E. T., p. 86—c. 1400). Chaucer's list of those who have been brought low is given in the *Monk's Tale;* they are Lucifer, Adam, Sampson, Ercules, Nabugodonosore, Balthazar, Zenobia, Petro (of Spayne), Petro (of Cipres), Barnabo, Hugilin, Nero, Oliphern, Antiochius, Alisaunder, Julius Cesar and Cresus. Hawes enumerates these whom Fame holds in remembrance: Hector, Josue, Judas Machabeus, Davyd, Alexander, Julius Sesar, Arthur, Charles and Godfrey (*Past. of Pleas.*) To illustrate the theme that all stand in change like a midsummer rose, Lydgate cites elsewhere David, Salamon, Jonathas, Julius, Pirrus of Vnd, Alexander, Nabigodonosor, Sadociopall, Tullius, Crisostomus, Omerus, Senec. and many knights (Min. P., p. 22; see also p. 122). Cf. the tone of the Roxbury Ballad *Farewell to the World:*
"For worldlie pleasure is but vanitie;
  None can redeeme this life from death, 1 see;
  Nor Cresus' wealth, nor Alexander's fame,
  Nor Sampson's strength, that could Death's fury tame." Rox. B. II. p. 25.
In that most doleful of poems Wigglesworth's *Vanity of Vanities* the motive is repeated in a new land:

"If Beauty could the Beautiful defend
From Death's dominion, then fair Absalom
Had not been brought to such a shameful end;
But fair and foul unto the Grave must come.

If Wealth or Scepters could Immortal make,
Then wealthy Croesus, wherefore art thou dead?
If Warlike-force which makes the World to quake,
Then why is Julius Caesar perished?

Where are the Scipio's Thunderbolts of War?
Renowned Pompey, Caesar's Enemy?
Stout Hannibal, Rome's Terror known so far?
Great Alexander, what's become of thee?
—Libr. Amer. Lit. II, p. 17.

See also Lydgate's *Dance of Macawbre* and *Story of Thebes,* fol. 387; Barclay's *Ship of Fools,* 1, p. 264; *Love's Labor's Lost,* VI, 130; V, Sc. 1, l. 130; Southwell's *Image of Death,* etc. Petrarch's *Triumph of Death* may also be compared.

P. 15, l. 470. *Nabügodónozór.* This is the pronunciation in Chaucer. The spelling *Nabuchodonosor* occurs in the Vulgate (Dan. I., iv); this is the usage of Gower (v. *Conf. Am.* Bk. I, near end), and Chaucer (*Monk's Tale,* l. 155; *Ho. of F.* l. 515), and Langland (*Piers Plow.* Pas. vii, l. 153).

l. 471. *Pharao* is the spelling of the Vulgate; Chaucer has Pharo (*Ho. of F.* l. 516) but Pharao in *Bk. of the Duch.* l. 282.

l. 490. *oldyrs.* The final s must be a scribal error; but cf. ll. 579, 599.

l. 492. Cf. Chaucer, *Knights Tale,* ll. 445 8:
"O cruel goddes, that governe
This world with byndyng of youre word eterne
And wryten in the table of athamaunt
Your parlement and your eterne graunt."

l. 493. *pesecoddys.* This is the form employed by Lydgate in Min. P. p. 105, *Secrees* l. 1374, and by Langland in *Piers Plow.* Pas. vi, l. 294, xiii (C), l. 221, and by Skelton *Why come,* etc., l. 108. The *Secrees* has
"Benys rype and pesecoddys grene."

P. 16, l. 499. *brayde*=started up. Cf. *Æsop,* Fab. 2, l. 90:
"Til sodainly al abrayde";
Temp. of Glas, l. 1054:
"Til at the last of routhe she did abraide";

Secrees, l. 308 :
   " Till I abrayde in purpoos to resorte."
See " braid," N. E. Dict.

l. 501. *boody, blood and boonys.* " Blood and bone " is a common formula in the Metrical Romances.

l. 503. *malapert.* Cf. Lydgate. Min. P., p. 23 :
   "Clatering pyes . . . .
   Most malapert there verdit to purpose ";
idem p. 166 :
   " Maleapert of chiere and of visage " (said of a jay).

l. 513. *leyte.* The other texts read " leytenynge "—which is, of course, meant.

l. 530. *hyt fell on a day.* Lydgate has this formula in Min. P., p. 74 : " It fil on a tyme."

l. 530. *wedyr.* Weddir is still the folk pronunciation in portions of Scotland. Cf. Barbour's *Bruce* III., l. 387:
   " Till wyntir weddir war away."

P. 17, l. 534. *dresse*=direct. See l. 1512 : " Myn ey gan I dresse." Cf. Chaucer, *Ml. Tale,* l. 282 :
   " And to the chambre dore he gan him dresse ;"
Gentl., l. 3 :
   " Must folowe his trace and alle his wittes dresse."

l. 550. *ray.* Ray means properly a ray, streak, stripe ; but was commonly used to designate a striped cloth (Skeat). See Lyd., *Lond. Lackpenny,* "a long gown of raye." The plural is found in *P. Pl.* Pas. v, l. 211, " Among the riche rayes." Barclay (*Ship of Fools,* 1, p. 35) refers to honest ray==striped cloth. See *Mem. of Lond.* ed. Riley. I. p. 109 for definition== " one piece of striped cloth." Cf. Peele, *Edward I.,* Sc. 6, l. 22 :
   " My milk-white steed treading on cloth of ray."

l. 561. Cf. Chaucer, *Man of L. Tale* l. 483:
" But tourne ayein I wil to my mateere ;"
Lydgate Min. P. p. 140 :
   " But to resorte ageyn to my mateere."

l. 562. And tó | begýn ' ne néw ' e whére | I léft. Few lines run as smoothly as this. The final *e* comes naturally into use.

l. 563. *besy peyn.* The phrases "besy peyn" and "besy cure" are very common in Lydgate and Chaucer. See Lydgate's Min. P., p. 87 ; *Æsop,* Fab. 2, l. 55, Fab. 6, l. 136 ; *Secrees,* l. 738, 1012 ; Chaucer, *Parl. of F.* l. 369 ; *Compl.* l. 2, 119, etc. This text has it again in l. 746. Spenser uses the phrase as in *Faerie Queene* V. xii. 26.

P. 18, l. 597. *nat worth a peere.* The writers of the period had a variety of expressions signifying worthlessness. See l. 493, not give 2 pesecoddes ; l. 560, rekke nat a strawe ; l. 1607, then a myte. Cf. *Mort. d'Art.* XV., cap. vi (ed. Southey, II. p. 254) :
   " Vayne glory of the world, the whiche is not worth a pere."
Chaucer has " Not worth a myte" in *Knights Tale,* l. 700, *Somp. Tale,* l. 253, *Sec. N. Tale,* l. 511, *Ch. Yem. Tale,* Pr. l. 80 ; " Not worth a flye " in *Parl. of F.,* l. 501 ; " Not worth a bene " in *Merch. Tale.* In the *Rom. of the Rose* are " Not worth a croked brere," l. 6191 ; and " Not worth an hen," l. 6856. In *Piers Plow.* is "She counteth nought a russhe," Pas. iii, l. 141. Gower uses "Not worth a kerse," *Conf. Am.* I, p. 334, and "Not worth a stre," I, p. 364. Skelton has "Set not a nut shell," *Col. Cl.* l. 1227. Cf. Dunbar, *Fre. Hon. and Nob.* l. 42 :
   " Set not by this warld a chirry."
Douglas says (Works II, p. 116, l. 19) : " I compt it neuir a myte."

l. 600. *dere*=injure. Cf. *Rom. of the Rose.* l. 4336 :
> " May falle a weder that shal it dere."

l. 601. *a son of myne.* With what an imperfect imagination Lydgate grasps the symbolism of his poem may be gathered by comparing this mere reference of Vice as the bastard son of Pluto with the mighty passage in Milton's *Par. Lost* (Bk. X) which describes the relationship of Satan and Sin and Death. Then I have misgivings for having attempted to revive this Lydgate ; one then realizes the force of Prof. Lounsbury's remark in his *Studies in Chaucer* that it is unfortunate that the dead past cannot bury not only its dead but its bores.

l. 602. *vaward*=reduction of vantward. Cf. Shakes. *Hen. V.* iv. 3 :
> " I beg
> My lord, most humbly on my knee
> The leading of the vaward."

This form is found as late as Drayton's *Agincourt,* Ode XII :
> " The eager vaward."

P. 19, ll. 610 *et seq.* the battle. Bunyan's *Holy War* offers many parallels to the conduct of this battle. Thus we are told that the Father appointed his Son to captain the forces of Good, that Emanuel chose five captains to accompany him, captains Credence, Good-hope, Charity, Innocent, and Patience, each with a standardbearer and holy escutcheon to advance ten thousand men. Emanuel rode at their head in a chariot. The army of Diabolus had set over it other captains : Diabolus the King, Incredulity, the Lord-general, the seven chief captains Beelzebub, Lucifer, Legion, Appollyon, Python, Cerberus and Belial, and minor captains Rage, Fury, Damnation, Insatiable, Brimstone, Torment, No-ease, Sepulchre and Past-Hope. This army, uncountable in number, set out from Hell-gate Hill and came by a straight course toward Mansoul, whose five gates (the five senses) they attack with varying fortune though with ultimate defeat. The general question of Bunyan's sources and models has not been fully considered. While it is apparent that he drew almost wholly from the Bible and his own conscience, yet his work must have been in part determined by the traditional accounts of Mansoul's Wars.

l. 612. *dereygne*=set in order, prepare. Cf. Chaucer, *Knights Tale,* l. 773 :
> " Bothe suffisient and mete to darreyne."

Cf. Spenser, *F. Q.* IV. iv. 26 :
> " Unable he new battell to darraine."

l. 617. *Vyce, etc.* It is possible to form from the drawings, Moral Plays and literature of the period a very accurate picture of the different vices as objectified in human symbol. If Lydgate is wanting here in descriptiveness it is probably because the work of delineation had been done before him and nothing more was needed beyond mere mention. Langland in *Piers the Plowman* (Pas. v) is especially realistic and dramatic :
> " Now awaketh Wratthe with two whyte even,
> And nyuelynge with the nose and his nekke hangynge ; "

> " Thanne come Sleuthe al bislabered, with two slymy eighen ; "

> " Eche a worde that he (envy) warpe was of an addres tonge,
> Of chydynge and of chalangynge was his chief lyflode,
> With bakbitynge and bismer and beryng of fals witnesse."

See especially Covetousness quoted below (l. 626).
In such character the Vices were kept constantly before the people in play and pageant, which practice was continued until late as witnessed by Richard Tarlton's play of the Seven Deadly Sins, in which Lydgate himself is presented as moving the scenes (cf. Collier, *Hist. Dr. P.* III, p. 304), and by such a remark as that made by Dick Bowyer in *Tryall of Chevalry* (c. 1605, Old Plays, ed. Bullen, III) : " If I had a pageant to present of the seven deadly sinnes, he should play Slouth." So long as these characters remained

before the people Lydgate's description was sufficient. I make this note because everywhere the relation between the pictorial, scenic and literary art of the period must be emphasized.

For the subjective conception see Chaucer's *Pers. Tale* and Gower's *Conf. Am.* etc. For a later characterization see Day's *Tractates* (c. 1600) ed. Bullen.

l. 617. *cure boyle.* This is one of many expressions relating to tournament which were introduced into literature, in this case from the French, during the Middle Ages. It means literally "boiled leather." It seems that the knights wore under their coat of mail a garment made either of silk and then called "wafenhemd" or of leather and called "curie." The latter garment was worn in France. It was made of strong leather made pliable by boiling. Chaucer in *Tale of Sir Th.* l. 164 uses the phrase, "His jambeaux were of quirboily," the term being interpreted as "tanned leather." Prof. Skeat (notes to *Pr. T.* p. 166) gives references to Marco Polo (ed. Yule, II, 49) where the men of Carajan are said to wear "armes cuiraces de cuir bouille;" also to Froissart (V. IV, cap. 19) who says the Saracens covered their targes with "cuir bouille." The term occurs in Barbour's *Bruce* XII l. 21-2:

> "And on his basnet hye he bar
> Ane hat off qwyrbolle ay-quhar."

In *Recuyell of the Hist. of Troye* "armed well with quyer boullye" translates the Fr. "armez de moult beaux habillemens courroyez."
See Cutts, *Scenes and Char. of M. A.,* p. 344.

l. 620. *croppe and roote.* Lydgate makes a very frequent use of this formula. See *Temp. of Glas,* l. 455:

> "Humble and benygne, of trouth crop and rote."

See Schick's references in notes to *Temp. of Glas,* p. 98. Chaucer has it in *Troyl. and Crys.,* II., l. 348:

> "And ye, that be of beaute crop and roote."

It occurs in Dunbar, *The Flyting,* l. 73:

> "Thow crop and rute of traitouris tressonable."

It is an expression still common in Scotland (W. Gregor). Dunbar has also "crop and grayne" (*The Warldis Instab.,* l. 99). Lydgate in Min. P. uses "roote and grounde" (p. 123), "gynnyng and roote" (p. 125), "gynnyng and ground" (238), and in this poem "roote and rynde" (l. 66). Caine in *The Manxman* (ch. xxii.) has "neck and crop" and Meredith the same phrase in *The Ordeal of Rich. Feverel.*

l. 621. *Pryde.* Pride is put the first as the master sin; by that sin fell the angels:

> "For Lucifer with hem that felle
> Bar Pride with him in to helle"—Gow., *Conf. Am.,* I., p. 153.

He appears again as General of the Army of Sin in Day's *Tractates* (Tract. 7, ed., Bullen, p. 55). See Introd. p. lxxii.

l. 622. *Pryde on a lyon, etc.* In the symbolism of the Middle Ages animals were used as signs of vices and virtues. The custom was started by the theologians, notably Jerome. In certain of the early *Bestiares,* as the *Renart le Nouvel* (1288) the animals were first associated with the Moralities. Dante in entering the dark wood was confronted by a leopard, a lion and a wolf, typical of certain sins. In the *Ancren Riwle* the symbolism is well established. In the processional described in the *Faerie Queene* (I., iv.) Idleness is seen riding upon an ass, Gluttony on a swine, Lechery on a goat, Avarice on a camel, Envy on a wolf and Wrath upon a lion. Bunyan makes some use of this traditional symbolism in the lions that guarded the palace Beautiful.

l. 622. *Envy.* Envy is personified in the *Temp. of Glas,* l. 147; cf. also *Rom. of the Rose,* l. 248; *Court of Love,* l. 1254, etc. For the portrait of Envy see Spenser, *F. Q.,* V., xii., 29-32.

l. 626. *Couetyse.* A fine description of Covetousness is drawn by Langland in *Piers Plow.* Pas. v., ll. 188–94 :

> "And thanne cam Coueytise . . . .
> So hungriliche and holwe, sire Hervy hym loked,
> He was bitelbrowed and baberlipped also,
> With two blered eyghen as a blynde hagge ;
> And as a letheren purs lolled his chekes,
> Wel sydder than his chyn thei chiueled for elde ;
> And as a bondman of his bacoun his berde was bidraueled."

This Vice is often mounted upon a horse that he may speed more quickly, as in *Evil Times of Ed., II.* (Polit. Songs, p. 326) :

> "Coveytise upon his hors he wole be sone there
> And bringe the bishop silver, and rounen in his ere."

Covetise is personified in the *Temp. of Glas*, l. 244. The fifth book of Gower's *Conf. Am.* is devoted to Avarice.

l. 627. *olyfaunt.* This is the spelling of Maundeville and Skelton. "Oliphantes" is found in Lyndesay's *Monarche*, l. 2295.

l. 631. *Slowthe.* Sloth is personified in *Temp. of Glas*, l. 244. See *Rom. of the Rose*, ll. 531, 593, 1273, etc. ; *Faery Queene*, I., iv, 18, etc.

l. 636. *Symony.* Note the feeling of Langland in this matter, *Piers Plow.*, Pas. ii., ll. 62–3, 86 :

> "Ac Symonye and cyuile and sisoures of courtes
> Were most pryue with Mede ;"

the priests wish to live in London

> "And syngen there for symonye for silver is swete."

See Dante's *Inferno* (c. xix.) for the punishment of the guilt of Simony.

P. 20, l. 640. *Ielacy.* Jealousy is personified in the *Temp. of Glas*, l. 148. See *Rom. of the Rose*, l. 3820 ; *Parl. of F.*, l. 252 ; *Quair*, 877.

l. 644. *Usury.* Usury was the special sin of Avarice (v. *P. Pl.*, Pas. v., l. 240-52). All usury was prohibited as a sin by the Canon Law (Southey, *Bk. of the Church*, p. 187). It was the theory of the schoolmen that the taking of interest was unholy since money was not of itself productive. Dante consigned usurers to one of the lowest regions of Hell. The continued prejudice in England against the money lender is testified by Shakespeare's *Merchant of Venice*, and Bacon repeated the old theory, "It is against nature for money to beget money." Cf. a Roxbury Ballad (I., p. 426):

> "The Usurers follow,
>   That pawnes have in hand ;
> With whoop and with hollow
>   They call for the Land
> Which spend-thrifts pawne to them
>   While for cash they hye ;
> To live to undoe them
>   This bargaine they'l buy."

l. 648. *Boldnes | in Yll with Foul | e Ry | baudy.* In this line the final *e* in foule seems to be pronounced. But Text B and the Prints read *Foule and Rybaudy.*

l. 655. *New-fangylnes.* The love of novelty seems to have been considered a special vice of the times. Lydgate in Min. P. (p. 71) speaks of "the serpent of newfangelnesse" and says (p. 60) :

> "I-bannysshed have newfangelnesse
> And put in his place perseveraunce."

Chaucer writes against "Women Unconstant" :

> "Madame, for your newe fangelnesse
> Many a servaunt have ye put out of grace . . . .
> To newe thing your lust is ever kene."

See also *An. and Arc.*, l. 141; *Leg. of G. Wom.*, Pr., l. 154. Nichol Newfangle is the "Vice" in the interlude *Like will to Like* (1568). This is also one of Stubbes' "Abuses" (p. 31).

l. 666. *Idylnesse.* Lydgate calls Idleness the "Moder to vices" (Min. P., p. 88) and the "Chief porteresse" of the vices (Min. P., p. 68). In *Æsop* he says again that "Vice alle proceden of idelnesse." Cf. Chaucer, *Sec. N. Tale*, ll. 1–3:

> "The ministre and the norice unto vices,
> Which that men clepe in English ydelnesse,
> The porter of the gate is of delyces."

l. 668. *but there was an [h]ost!* Considering the chief vices as roots and stems, the secondary branches and twigs become innumerable. Thus Chaucer enumerates in the *Pers. Tale* among the twigs from the root of pride inobedience, avaunting, ypocrisye, despit, arragaunce, impudence, swellyng of hert, insolence, elacioun, impacience, strif, contumacie, presumpcioun, irreverence, pertinacie, and veinglorie. This gives material and scope for incalculable growth and differentiation. Give the fancy play and in a moment one exclaims with Barclay (*Ship of Fools*, I., p. 4):

> "For yf I had tunges an hundreth : and wyt to fele
> Al thinges natural and supernaturall,
> A thousand mouthes : and voyce as harde as stele,
> And sene al the seven sciences lyberal,
> Yet cowde I neuer touche the vyces all,
> And syn of the worlde : ne theyr braunches comprehende :
> Nat thoughe I lyued vnto the worlds ende."

For the abundance of vices of the time of Henry VIII., v. *The Hy Way to the Spitl-house* (Bartholomew's Hospital, London): description in Furnivall's ed. of *Capt. Cox, etc.* (Ballad Soc.) p. ci–ciii.—twenty-three sets of unfortunates. See especially the list of "unthrifts," p. ciii. Cf. Wyclif's list of sins in *Fifty Heresies and Errors of Friars* (ed., Arnold, III., p. 366). Cf. the vices that voyage in Barclay's Ship of Fools ; also those satirized in Skelton's *Bowge of Court* and the list of rogues in the Miracle Play, *The Last Judgment* (Roxburge Club). For the species of rogues and vagabondes in Elizabethan England, cf. Thornbury, *Shaks. Engl.*, I., ch. viii.; Decker's *English Villanies*, Harrison's *England*, II., ch. xi., *passim;* *Three Tracts about Old Rogues*, ed. by Viles and Furn. (N. Shaks. Soc.); Stubbes' *Anatomy of Abuses* (N. Shaks. Soc.). These enumerations throw much light upon the practical life of the time. Many of the Commons in Lydgate's list are not known to us even by name.

P. 21, l. 673 *et. seq.* Langland groups "bakbiteres, breke-chestes, brawleres and chideres" (*P. Pl.*, Pas. xvi., l. 43).

ll. 674, 676. *fasers=*boasters, *crakers=*vaunters. See Skelton, *Garl. of Laur.*, ll. 188–9:

> "Some lidderons, some losels, some noughty packis ;
> Some facers, some bracers, some make great crackis ;"

Borde, *Bk. of Knowl.:*

> "I wyll boost myselfe, I wyll crake and face ;"

Barclay, *Ship of Fools*, I., p. 198:

> "For greatest crakers ar nat ay boldest men.

l. 679. *scismatykes.* Cf. *Piers Plow.*, Pas. xi., l. 114–15:

> "For Cryste cleped vs alle come if we wolde,
> Sarasenes and scismatikes and so he dyd the Iewes."

l. 681. *coyn wasshers and clyppers.* For the evil of counterfeiting, etc., cf. Hoccleve's *Complaint*, Min. P., xxi.

l. 685. *tregetours.* For the pretentions of these tricksters see *Frank. Tale*, ll. 413–20:

> "Which as the subtile tregetours pleyen
> For oft at festes have I herd seyen,
> That tregettoures, withinne an halle large,
> Han made in come water and a barge,
> And in the hall rowen up and doun:
> Sometyme hath semed come a grym leoun
> Som tyme a castel al of lym and ston,
> And whan hem liked voyded it anon."

l. 691. *stalkers by night.* A proclamation was made in London in 1329 to the effect that no one should be so daring as to go wandering about the city after the hour of Curfew (see *Memor. of Lond.*, ed. Riley, I, p. 173; II, p. 482).

l. 692. *brekers of lofedayes.* Love-days were days fixed for settling differences by umpire. Cf. *Cov. Myst:*

> "Now is the love-day mad of us foure fynially,
> Now may we leve in pes as we were wonte."

A passage in Wyclif's Tracts (Works, ed. Arnold III, p. 322) throws light upon the custom. We see knights and yeomen kneeling in the castle chapel, a general gathering in the hall, statements from both sides, arbitration and reconciliation (Arnold).

l. 693. *getters.* Cf. Barclay, *Ship of Fools.*, I, p. 146:

> "Ye wasters and getters by nyght."

In Bunyan's *Pilg. Prog.* is a schoolmaster who taught the art of "getting" either by violence or cozenage, flattery, lying, etc.

l. 694. *Tytyuyllys.* Any person with evil propensities (Collier). Douce derives the name from *Titivilitium,* a word used by Plautus. Collier suggests its derivation from *totus* and *vilis.* He appears in *The Mirroure of Oure Ladye* (E. E. T. p. 54) saying "I am a poure dyvel and my name ys Tytyvyllus." His office was to bring to his master every day one thousand bags of syllables skipped in reading and singing the divine service in the churches. He appears in this character in MS. Lansd. 762 (quoted by Wright):

> "Hii sunt qui Psalmos corrumpunt nequitur almos:
> Jangler cum jasper, lepar, galper quoque, draggar,
> Momeler, for-skypper, for-reynner, sic et over-leper,
> Fragmina verborum *Tutivillus* colligit horum."

He became a common figure in the plays as any evil fellow. He is one of the devils in the play of *The Last Judgment,* where he seems to be a churchman opposing the heresy of Wyclif. He is a fiend in a Towneley Mystery (pp. 310, 319) and a lawless fellow in *Ralf Roister Doister.* He is a fiend in *Mankind* representing the sin of the flesh. Skelton (*Col. Cl.* l. 418) uses the phrase "and talkys lyke tytyvelles," probably here a tale-bearer, in which character he appears in *Rogues and Vag.* (N. Shaks. Soc. p. 15). In Stubbes' *Anat. of Abuses* he is a flatterer (p. 122). The word occurs again in Skelton's *Garl. of Laur.,* l. 642. See Collier, *Hist. Dr. P.* II, pp. 146, 207, 223; Dyce's notes on Skelton; notes to *Myrrour of O. Ladye,* p. 342.

l. 696. *carders*—card-players. For the punishment for cheating at play see *Mem. of Lond.* (ed. Riley, II, p. 395). "Turning the tables" was one method of cheating.

l. 696. *closshers.* This was a kind of game. Cf. Stubbes' *Anat of Ab.* notes p. 316: an act of Hen. VIII. — "noe manner of person shall . . . . kepe . . . any alley or place of bowlinge Coytinge, Cloyshe, Coyles, etc."

l. 697. *Tyburne.* The place of execution in London. Cf. Rowland's *A Fooles Bolt is soone Shot:*

> "Of Tybourne (i. e. the gallows) common hye-way cannot fayle."

Harrison (*England* II, ch. 16) calls the halter a "Tiburne tippet." This was also the name of a prison in London. *Coloppys* means pieces of meat, used figuratively often for children (as in *I. Hen.* vi, v. 5). "Tyburne coloppys" may have been a slang phrase. Cf. *Cocke Lorelles Bote,* C. *i. a.*

l. 698. *double tollyng myllers* = those millers who tolled with a too "golden thumb."

l. 702. *brokers* = receivers of stolen goods etc. Cf. Stubbes' *Anat. of Ab.* Pt. II., p. 40.

l. 707. *sotyll ambidextres* = Jacks-of-both-sides. "Ambidexter is that jurous or embraceour that taketh of both parties for the giving of his verdict" (Cowell'r *Interpreter*). A tricksey character called Ambidexter appears in Bullein's *Dialogue against the Fev. Pest.* (E. E. T. p. 20), Cf. Middleton, *Fam. of Love,* V, 3: "I'll play Ambidexter"; also Peele, *Sir Cly. and Sir Clam.,* sc. vi, l. 77. In an early American poem by Ebenezer Cook reference is made to
"an ambidexter Quack
Who learnedly had got the knack
Of giving glisters, making pills,
Of filling bonds and forging wills "—*Libr. of Amer. Lit.* II, 273. Stubbes in his *Anatomy of Abuses* speaks of "doble dealing ambodexters" (p. 141).

l. 708. *Sodomytes.* Used by Stubbes to signify fornicators (*Anat of Ab.* l. p. 145).

P. 22, l. 710. *wetewoldes that suffre syn in her syghtes.* A wittol was a tame "cuckold"—one who had knowledge of his wife's infidelity. Skelton, *Garl. of Laur,* l. 187, refers to "wetewoldis." Middleton in *Chast Maid of Cheapside* gives a picture of one. Cf. Shaks. *Mer. W. of Wind.,* II, 2:
"But cuckold! wittol-cuckold! the Devil himself hath not such a name." Cf. *Loves's Labour's Lost,* v, 904 12:
"When Daisies pied and Violets blew
And Cockow-buds of yellow hew
And Ladie-smokes al silver white,
Do paint the Meadowes with delight,
The cuckow then on everie tree
Mocks married men; for thus sings he.
Cuckow!
Cuckow! Cuckow! O worde of feare,
Unpleasing to a married eare."

l. 711. *abhominable.* This is the regular spelling of the N. E. abominable in O. Fr. and in English from Wyclif to the seventeenth century. This spelling is defended by Holofernes in *Love's Lab. Lost* against the "racker of orthography" who would say abominable.

l. 711. *auauntours.* Cf. Chaucer, *Pers. Tale*: "Avauntour is he that bosteth of the harm or of the bounté that he hath don."

l. 713. *vnthryftys.* Cf. Barclay, *Ship of Fooles,* I, p. 2:
"But such Unthriftes as sue theyr carnal lust."

l. 714. *loselles.* Cocke Losel or Lorel was a generic term for a rascal. Cf. Browning, *Strafford.* III, 2, l. 170.

l. 717. *for to say.* The common M. E. usage. "For to fet," l. 1155.

l. 727. *I will auauntage take where I may.* Cf. the words of Legion in Bunyan's *Holy War:* "Therefore let us assault them in all pretended fairness, covering our intentions with all manner of lies, flatteries, delusive words."

l. 732. *mortall* = equivalent to "lethalis," deadly. Cf. *Æsop,* Fab. 4, l. 34, "Of mortal hunger."

l. 732. *shoure* = conflict, struggle. O. E. scûr. Commonly applied to the assault of battle. See line 1042.

l. 742. *to me ward.* Toward was frequently divided and the object inserted between the parts as here. Cf. II Cor. 3:4: "And such trust have we through Christ to God-ward."

P. 23, l. 748. *Ymaginacion.* Note the part played by Imaginative in *Piers Plow.* Pas. xii.

l. 760. *mowte.* Mowe and mowte are common in M. E. See l. 264 where mought rimes with fought.

l. 766. *lest and moost.* A common formula in Lydgate, Chaucer and other writers. Cf. *Ck. Tale*, l. 460:
"Faire they were welcomed bothe lest and meste."
Langland (*Piers Plow.*, Pas. ii, l. 45) has "the lasse and the more."

l. 773. *trayne.* Cf. Fairfax's Tasso, II, l. 89:
"So lions roar, enclos'd in train or trap";
Fairy Queene, Bk. I, c. iii, st. 24:
"By traynes into new troubles to have toste."
Milton has "wily trains" in *Comus*, l. 151. Shakespeare uses it once in this sense in *Macbeth*, IV. 3.

l. 773. *coltrop* = a pointed iron instrument strewn in battle fields to hinder cavalry. Cf. Beaumont and Fletcher, *Love's Pilgrimage:*
"I think they ha' strew'd the highways with caltraps,
No horse dares pass 'em."
It occurs in Middleton, *Women Beware Women.* Cf. the proper name Caultrap.

l. 776. *Iyce hys.* See "Vertew hys," l. 798 etc. The corruption of his for O.E.-ës, the genitive termination, is found as early as Layamon's *Brut;* "For Gwenayfer his love." "Ine was the forste mon that Peter his peny bigan" *Brut,* (B.) III., l. 285. The *Prayer Book* has "For Christ his sake." Cf. Stubbes' *Anat. of Abuses* (1583) p. 75: "Every poore Yeoman his daughter, every Husbandman his daughter, and every Cottager his daughter." This use occurs in Spenser, Shakespeare and Bacon and did not die out until the eighteenth century. Ben Jonson, English Grammar XIII. calls it "the monstrous syntax of the pronoun *his* joining with a noun betokening a possessor"; and yet Addison, *Spectator No. 135,* writes that "the same single letter (s) ... represents the *his* and *her* of our forefathers"; v. Marsh *Lectures* XVIII (Percival). In *Guardian No. 98* Addison writes: "My paper is the Ulysses *his* bow." The use extended to the feminine gender and the plural number (v. *Cent. Dict.* under *his²*).

l. 776. *purseuaunte.* Cf. Chaucer, *Ho. of Fame,* l. 1321: "The pursevauntes and heraudes"; *Flow. and Leaf,* l. 232: "Of heraudes and pursevauntes eke." Shakespeare has: "These gray locks the pursuivants of death" (*Henry VI,* II, 5, 5). Browning uses it in *Blot in the Scut.,* Act I, l. 4; and Tennyson in *Balin and Balan:* "A spangled pursuivant."

P. 24, l. 792. *foure dowty knyghtys* = the virtues called "Cardinal" in accordance with the Platonic Ethics. These virtues together with the theological triad appear as maidens in Dantes *Purg.* (c. xxix) accompanying the chariot of the Church. This pageant of the advance of Virtue suggests that of the last five cantos of the *Purgatorio.* No doubt, such scenes occurred in the street processional plays. Note the pageant in the *Anti-Claudianus* with Reason as charioteer. (There is a vicar in *Piers Plow.* who said the only cardinals he knew were those sent by the Pope.)

l. 808. *Pacyence.* In *Piers Plow.* Patience is described as a tree which grows in the heart and bears fruit of Charity. The tree is supported against the winds of the world, the flesh, and the devil by three props denoting the Trinity.

P. 25, l. 815. This line seems to be corrupted in the *MS.* which reads "was tra-
pure was gay." *Trapure* refers to the "trappings" of the steed. Cf. *Flow.
and Leaf,* ll. 244-5:
"With cloth of gold and furred with ermine
Were the trappores of here stedes stronge,
Wide and large, that to the ground dide honge";
Lydgate, *Min. P.,* p. 118:
"Trappours of golde ordeyned were for stiedis";
Hawes, *Past. of Pleas.,* p. 132:
"Wyth haute courage betrapped fayre and gaye
Wyth shyning trappers of curiositie."

l. 824. *to steuyn.* Stevene is always employed by Chaucer as a noun. It
has here a verbal use probably from the necessity of the rime. There was,
however, the older verb from stefnen (cf. *M. E. Dict.,* Strat.-Brad.).
Douglas has (II., p. 225, l. 8): "towart the port thai stevin"—directed
their ship; but this is from the Icl. stefna - prow. Chaucer has this set of
rimes in *Kn. Tale,* ll. 1720-21; *Troil. and Cris.,* III., ll. 1723-25; *Leg. of
G.W.,* ll. 1218-19.

l. 844. *Pouerte.* Poverty was a highly praised virtue in the Church. It is
said in *Piers Plow.,* Pas. xiv., that this virtue preserves men from the Seven
Sins, for it (1) is hateful to Pride, (2) has few responsibilities, (3) does not
win wealth falsely, (4) is the gift of God, (5) is the mother of health, (6) is
without peril of robbery, (7) is a source of wisdom, (8) deals fairly with
others, (9) is without care. Feigned Poverty is one of the Vices, l. 657.

P. 26, l. 854. *Konnyng with hys genalogy.* That is to say the Seven Arts and
Sciences. The seven sciences as originally distinguished were Mathematics,
Geometry, Astronomy, Music, Ethics, Physics and Metaphysics. The seven
arts were: Grammar, Dialectics, Rhetoric (the trivium) and Arithmetic,
Music, Geometry, and Astronomy (the quadrivium). These are mentioned
familiarly by all the learned writers of the Middle Ages. They were char-
acterized also in the plays and pageants and such objectification gives
meaning to the processional of the poem. In Lydgate's description of the
King's entry into London there is an account of a spectacle representing the
Seven Sciences. The name of Priscian is associated with Grammar ("the
roote of alle connyng"), Aristotle with Logic, Cicero with Rhetoric, Boethius
with Music, Pythagoras with Arithmetic, Euclid with Geometry, and Albu-
masar with Astronomy ("alder-highest"). In *Piers Plow.,* the sciences ap-
pear as sons of the Clergy, serving the Lord of Life in a castle (Pas. xiii).
See Gower, *Conf. Aman,* Lydgate's *Pur le Roy, Chestre Plays* (Wright, p. 241),
Hallam, *Lit. of Europe,* etc.

ll. 867-870. The Magical and Black Arts. The specific "Black Arts" were
commonly five: Necromancy, Pyromancy, Geomancy, Hydromancy, and
Aerimancy, signifying divination by means of the dead, fire, the earth, water,
and the air respectively. These species are indicated by Huge de S. Vic-
tore (see Skeat's Notes to *Piers Plow.,* p. 246). Gower *Conf. Aman.,* III.,
p. 45, describes these five kinds in detail; see also Lydgate's *Secrees.* As
to the merits of the magical arts, opinion was divided. The Black Arts
were almost universally denounced in this period in England. Alchemy
and Physiognomy were, however, often employed. It seems that there was
a revival of Magic, and especially of Alchemy, during Chaucer's and Lyd-
gate's lifetime. But we find that sorcery, soothsaying and magic were pun-
ished in London as early as 1382, the affirmation being that "the art of
magic redounds against the doctrine of Sacred Writ"; the punishment was
exposure upon the pillory (*Mem. of Lond.,* ed. Riley, II., pp. 462, 472, 518).
A statute forbidding the practice of Alchemy was passed in 1403. The art
was revived again at about the end of the century, so that Henry VI.
appointed three Royal Commissioners to investigate the subject. Their
report is dated 1456 (see *The Antiquary,* Sept. 1891, for documents illus-

trating the revival of Alchemy at about the middle of the fifteenth century). We find that Alchemy was condemned by Gower (*Conf. Am.* II., p. 88); Alchemy and other arts by Langland (*Piers Plow.*, Pas. x., ll. 207–15); the magical arts in general by Chaucer (in *Ch. Yeo. Tale*, and *Pers. Tale*) and Lydgate (in the present instance and *Secrees* st. 82–84 though favorable to physiognomy, st. 353 54, and in *Story of Thebes* [fol. 390], where he condemns Bishop Amphiorax to hell as the mede of his idolatry and magic) and Barclay (*Ship of Fools*, II., pp. 18, 191, 219). As a matter of fact, Alchemy flourished in spite of condemnation and belief in it continued far into the seventeenth century (see *Faery Queene*, I., c. i., st. 36–37 and Sir Th. Browne, Works I., ch. x.). In Ward's *O. E. Drama*, Introduction to Marlowe's "Dr. Faustus," the general attitude of the M. Ages toward magic and magicians is shown. See *Secrees*, notes, p. 93–95.

l. 868. *Glotony.* This must be a mistake of the scribe for Alchemy.

l. 870. *Pawmestry.* Divination by the lines of the hand.

l. 882. *Ches.* Cf. *Æsop*, Fab. 5, l. 71:
"The crane chase a surgeon to be";
Temp of Glas., l. 214, 336:
"Would freli chese."
Note *leese* l. 1100.

l. 886. *ware of contagious geere.* Contagious geere ═ ?

P. 27, l. 887. *lere.* "Lere" here means learn; "lerne" in l. 957 means teach. Cf. *Temp. of Glas.*, l. 297, 1021 learn:
"Fro dai to dai that I myghte lere";
idem, l. 656 — teach:
"Than cometh dispeire and ginneth me to lere."
Cf. *Story of Thebes*, fol. 378:
"The which beasts as the story leres."

l. 895. *secte.* Cf. *Rom. of the Rose*, l. 5745:
"Eke in the same secte or sette."

l. 896. See note on l. 1097.

P. 28, l. 925. *then I reherse can.* Cf. *Temp. of Glas.*, l. 560: "as I reherse can" and often.

l. 932. *Macrocosme.* I interpret this to mean Microcosm from the interpretation by Doctrine, st. 262. For the conception of Microcosm see *Secrees*, ll. 2313–17:
"In beeste nor thyng vegitable,
No thyng may be vnyuersally
But yif it be founde naturally
In mannys nature. Wherfore of oon accoord
Oold philisoffres callyd hym the litel woord (worlde)."
See also Stubbes, *Anat. of Abuses*, p. 111:
"And therfore, wheras in making of other things he used only this Woord, FIANT, be they made or let them be made, when he came to make Man, as it weare advysing himselfe and asking councell at his wisdome, he said FACIAMUS HOMINEM, let us make Man; that is a wonderful Creature: and therfore is called in Greek MICROCOSMOS, a litle world in himself. And truely he is no lesse, whether we consider his spirituall soule, or his humaine body, etc."
For a fuller account of Man, the Microcosm, assailed by Vices and defended by Virtues, see Fletcher's *Purple Island*, the most dreadful of all the Holy Wars.

l. 939. *hygh weyes fyue.* All the old books make much of man's five senses, the high-ways of Mansoul. Note the use made by Bunyan of this conception in *Holy War:*

"The famous town of Mansoul had five gates at which to come, and out at which to go; and these were made likewise answerable to the walls, to wit, impregnable, and such as could never be opened nor forced but by the will and leave of those within. The names of the gates were these: Eargate, Eye-gate, Mouth-gate, Nose-gate, and Feel-gate."

l. 941. *blyue.* Cf. Chaucer, *Bk. of the Duch.* l. 152:
"Go now faste, and hy thee blyve;"
Æsop, Fab. 4, l. 206:
"With ravenous feete, wynged to flee blyue."

P. 29, l. 957. *lerne hem a new daunce.* A common saying with Chaucer and others. Cf. *Rom. of the Rose,* l. 4300:
"For she knew alle the olde daunce."
Cf. Chaucer, *Troyl and Crys.* II. l. 554; *Dr. of Ph. Tale,* l. 79; *Cant. Tales,* Pr. l. 470. Cf. Gower *Conf. Aman.,* I., p. 260:
"Now shalt thou singe an other songe."

l. 974. *dubbyd.* Cf. *Piers Plow.,* Pas. i., ll. 102-3:
"For Dauid in his dayes dubbed knightes
And did hem swere on here swerde to serue trewthe euere."
In *Ad. Dav. Dream* (E.E. T., l. 76) "dubbing" is a substantive and means decoration.

P. 30, l. 998. *Reson.* Reason is a common personification. See *Rom. of the Rose,* 3034, 3193; Lydgate's Min. P., p. 219; *Piers Plow.* Pas. xv., xvi.; Dunbar's *Gold. Targe,* 151, etc. In *Piers Plow.* Reason has many names: anima, animus, mens, memoria, ratio, sensus, conscientia, amor, spiritus. He plays an important part in the poem.

l. 1009. One instance of a double negative. Cf. *Æsop,* Fab. 4, l. 53:
"I may no favour do to nowther side."

l. 1012. *hyng in hys balaunce.* A very common figure. Cf. *Temp. of Glas,* ll. 641, 348; Chaucer, *Troyl. and Crys.* II., l. 466:
"And ek myn emes lyf is in balaunce."
In Barclay's *Ship of Fools* is a wood-cut showing the world and things eternal in a balance. Cf. Spenser's figure in *Faerie Queene* V., ii., 30-49.

l. 1012. *ambygnyte.* Chaucer has amphibologyes, *Troil. and Cris.,* iv., l. 1406.

P. 31, l. 1023. *sewe the felde.* Lydgate probably had in mind the parable of the Sower. Langland has a parable of the ploughman in Pas. xix.; there the weeds of vice grow in the field but they are uprooted by the harrow of the Law.

l. 1038. *swage.* I define as "discharge" but find no authority for it except the context.

l. 1038. *gonnes.* The first mention of guns or "gonnes" as being in use in England is found in an inventory of munitions of war in a London document dated 1339 (see *Mem. of London,* ed. Riley, I., p. 205). These "gonnes" were made of brass or "latone" and fired "pellets of lead," using gunpowder. Cf. Chaucer *House of Fame,* III., l. 553:
"Swift as a pellet out of a gonne,
When fire is in the powder ronne";
Lydgate's *Story of Thebes,* fol. 392:
"Noise more hideous then thunder
Of gonne shot."
The word was also employed to designate a machine that cast stones. Cannon is mentioned in Barbour's *Bruce* (1375) Bk. XIX., l. 399. Cannon had been used in Florence in 1326.

P. 32, l. 1063. *abew*=a beu. Gower has the phrase in *Conf. Aman.*, III., p. 356:
> "Er thou make any such assaies
> To love and faile upon thy fete
> Better is to make beau retrete."

The word beau was commonly used in address as in *Rom. of the Rose*, l. 800:
> "What do ye there, beau sir ?"

Sir Gawain, E.E. T., l. 1222:
> "Nay, for sothe, beau syr ";

also *House of Fame*, l. 643. Cf. *Rich. Rede.*, Pas. iii., l. 1:
> "Now leve we this beu brid."

l. 1063. *lytyll tyne*. Cf. Skelton, *Garl. of Laur.* l. 505:
> "A lytyll tyne stande backe ";

Heywood, *Dialogue:*
> "For when prouender prickt them a little tine."

The two words generally occur together. See l. 1283.

l. 1066. *by lyklynes*. Cf. *Temp. of Glas.*, l. 18; Chaucer. *Am. Compl.* l. 15
Cl. Tale, II., l. 200, etc.

l. 1089. *lowte*. Cf. *Æsop*, Fab. 2, ll. 17–18.
> "Whan sulphur toward the dawenyng
> Lowtith to the oryent ";

Piers Plow., Pas. iii., l. 115:
> "Knelynge, Conscience to the kynge louted."

See also text, ll. 1439, 1925, vnderlowte 1273.
Cf. Browning, *Ring and Book:*
> "I have louted low."

P. 33, l. 1094. *Perséueraunce.* The accent as in Chaucer.

l. 1095. *hogy.* Cf. Marlowe, *Tamb. the Gt.:* "my hugy host." This was Dryden's usage.

P. 34, ll. 1142–6. The way of repentance is made clear by Chaucer's Parson : "Now shalt thou understonde what bihoveth and is necessarie to verray parfyt penitence ; and this stondith in thre things, contricioun of hert, confessioun of mouth, and satisfaccioun." The first, said Patience in *Piers Plow.* (Pas. xiv.), saves men, the second slays sins, the third uproots sin altogether. Contrition and Confession appear as two horses that bear ripened grains to the house of Unity (*Piers Plow.* Pas. xix.). They are good dames in Hawes' *Past. of Pleas.*, giving sure passage to Purgatory to Graunde Amour. They are characters in the Moralities. The trinal stairs in Dante's *Purgatorio* (c. ix.) refer to these stages of repentance. All these figures refer to the creed of the Church as expounded for instance by Thomas Aquinas in his great work *Summa Theologica* (III. p. 90).

l. 1147. *fro poost to pylour.* Cf. Barclay, *Eclogues:*
> "From post unto piller tost shall thou be."

l. 1154. Despair appears in *Temp. of G.* l. 656. He was a common figure in the mediaeval imagination. Cf. Spenser's treatment of Despair. (See a paper by Dr. F. I. Carpenter reported in Univ. of Chicago Cal. Aug. '05.)

l. 1158. *Alpha and Oo.* This occurs in the *Creation*, sc. I., York Plays, in the address of the Deity :
> "I am Alpha and O."

P. 35, l. 1167. *borow*--verbal. Cf. Chaucer, *Ck. Tale* l. 204 :
> "For he hath slayn my two sones, but if God hem borwe ";

the old play, *World and Child :*
> "Some good word that I may say
> To borow man's soul from blame."

See also *Piers Plow.* Pas. iv, l. 108–9.

This word was often used as a noun as in *Tem. of Glas*, l. 1145:
> "And as for him I will bene his borow,"

and in the phrase "to borow" (=for a security).

l. 1169. *tenebrus*, Cf. Hawes' *Past. of Pleas.* p. 15, 74:
> "Auster gan cover with clowde tenebrus";
> "The night was wete, and also tenebrous."

l. 1185. *fly*. This is the reading of MS. B. A has sty from stigen, to ascend.

P. 36, l. 1204. *bettyr late then neuer.* Cf. Chaucer, *Ch. Yeo. Tale*, l. 399:
> "For bet than never is late."

l. 1226. *sothe.* Cf. Chaucer, *Parl. Fou.*, l. 578, "sothe sadde"=sober truth.

l. 1232. *as a pleyer.* Collier in a note on this passage (*Annals of the Stage*, p. 31) refers to player as an actor, interpreting the line to mean that Sensuality must change his character like an actor. But "to drawe a draught" is used of games as chess. Thus Chaucer (*Bk. of the Duch*, l. 682) has
> "I wolde have drawe the same draughte."

In a work described by Collier (*An. of Stage*, p. 63) entitled *The Church of Yvell men and women* players refers to gamesters, dicers, etc.
"Player" would seem to mean here "gamester"; though it is possible that "draught" may be used here figuratively for "character" as Collier suggests.

P. 37, l. 1242. *finaunce.* Cf. Skelton, *Erle of Nh.*, l. 195:
> "With thy bloud precious our finaunce thou did pay";

the same line occurs in Percy's *Reliques*, l, p. 125.

l. 1255. Reason in Microcosm. Cf. description of Reason in the *Romaunt of the Rose*, ll. 3193 *et seq.*, where she warns against the follies of Love. Chaucer's Parson says:
> "For it is soth, that God, and reasoun, and sensualité, and the body of man, be so ordeyned, that everich of these four thinges schulde have lordschipe over that other, as thus: God scholde have lordschip over reasoun, and reasoun over sensualité, and sensualité over the body of man."

Cf. Lydgate Min. P., p. 219:
> "Sith thu were wroughte to be celestial,
> Let reson brydle thy sensualite."

l. 1256. *recreaunt.* This was a word which Knights uttered in acknowledging defeat. "Yelde hym recreaunt" = yielded himself as a defeated knight. The oath taken by a combatant ran thus: "Je suis prest de le prouver de mon corps contre le sien, et le rendre mort ou recreant . . . et véez çy mon gage." The customary form of demanding surrender was: "And but thou yeeld thee as overcome and recreaunt thou shalt die." Cf. *Sir Gawayne*, E. E. T., l. 456:
> "Therfore com other recreaunt be calde."

Piers Plow. (Pas. xv, l. 133) has "yelde hym creaunt" (as a believer?); "creaunt" is sometimes used for recreaunt in the sense explained above.

l. 1267. *astert.* Cf. Chaucer, *Fr. Tale*, l. 294:
> "He seith, he may not fro his deth asterte."

P. 38, l. 1268. *Nature.* Nature was given especial personification by Alanus de Insulis in his *Planctus Naturæ* (Wright ed., Rec. Ser., pp. 431–456). Chaucer in the *Parl. of Foules* describes her as a Queen surrounded by the animals of the earth and air (ll. 298–301, etc.). In Langland's dream Nature appears and shows the wonders of the world (Pas. xi, l. 311–25). She was an empress in the pageant that welcomed Henry VI. to London (*Pur Le Roy*). See the *Faerie Queene* VII, vii.

l. 1274. *shoo clowte*=shoe-cloth. Cf. Skelton, *El. Rum*, ll. 143–4 :
"Some wyth a sho clout
Bynde theyr heddes about."
Browning his "clouted shoon" (Ring and Book, p. 321).

l. 1299. *blere.* Cf. *Rom. of the Rose* l. 3912 :
"That almoost blered is myn yhe ";
Chaucer, *Maun. Tale*, l. 148 :
"Far al thy waytyng, blered is thin ye."
See also *Rv. Tale*, l. 129; *Piers Plow.* Pr. l. 74; *Rox. Ballads* 1, p. 163;
Milton's *Comus*, ll. 153–6 :
"To cheat the eye with blear illusion ";
Shaks. *Tam. of Shrew*, V, i :
"While counterfeit supposes blear'd thine eyne."

P. 39, l. 1311. *astonyed.* Cf. *Tem. of Glas*, l. 24 :
"I wex astonyed."

l. 1317. *howe a devyll way!* Cf. Chaucer, *Ml. Tale*. Pr., l. 26 :
"Tel on, a devil way!";
idem, l. 527 :
"And let me slepe, a twenty devyl way";
Ch. Yeo. Tale, Pr. ll. 229–30 :
"And al the cost on twenty devel waye
Is lost also";
Leg. of G. Wom., VI, l. 292 :
"A twenty devel way the wynde him dryve."

l. 1327. *longeth.* Cf. *Secrees*, l. 1029 :
"Of all such vertues as longe to a kyng."

P. 40, l. 1340. *Resydynacion* = back-sliding. The term occurs again in **Skelton**,
Col. Cl. ll. 523–5 :
"And of resydeuacyon
They make interpretacyon
Of an aquarde facyon."

P. 41, l. 1384. *wysshe.* Cf. Chaucer, *A. B. C.* l. 155; *Ho. of Fame* ll. 489–91;
Temp. of Glas l. 637 :
"So wisse me now what me is best to do ";
Piers Plow. Pas. v, ll. 540–562 :
"I shal wisse you witterly the weye to his place."

l. 1386. *as I gesse.* Cf. Chaucer, *Bk. of Duch.* l. 35; *Compl. of M.* l. 195;
Parl. of Fou. ll. 160, 200, 223; *Cant. Tales*, Pr. l. 82; *Knight's Tale*, l. 192;
Lydgate, Min. P., p. 54. Cf. Dunbar, *Gold. Targe*, l. 230 :
"God Eolus, his bugill blew I gesse."

l. 1403. Death and dread. Among the Roxburge Ballads (I, p. 312) is
one which runs as follows :
"Lament your sinnes, good people all, lament,
You plainly see the Messenger is sent, -
I meane grim Death, and he doth play his part;
He stands prepar'd to strike you to the heart."
This is accompanied by the cut of a hideous skeleton with a dart. Cf. *Piers
Plow.* Pas. xx, ll. 198 -200:
"And as I seet in this sorwe I say how kynde passed,
And deth drowgh niegh me, for drede gan I quake,
And cried to kynde out of care me brynge."

P. 43, l. 1448. *vre.* This word occurs in French law — *mis en ure* (Kelham).
Its use was maintained in England through the 16th century. I find it in
an early American poem, Wigglesworth's *Day of Doom* (1662) :
"The best of men had scarcely then
Their Lamps kept in good ure."

l. 1455. *sesyne.* A law term denoting the ownership of property. To take seizen refers to the ceremony of taking possession of one's freehold. Cf. R. of G. *Chr.* Reign of Wm. 1. 528:

"Ac wende him out of Normandie anon to Engelande
Vorto nime hastliche seisine of is lande."

See *Morte Arthur* (Th. MS.), l. 3589.

l. 1463. *fyn fast shut.* I make fyn an adverb with the force of very or completely. The word finliche in the phrase "finliche well" (= very well) occurs in *Sir Bevis of Hamtoun* l. 4052; also afin with the same meaning in l. 2577: "The beschop was glad afin." Chaucer uses fyn as an adj. in *Troil. and Cris.* V. 421: "of fyne force" (= of very need). Cf. our use of clean — completely, as in "clean laid aside," and of pure as "the pure death" (= death itself).

P. 44, 1479. *herber wallyd round about.* Doctrine's arbor is probably in imitation of the Garden of Mirth in *Rom. of the Rose:*

"And when I had a while goon,
I saugt a gardyn right anoon,
Ful long and brood, and every delle
Enclosed was, and walled welle,
With highe walles enbatailled,
Portraied without and wel entailled
With many riche portraitures."—ll. 135-141.

Cf. the Tower of Doctrine in Hawes' *Pastime of Pleasure,* written in imitation evidently of Lydgate's arbor: Graunde Amour is taught wisdom by learned dames, the Seven Sciences. All these may be suggestions of the Noble Castle of Learning in Dante's Inferno (c. iv) with its scholastic walls.

l. 1483. *Wytte.* In the homily of the *Sawles Warde* man is described as a house whose master is Wit. Wit's wife is named Will.

l. 1491. *perfyte.* Cf. *Secrees,* ll. 365, 387, 273: "In parfight clernesse."

l. 1509. *dalyaunce.* Dalyaunce in Lydgate seems always to refer to speech. See Schick's quotations, notes p. 91. In the *Pilgrimage of Man* "longe dalyaunce" translates the French "long parlement." Cf. *Temp. of Glas,* l. 291:

"Of port benygne, and of *daliaunce* (address);"

Æsop, Fab. 6, l. 93:

"That we togydre may have oure daliaunce;"

Min. P., p. 71:

"Countrefeteth in speche and daliaunce;"

Secrees, l. 2706:

"Lawhyng visage is good in daliaunce."

l. 1512. *myn ey gan I dresse.* Cf. *Temp. of Glas,* l. 850:

"Gan cast hir eyen."

P. 45, ll. 1515 *et seq. on tho walles was made memory,* etc. Douglas evidently imitates these pictures of sacred history in his account of the reflections seen in the mirror of Venus (Works I., pp. 57-59)—another poetical device of the same kind. See Introd., p. lvii.

l. 1538. *Iudyth.* Judith is often mentioned in M. E. Lit. Cf. Chaucer, *M. of L. Tale,* 841; *March. Tale,* l. 122; *Monks Tale,* ll. 561-584; *Piers Plow.,* Pas. xvii., l. 21, etc. The account of the O. E. epic of Judith was probably known by the side of the version in the Vulgate.

P. 46, ll. 1562 *et seq.* These pictures are drawn from the frescoes on monastery walls whereon it was customary to present the saints with their traditional attributes. Lydgate's descriptions represent late traditions those of the 13th and 14th centuries (note the attribute of St. James the scallop shell, given him after the 13th century). The attribute of Peter was the key;

Paul held a sword; James the Great was a pilgrim with a long staff, wearing a cape with a scallop shell on his shoulder or hat, etc. Other pictures were the "Martyrdoms" which represented the manner in which the saints were slain: Thomas by a spear, Philip on the cross, James the Less by a club, Bartholomew by flaying, Simon and Jude, always together, by a sword and club, etc. There will be remembered in this connection Albert Dürer's picture of St. Thomas who is seen holding a lance, and Angelo's Last Judgment where Bartholomew appears holding his skin in one hand and the knife with which he was flayn in the other. Many other pictures will be recalled and this is a necessary process in reading Lydgate—of the Apostles and Fathers as here displayed. For the emblems of the Apostles and Saints cf. Jameson, *Sacr. and Leg. Art.* Cf. the *Ormulum* V. i., p. 201 and note; *Curs. Mun.*, p. 1218; Lyndesay's *Monarche*, II. 2279 *et seq.*

P. 47, l. 1583. *Beede.* One does not meet with many late references to Baeda. He is mentioned however, by Dante in *Par.* c. x., l. 131; and by Wyclif (*Works*, I., p. 35; III., p. 477).

l. 1584. *Orygene.* An Alexandrine Greek, born A. D. 185. Bitter controversy arose regarding his views on the final salvation of men, the transformation of man's earthly body at the resurrection, etc. His "errors" are contained chiefly in his work, περὶ ἀρχῶν. A private "error" is also recorded of Origen to which reference here may be made. See Butler's *Lives of Saints*, ix., p 360.

l. 1589. *Sybyll.* "The pictures of the Sybils are very common, and for their prophecies of Christ in high esteem with Christians." —Sir Th. Browne. In the account of Varro the sybils numbered ten.

l. 1608. *houyd.* Cf. *Chorl and Bird*, 187: "Hovyng above his hedde" (said of a bird).

l. 1611. *gall.* Gall-trees were those that, like the oak, bear bitter galls. Spenser has "trees of bitter gall" (*Faery Queen*, II., vii., st. 52).

P. 48, ll. 1618 *et seq.*
The whole discourse of Doctrine is written in the light of Catholic doctrine and practice. There is a certain kind of ingenuity exercised in the handling of the materials, but beyond a skillful presentation of doctrine there is not the least display of poetic genius in all this part.

P. 49, l. 1657. *made her beerdys on the new gete* —changed their purpose. Palsgrave defines "new get" as "guise nouvelle." Cf. Chaucer, *Cant. Tales*, Pr., line 682 :
"Him thought he rood al of the newe get:"
All. Tale, l. 136 : (a kirtil)
"Schapen with goores in the newe get;"
Skelton, *Magnif.*, l. 458 :
"The courtly gyse of the newe iet."
Those who cut their beards in the latest fashion had a place in Barclay's *Ship of Fools* (I., p. 35). Cf. the phrase, "To make one's beard" == to deceive; as in Chaucer, *Reeves Tale*, l. 176 :
"Yet can a miller make a clerkes berd."
Cf. *Ho. of Fame*, l. 689; *W. of B. Tale*, Pr., l. 361.

P. 50, l. 1714. *habundaunce.* So in Chaucer's *Fortune*, l. 29.

l. 1718. *gryffyng.* Cf. *Seeres*, l. 2373 :
"Which gryffyd on stokkys haue many braunchys."

P. 51, l. 1728. Cf. *Æsop.* Fab. 7, ll. 64–5 :
"Men may at the ie se a pref
Of this matere."

ll. 1737 *et seq.* The Times. In the Calendar of the *Cursor Mundi* there are seven ages : (1) from Adam to Noah ; (2) from Noah to Abraham ; (3) from Abraham to David ; (4) from David to Solomon ; (5) from Solomon to the birth of Christ ; (6) from the birth to the death of Christ ; (7) from the death of Christ to the Day of Doom, the period of Antichrist.
Cf. also Wyclif, *Works*, I., p. 99.
Gower has a reading of the Times similar to Lydgate (Prol. *Conf. Am.*), agreeing especially in the Time of War.

P. 52, l. 1772. *that ys to sey.* Very common in Lydgate. Cf. *Temp. of Glas*, ll. 311, 426, 512, 715, 1124, etc.

l. 1784. *prynte hit in thy mynde.* A favorite phrase with Lydgate. Cf. Min. P., p. 36.

P. 53, l. 1805. *cast in a boon.* Cf. Chaucer, *Kn. Tale*, l. 319 :
   " We stryve, as doth the houndes for the boon."

P. 54, l. 1829. *the lesse worlde.* This is Milton's "less universe" (*Par. Reg.*, iv., l. 458). Said Sir Th. Browne (*Relig. Med.*) : " That we are the breath and similitude of God, is indisputable and upon record of Holy Scripture ; but to call ourselves a microcosm, or little world, I thought it only a pleasant trope of rhetorick, till my near judgment and second thoughts told me there was a real truth therein."

l. 1844. *dampnacion.* So Chaucer in *Pd. Tale*, l. 38 ; *A. B. C.*, l. 167.

l. 1852. *inwarde wyttes.* Man was regarded as having five outward and five inward wits. Cf. *World and Child*, Dods, I., p. 273 :

Age	" Of the five wits I would have knowing.
Pres.	Forsooth, sir, hearing, seeing, and smelling,
	The remenant tasting and feeling :
	These being the five wits bodily,
	And, sir, other five wits there been.
Age.	Sir Perseverance, I know not them.
Pres.	Now, Repentance, I shall you ken,
	They are the power of the soul :
	Clear in mind, there is one
	Imagination, and all reason,
	Understanding and compassion."

Hawes, in *Pastime of Pleasure*, enumerates the five inward wits as common-wit, imagination, fancy, estimation and memory. The five senses perform the outward offices, being simply receptive gates, but the wits perceive and judge. From this distinction arose the figure of the senses as gates, or as highways of the soul.
   " Thet inewyt hvs the dore-ward,
      The doren wyttes fyve " — Shoreham, Per. Soc., p. 55.
" For tho (the five wits) be properly the gates,
      Through which as to the hert algates
      Cometh all thing unto the feire,
      Which may the mannes soule empeire " — *Conf. Am.*, I., p. 52.
The inward senses were then the faculties of the mind. Thus Lydgate says (*Temp. of Glas*), ll. 380-1 :
" With al my reson and alle my ful mynde, and five wittes."
The Five Senses were personated in Middleton's *Triumph of Truth* (1613). They appeared in character at the King's entry into London in 1603 and again at the Lord Mayor's Pageant in 1681 (Bullen).
The different senses are enumerated in Ælfric's Homilies, O. E. Homilies, Sawles Warde, etc. Cf. *Piers Plow.*, Pas. i., ll. 15-16 ; Wyclif's Tracts (III., p. 117) ; *Tale of Mel.; An Orysoun for sauynge of the fyve wyttes* (Vern. MS. E. E. T., xvii) ; *Interlude of the Four Elements;* Lydgate's Min. P., p. 253 ; *Faery Queene* (II., xi., st. 7) ; Fletcher's *Purple Island;* Bunyan's *Holy*

War, etc. Cf. a modern book entitled *The Five Gateways of Knowledge*, by
Dr. Geo. Wilson, and *Lect. and Addresses*, by Sir W. Thomson, on the *Six
Gateways of Knowledge.*

P. 54, l. 1855. *stremes.* Cf. *Temp. of Glas*, ll. 702, 582 :
> " For with the stremes of hir eyen clere."

l. 1858. *sauns.* Commonly found in the phrase "sauns faille," as in
Chaucer, *Ho. of Fame*, ll. 188, 429 ; *Man of L. Tale*, l. 403; the *Court of
Love*, l. 117 (" withouten faille," l. 710); Rob. of B. *Chron.*, l. 4507. *Piers
Plow.* (Pas. xii, l. 280) has "saunz reule;" Skelton, *Why Come*, l. 426.
" saunz aulter remedy."

l. 1860. *blyn.* Cf. Rob. of B. *Chron.*, l. 2263 :
> " Evere to brenne and nevere to blynne ; "

Percy, *Reliq.*, III, p. 46 :
> " On thy striking doe not blinne."

P. 55, l. 1872. *wyre.* Cf. Chaucer, *Ho. of Fame*, l. 979 :
> " Tho gan I wexen in a were ; "

Rom. of the Rose, l. 4468 :
> " Withoute deceyte or ony were ; "

Piers Plow., Pas. xi, l. 111 ; xvi, l. 3 ; *Temp. of Glas*, ll. 651, 906 and see
Schick's notes p. 104. Cf. Dunbar's *Man, sen thy Lyfe is ay in Weir.*

l. 1886. *daryng as a dastard.* Said in irony.

l. 1887. *Come of* — make an end. Probably our modern slang phrase
" come off." It was in common usage in M. E. Cf. Chaucer, *Troil. and
Cris.*, II, 310 :
> " Com of, and tel me what it is."

Temp. of Glas, l. 1272 :
> " Cometh off at ones, and do as I haue seide."

See Schick's notes, p. 119, for further references ; also Skelton, *Magnif.*,
l. 103 :
> " Come of, therefore, let se."

l. 1887. *thy wytte stant a crooke.* See also ll. 1918, 1932. Cf. Chaucer,
Ho. of Fame, l. 621 :
> " Although that (wit) in thy hede full lyte is ; "

Lydgate, *Chorl and Bird*, Min. P., p. 191 :
> " Thy brayne is dul, thy witte is almoste gone ; "

Piers Plow., Pas. i, l. 138 :
> " ' Thow doted daffe,' quod she, ' dulle arne thi wittes ; ' "

and cf. Emerson, *The Sphinx* :
> " Dull Sphinx, Jove keep thy five wits."

l. 1897. *tonne.* Lydgate has again (Min. P., p. 176) the rime tonne, sonne,
and in *Secrees*, ll. 249-50. Referring to Diogenes Lydgate says :
> " His paleys was a litel poore tonne."

P. 57, l. 1952. *as blak as a coole.* Other objects of comparison with blackness
were raven, crow, the devil, jet, ink and soot. Cf. *Conf. Am.*, II, p. 335 :
> " With fethers blacke as any cole."

l. 1953. *cropyn in a mouse hoole.* Cf. Skelton, *Why Come*, ll. 289-91 :
> " Our barons be so bolde,
> Into a mouse hole they wolde
> Rynne away and crepe."

P. 58, l. 1997. *my wyt ys soo thynne.* See l. 896. Middle Engl. writers were fond
of acknowledging the weakness of their wits. Thus Chaucer confesses in
the Prol. of the Tales (l. 746) "My wit is short." His Marchant said (l.

438) "My tale is doon, for my wit is thinne." Again the poet writes (*Ho. of Fame*, ll. 1179-80:
> "Ne can I not to yow devyse (Temp. of Fame)
> My wit ne may me not suffyse;"

and to describe the beauty of his lady (*Bk. of the Duch.*, l. 898):
> "Me lakketh bothe English and wit."

Lydgate was even more self-depreciatory (for references see *Temp. of Glas* Introd. p. cxl-cxli and *Secrees*, p. xx).
"Make his wittes thynne" occurs in *Ch. Yeo. Tale*, Pr. l. 189; cf. R. of B, *Chron.* l. 113.

P. 59, l. 2008. *knette.* See line 991 knyt, 1186 knet. Cf. *Temp. of Glas*, l. 1230, "The cnott is knytt."

P. 60, l. 2065. *God knoweth and nat I.* An allusion to Paul's saying, II Cor. xii, 2-3.

l. 2070. *take the best, etc.* Cf. Chaucer, *N. Pr. Tale*, l. 623:
> "Takith the fruyt and let the chaf be stille;"

Conf. Aman. 1, Pr. p. 32:
> "The chaf is take for the corne;"

Lydgate's *Min. P.* p. 149:
> "Cheese we the roosys, cast away the thorn;"

idem, p. 173:
> "Wedyde the cokkelle frome the puryd corne;"

Secrees, l. 734:
> "As vndir chaaf is closyd pure corn;"

idem, l. 1224.
> "Woord is but wynd; leff woord and take the dede;"

Story of Thebes fol. 370:
> "Avoiding the chaffe . . .
> Enlumining the true piked graine."

P. 61, l. 2079. *three enymyes.* The World the Flesh and the Devil were figuratively spoken of as foes or robbers or wild beasts or adverse winds etc. In O. E. Homilies (Morris p. 241) they are described as foes and again as robbers. According to Boccaccio the three beasts which hindered Dante's progress represented these forces. In *Piers Plow.* (Pas. xvi) these are winds that blow against the tree of Patience. Chaucer's *Tale of Mel.* reads "Thou hast doon synne ageinst oure Lord Crist, for certes the thre enemyes of mankinde, that is to saye, thy flessche, the feend, and the world, thou hast y-suffred hem to entre into thin herte wilfully, by the wyndow of thy body, and hast nought defended thiself sufficiently agayns here assautis, and here temptaciouns, so that they have woundid thi soule in fyve places, that is to sayn, the dedly synnes that ben entred into thin herte by thy fyve wittes."
> "And thus it falleth
> That thorugh the fende and the flesshe and the frele worlde
> Synneth the sadman a day seuene sythes" (*P. Pl.* Pas. viii, l. 38-44).

The Devil was thought to work by Pride, Wrath and Sloth; the World by Covetousness and Envy; the Flesh by Gluttony and Lechery. Hawes gives a similar exhortation in *Past. of Pleas:*
> "Than in your mynde inwardly despyse
> The brytile worlde, so full of doublenes,
> With the vyle flesshe, and ryght sone aryse
> Out of your slepe of mortall hevynes;
> Subdue the devill with grace and mekenes,
> That after your lyfe frayle and transitory,
> You may than live in joye perdurably."

l. 2087. *guerdoun.* A favorite word of Lydgate's. Cf. *Æsop*, Fab. 3, l. 64; Fab. 5., ll. 21, 25, 35; Fab. 6., ll. 145, 165; Min. P. p. 76, "a gwerdonles guerdone"; *Temp. of Glass*, ll. 806, 1139; *Secrees*, l. 900, etc.

l. 2105. *benygne Ihesu.* Cf. Lydgate's *Testament* Min. P. p. 236: "O gracious Ihesu! benygne and debonayre." No one can question the piety of these monkish writers. Cf. Hawes' closing, the *Past. of Pleas.:*

> "Nowe blessed lady of the health eternall,
> The quene of comfort and of heavenly glory,
> Praye to thy swete sonne whiche is infinall,
> To geve me grace to wynne the victory
> Of the devill, the worlde, and of my body,
> And that I may my selfe well apply
> Thy sonne and the to laude and magnifie."

Skelton, looking back upon such writers, especially upon Lydgate and his *Assembly of Gods,* acknowledges their authority — those poets

> "Whyche full craftely,
> Vnder as couerte termes as could be,
> Can touch a trouth and cloke it subtylly
> Wyth fresshe vtteraunce full sentencyously;
> Dyuerse in style, some spared not vyce to wryte,
> Some of moralyte nobly dyde endyte."
> —*Bowge of Court, Pr.*

To conclude, the significance of Lydgate in the history of literature I under-stand to be this: Taking his work in its entirety he seems to embody the forces that were shaping England during the late Middle Age in a more conspicuous manner than any other Middle English author. Chaucer stands out, of course, the supreme genius of the period, original and creative, the glory of the Court, the herald of the Renaissance. After Chaucer, in point of creativeness, ranks Lang-land the mystic, the scholar, the churchman, the prophet of the Reformation. Now the progress of literary history is often most clearly marked, as Mr. Gosse well maintains, in the less monumental figures of any period. The very genius of Chaucer and Langland removed them somewhat from the effects of environment. With Lydgate there is not much question of personal force. What is valuable in his work arises from his lack of originality and very incapacity as a poet. He is the product of his age — at one time yielding himself to the Romantic tendency, spending his youth in pleasure, writing ballads, romances, plays and histories for the King and Court. Then the love of Mother Church detains him, he assumes the cowl, and lives and dies at Bury St. Edmund. As a result of living in his environment no other early English author can equal him in the scope of his interests. He copied and translated everything that came to his hand. His work embraces ballads, lyrics, epics, allegories, fables, moral romances, social satires, histories, philosophical and scientific treatises, hagiologies and devotional manuals. The Romantic and the Scholastic blend in him in this remarkable manner. Because of his contemporaneity his rewards accrued to him in his lifetime. He was patronized by the Court and lived in the favor of his fellow-poets. For a century his fame was maintained, and his influence was even stronger than Chaucer's upon Burgh, Hawes, the Scottish poets, and laureate Skelton — his fame and influence passing with the traditions that gave them effect.

In the matter of language Lydgate is perhaps more typical of his period than Chaucer. Chaucer's whole linguistic system is for his time forced and artificial. Middle English does not have the regularity and certainty which Chaucer's usage seems to imply. Not a one of his successors could support his literary dialect. James's Quair, purposely composed in the Chaucerian manner, is artificial to the extreme. Lydgate's poetic incapacity compelled him to fall back upon the current speech. In short, in this, as in all other respects, Lydgate was the immediate product of his environment. He wrote not for all time but for an age.

CATALOG OF PERSONS.

(The numbers refer to lines except those marked st.=stanza).

LYDGATE.

The poet performs a twofold function; he is one of the prime movers in the vision (v. especially his fear of Death, st. 277-286) and at the same time the conscious teller of the story, never forgetting the "gentle reader." (*a*) As an actor: goes forth to the lake's side and dreams, st. 1, 2; accompanies Morpheus to the Court of Minos, st. 3-5; attends the banquet given to the gods, st. 27-87; a spectator on the field of battle, st. 88-210; at the school of Doctrine, st. 211-290 (fears Death, st. 277-286); returns to his bed, st. 291, 292; awakes and writes st. 293-296.

(*b*) References to himself as narrator, st. 76, 81, 160, 171, 214, 222, 228, 229, 230, 294-301.

THE DIVINITIES (AT THE ASSEMBLY).

Apollo, the God of Light, the giver and director of the banquet, st. 24, 25, 27, 28, 30, 32, 34, 35, 36, 37, 55, 73, 103, 189; interpretation by Doctrine, 237.

Atropos, the God of Death; is met by Discord, st. 60; makes complaint to the gods, st. 61-71; is promised aid against Virtue, st. 72-75, 81-87; threatens the gods, st. 138; is angered at the success of Virtue, st. 188-192; seeks the Lord of Light, st. 198-199; is called Death, st. 201; is made master of Microcosm, st. 203, 207-209; vanishes, st. 210; interpretation by Doctrine, st. 257-260; makes Lydgate to fear, st. 277-279; the fear of Death explained, st. 280-288.

Aurora, the Goddess of the Dawn, the companion of Apollo at the banquet, st. 37, 55.

Bacchus, the God of Wine, at the banquet, st. 51.

Cerberus, the Porter of Hell; brings Eolus to the Court, st. 6, 79; to the banquet, st. 27; is sent to summon Vice, st. 87-88; porter of Hell, st. 167.

Ceres, the Goddess of Corn, at the banquet with Cupid, st. 42; said to be influenced by Phœbe, st. 52; interpretation by Doctrine, st. 245.

Cupid, the God of Love, at the banquet, st. 43.

Diana, the Goddess of the Wood and the Chase, complainant at the Court of Minos, st. 6-11, 22, 80; dismisses the case to attend the banquet, st. 25-27; is persuaded by Apollo to forgive Eolus, st. 28-34; at the banquet with Mars, st. 38-39; interpretation by Doctrine, st. 235-239.

Discord, the Goddess of Strife, comes to the banquet but is given no seat and departs in anger, st. 59-60; conspires with Atropos, st. 60-62; interpretation by Doctrine, st. 257-260.

95

Eolus, the God of the Winds, a prisoner at the Court of Minos, st. 6-26, 76-80; judgment is suspended for the banquet, st. 28-35; is forgiven, provided he give aid to Atropos against Virtue, st. 75, 81-84; interpretation by Doctrine, st. 233-234.

Fortune, the Goddess of Chance, at the banquet, st. 46; interpretation by Doctrine, st. 246.

Isis, the Goddess of Fruit, at the banquet, st. 48; interpretation by Doctrine, st. 246.

Juno, the Goddess of Riches, at the banquet, st. 40.

Jupiter, the God of Wisdom, at the banquet, st. 39.

Mars, the God of War, at the banquet, st. 38; agrees to assist Atropos, st. 73-74.

Mercury, the God of Language, at the banquet, st. 53; agrees to assist Atropos, st. 74.

Minerva, the Goddess of War, or of Harvest, at the banquet, st. 50.

Minos, the Judge of Hell, in Court, st. 4, 6-26, 79-80.

Morpheus, the Shewer of Dreams (dwells in Fantasy l. 35); leads Lydgate to the Court of Minos, st. 2-5, 79, to the palace of Apollo, st. 27; is sent to warn Virtue, st. 103-107; is given care of the five gates of Microcosm, st. 184-186; conducts Lydgate to the School of Doctrine, st. 210-212, 223, 231, 268, 270, 277; interpretation by Doctrine, st. 265; leads Lydgate to his bed, st. 290-292.

Neptune, the God of the Sea, complainant at the Court of Minos, st. 6-7, 12-20, 80; dismisses the case to attend the banquet, st. 25-27; accepts Phœbe as arbitress, st. 34-35; at the banquet, st. 49; said to be ruled by Phœbe, st. 52; agrees to aid Atropos, st. 73; is requested by Phœbe to forgive Eolus and complies, st. 82-83; interpretation by Doctrine, st. 235-239.

Othea (Athena), the Goddess of Wisdom, at the banquet, st. 44; counsels the gods, st. 75; is referred to, st. 82.

Pan, the God of Shepherds, at the banquet, st. 47; serves as minstrel, st. 58; interpretation by Doctrine, st. 246.

Phœbe, the Goddess of Waters, the Moon; the mistress of Neptune, st. 35; at the banquet, st. 52; entreats Neptune, st. 81-83.

Pluto, the God of Hell, father of Vice, st. 86-87; at the Court in Hell, st. 4, 6-24; dismisses the Court for Apollo's banquet, st. 24-27; declares the complaint against Eolus, st. 29; at the banquet, st. 45 (how Eolus came into Pluto's power, st. 76-79); sends for his son Vice to overthrow Virtue, 85-87; commands Vice, st. 138; "On in Pluto's name," l. 1077.

Saturn, the God of Cold, at the banquet, st. 40, 41; agrees to assist Atropos, st. 74.

Venus, the Goddess of Love, at the banquet, st. 54.

POETS AND PHILOSOPHERS.

(WAITERS AT THE BANQUET, ST. 56-58; INTERPRETATION BY DOCTRINE= FEIGNERS OF FABLES, ST. 241-249.)

Albert, 398.
Arystotyll, 390.
Aueroys, 394.
Auycen, 394.

Dorothe, 391.
Dyogenes, 391, 1397, 1399.
Esculapion, 396.
Euclyde, 398.

Galyen, 395.
Hermes, 393.
Ipocras, 395.
Messehala, 392.
Omere, 397.
Orace, 397.
Orpheus, 400.
Ouyde, 397.

Plato, 392.
Saphyrus, 393.
Socrates, 392.
Sortes, 393.
Sychero, 390.
Tholome, 391.
Virgyle, 397.

THOSE SLAIN BY ATROPOS WITH HIS DART (ST. 64-69)

Achilles, 474.
Alexaunder, 464.
Artour, 466.
Cesar, Iulius, 465.
Charles, the Noble, 467.
Cirus, 474.
Cosdras, 473.
Dauid, 466.
Ector of Troy, 463.

Godfrey of Boleyn, 469.
Hanyball, 473.
Hercules, 472.
Iason, 472.
Iosue, 466.
Iudas Machabee, 468.
Nabugodonozor, 470.
Pharao, 471.
Sypio, 473.

THE MORALITIES.

Virtue, Christ's Champion (l. 1103). Atropos complains to the gods that Virtue escapes his dart, st. 69-70; the gods conspire to conquer, st. 72–75, 81-87; is warned by Morpheus to prepare for the battle with Vice, st. 103-105; gathers his hosts, st. 107-133; hastens to the field Microcosm, st. 135; charges his men to be guided by Grace, st. 136; gives knighthood to fourteen captains; sends embassadors to Freewill; engages in battle, st. 148-162; is compelled to retreat, st. 152; returns to the field, st. 160; overthrows Vice with the help of Preserverance, st. 162; is rewarded and blessed by Predestination, st. 168-169; thanks God for the victory, st. 170; is sought for by some of Vice's host, st. 171-174; seeks recompense from Freewill, st. 174-179; puts Reason and Freewill in charge of Microcosm, st. 180; charges Sensuality to be guided by Sadness, st. 181-183; gives to Morpheus the care of the five gates, st. 184-186; returns to his castle, st. 187; (Apollo informs Atropos that Virtue is not in his jurisdiction, st. 190); sends messengers to Microcosm, st. 197; prepares the field against the coming of Death, st. 204-207; is exalted above the firmament, st. 210; interpretation by Doctrine, st. 261-266; the moral, st. 297-301.

Virtue's host, st. 109-132, pauses under the Sign of the Rood, st. 149; is protected by the Shield of the Holy Trinity, st. 150.

Imaginacion, messenger of Virtue, 748, 757.

Messengers=
Prayer, 1377.
Fastyng, 1377.
Penaunce, 1377.
Almesdede, 1378.

Baptyme, the leading captain, 951, 1081, 1090, 1105, 1198, 1211, 1216.

Perseueraunce, captain of the rearguard, 1094, 1115, 1125, 1129.

Constaunce, 1128.
Knights, guides of Virtue's car=
Ryghtwysnes, 795, 1385, 1394, 1401,
1418.
Prudence, 796.
Streyngth, 797.
Temperaunce, 798.
Seven chief captains=
Humylyte, 801, 1142.
Charyte, 804, 1435.
Pacyence, 808.
Lyberalyte, 811.
Abstynence, 814.
Chastyte, 818.
Good Besynesse, 821.
Embassadors sent by Virtue to Freewill=
Reson, 998.
Discresion, 998.
Good Remembraunce, 998, 1452.
Minor captains dubbed knights by Virtue
(14)=
Feythe, 986, 1082, 1089, 1105, 1196,
1208, 1210, 1435.
Hope, 986, 1082, 1089, 1105, 1196,
1435.
Mercy, 986, 1194.
Trouthe, 986.
Ryght, 986.
Resystence of Wrong, 987.
Confession, 988.
Contricion, 988.
Satisfaccion, 988.
Verrey Drede of God, 989.
Performyng of Penaunce, 989.
Perfeceyon, 990.
Konnyng, 990.
Good Dysposicion, 990.
The minor captains led by Grace; 1st
group (57)=
Grace, 853, 948.
Trew Feythe, 828.
Hoope, 828, 986, 1082, 1089, 1105,
1196, 1435.
Mercy, 828, 986.
Pecse, 828.
Pyte, 828.
Ryght, 829.
Trowthe, 829, 986.

Mekenesse, 829.
Good Entent, 829.
Goodnes, 830.
Concorde, 830.
Parfyte Vnyte, 830, 1082, 1105.
Honest Trew Loue, 831.
Symplycyte, 831.
Prayer, 832, 1377.
Fastyng, 832, 1377.
Preuy Almysdede, 832, 1378.
Artycles of the Crede, 833.
Confession, 834, 988, 1143, 1429.
Contrycion, 834, 988, 1145, 1429.
Satysfaccion, 834, 988, 1146, 1429.
Sorow for Synne, 835, 1430.
Gret Repentaunce, 835, 1430.
Foryeuenes of Trespas, 836.
Good Dysposicion, 836, 990, 1431.
Resystence of Wrong, 837, 987.
Performyng of Penaunce, 837, 989,
1148, 1377, 1432.
Hooly Deuocion, 838, 1431.
Good Contynuaunce, 838.
Preesthood, 839, 1424, 1426.
Sacramentes, 839; the Sacrament of
Eukaryst, 1428, 1439; Holy Vnccion,
1444.
Sadnesse, 840, 1233, 1265, 1279,
1349, 1355, 1361, 1374, 1380, 1436.
Commaundementes, 840.
Sufferaunce in Trowble, 841.
Innocency, 841.
Clennesse, 842.
Continence, 842.
Virginite, 842.
Kyndnesse, 843.
Reuerence, 843.
Curtesy, 843.
Content, 844.
Plesyd with Pyteous Pouerte, 844.
Entendyng Well, 845.
Mynystryng Equyte, 845.
Hooly Indyfferency, 846.
Laboryng the Seruyce of God to
Multyply, 847.
Refuse of Rychesse, 848.
Perfeccion, 849, 990.
Parfyte Contemplacion, 849.

interpretation by Doctrine, st. 261–
   266 ; moral, st. 297–298.
Vice's host, st. 89-103.
Oryginal cryme =
   Messenger of Vice, 776, 781, 950,
   955.
Seven chief captains =
   Pryde, 621.
   Enuy, 622.
   Wrethe, 624.
   Couetyse, 626.
   Glotony, 628.
   Lechery, 630.
   Slowthe, 631.
Embassadors sent by Vice to Freewill =
   Temptacion, 1004.
   Foly, 1004.
   Sensualyte, 1004.
Minor Captains dubbed Knights by Vice
   (14) =
   Falshood, 974, 643.
   Dyssymulacion 974, 636.
   Symony, 975, 636.
   Vsure, 975, 644.
   Wrong, 975, 645.
   Rebawdy, 975, 648.
   Malyce, 976, 640.
   Deceyte, 976, 647.
   Ly, 976, 644.
   Extorcion, 976, 637.
   Periury, 977, 644.
   Diffidence, 977, 652.
   Apostasy, 977, 657.
   Boldnesse in Yll, 978, 648.
The Minor Captains (75) =
   Sacrylege, 636.
   Symony 636, 975.
   Dyssimulacion, 636, 974.
   Manslaughter, 637.
   Mordre, 637.
   Theft, 637.
   Extorcion, 637, 976.
   Arrogaunce, 638.
   Presumpcion, 638.
   Contumacy, 638.
   Contempcion, 639.
   Contempt, 639.
   Inobedience, 639.

Malyce, 640, 976.
Frowardnes, 640.
Gret Ielacy, 640.
Woodnesse, 641.
Hate, 641.
Stryfe, 641.
Impacience, 641.
Vnkyndnesse, 642.
Oppression, 642.
Wofull Neglygence, 642.
Murmour, 643.
Myschyef, 643.
Falshood, 643, 974.
Detraccion, 643.
Vsury, 644, 975.
Periury, 644, 977.
Ly, 644, 976.
Adulacion, 644.
Wrong, 645, 975.
Rauyne, 645.
Vyolence, 645.
False Iugement, 646.
Obstynacy, 646.
Dysseyte, 647, 976.
Dronkenes, 647.
Improuydence, 647.
Boldnes in Yll, 648, 978.
Foule Rybaudy, 648, 975.
Fornycacion, 649.
Incest, 649.
Auoutry, 649.
Vnshamefastnes, 650.
Prodygalyte, 650.
Blasphemie, 651.
Veynglory, 651.
Worldly Vanyte, 651.
Ignoraunce, 652.
Diffydence, 652, 977.
Ipocrysy, 652.
Seysme, 653.
Rancour, 653.
Debate, 653.
Offense, 653.
Heresy, 654.
Errour, 654.
Idolatry, 654.
New Fangylnes, 655.
False Pretense, 655.

Inordinat Desyre of Worldly Excel-
lense, 656.
Feynyd Pouert, 657.
Apostasy, 657, 977.
Disclaundyr, 658.
Skorne, 658.
Ielousy, 658.
Hoordam, 659.
Bawdry, 659.
False Mayntenaunce, 659.
Treson, 660.
Abusion, 660.
Pety Brybery, 660.
Vsurpacion, 661.
Horryble Vengeaunce, 661.
Idylnesse, 666.
Captains refused by Virtue who enter the
service of Vice (st. 124-126)=
Nygromansy, 867.
Geomansy, 868.
Magyk, 868
(Glotony), 868.
Adryomancy, 869.
Ornomancy, 869.
Pyromancy, 869.
Fysenamy, 870.
Pawmestry, 870.
The Commons with Vice led by Idleness=
Bosters, 673.
Braggars, 673.
Brybores, 673.
Praters, 674.
Fasers, 674.
Strechers, 674.
Wrythers, 674.
Shakerles, 675.
Shaueldores, 675.
Oppressours, 676.
Crakers, 676.
Meyntenours of querelles, 677.
Lyers, 677.
Theues, 678.
Traytours, 678.
Herytykes, 678.
Charmers, 679.
Sorcerers, 679.
Scismatykes, 679.
Symonyakes, 680.

Vsurers, 680.
Multyplyers, 681.
Coyn wasshers, 681.
Coyn clyppers, 681.
Vsurpers, 682.
Extorcioners, 682.
Bakbyters, 683.
Glosers, 683.
Flaterers, 683.
Murmurers, 684.
Claterers, 684.
Tregetours, 685.
Tryphelers, 685.
Feyners of tales, 685.
Lurdeyns, 686.
Pykers of males, 686.
Rowners, 687.
Uagaboundes, 687.
Forgers of lesynges, 687.
Robbers, 688.
Reuers, 688.
Ryfelers, 688.
Choppers of churches, 689.
Fynders of tydynges, 689.
Marrers of maters, 690.
Money makers, 690.
Stalkers by nyght, 691.
Euesdroppers, 691.
Fyghters, 692.
Brawlers, 692.
Brekers of lofedayes, 692.
Getters, 693.
Chyders, 693.
Causers of frayes, 693.
Tytyuyllys, 694.
Tyrauntes, 694.
Turmentoures, 694.
Apostates, 695.
Relygyous dyssymulers, 695.
Closshers, 696.
Carders, 696.
Hasardoures, 696.
Tyburne coloppys, 697.
Pursekytters, 697.
Pylary knyghtes, 698.
Double tollyng myllers, 698.
Tapsters, 699.
Hostelers, 699.

IN THE FIELD OF MICROCOSM (MS = MACROCOSM).

The Field : is named Microcosm, 932 ; in the midst = Conscience, 934, Synderesys, 937 ; its lord = Freewill, st. 143; approached by five highways open to the Vices and Virtues, st. 135 ; interpretation by Doctrine, st. 262, 265.

The battle : the field, first entered by Original Crime, st. 111 = driven out by Baptism, st. 112 ; sowed with evil seeds by Sensuality, st. 146-148; the battle between the vices and virtues, st. 148-162 (won by Perseverance, st. 157-162).

Freewill, Lord of Microcosm, st. 143 ; receives embassadors from Virtue, st. 143, from Vice, st. 144 ; gives an ambiguous answer, st. 145 ; takes the part of Vice, st. 151-152, 155 ; repents and seeks the counsel of Conscience, st. 163 ; is sent to Humility, Confession, Contrition, Satisfaction and Penance, st. 164 ; appears before Virtue, st. 174 ; blames Sensuality, st. 175-176 ; in recompense yields Microcosm to Virtue, st. 178-179 ; is made bailiff under Reason, st. 180.

Prescience, sent from above the firmament by Alpha and Omega (v. l. 1158, 1176, 1467) to punish Vice, st. 166-167.

Predestinacion, sent to reward Virtue, st. 168-169 ; they vanish, st. 170.

Vice's host ; scourged by Prescience, st. 167 ; some seek Peace, Mercy, Faith, Hope, Baptism, Confession, Conscience, Circumcision, st. 171-174.

Sadnesse, takes Sensuality prisoner, st. 177 ; is given the guidance of Sensuality in Microcosm, st. 181, 183, 193; with Reason clears Microcosm of the evil weeds of Sensuality, st. 195 ; with Reason prepares the field for the coming of the Lord of Light, st. 206.

Reason, rules in Microcosm, st. 180, 187, 193, 195, 197, 206.

Nature (has jurisdiction over living creatures, st. 65, 69, 190; has "carnal might," l. 1381) requires that Sensuality be given his liberty, st. 182; is powerless to help Atropos against Virtue, st. 194.

Morpheus, is given charge of five gates of Microcosm, st. 185-186.

Atropos, resolves to enter the service of God, st. 191 ; inquires the way to

Righteousness, st. 198, 199; is called Death, st. 201; is given power in Microcosm, st. 203, 207–209; vanishes, st. 210.

The Lord of Light, received in Microcosm, st. 204–206.

Resydyuacion, enters Microcosm but is repulsed, st. 192–195; interpretation by Doctrine, st. 266.

THE ACCORD OF REASON AND SENSUALITY.

Reason, an embassador of Virtue and ruler in Microcosm; Lydgate muses how he may make Reason and Sensuality to accord, st. 1; Reason is sent by Virtue as an embassador to Freewill, st. 143; has no fear of Sensuality, st. 176; is given charge of Microcosm, st. 180; has guard over Sensuality, st. 187, 193 (v. 266); is superior to Nature, st. 194; with Sadness clears Microcosm of weeds, st. 195; is directed by Prayer, Fasting, Penance and Almsdeed st. 197; shows Atropos the way to Righteousness, st. 198–199; with Sadness, cleanses the field against the coming of the Lord, st. 206; comes with Sensuality to Doctrine to clear up Lydgate's doubt, st. 276–279; Reason and Sensuality agree as to the fear of Death, st. 280–282; vanishes, st. 283; interpretation of the concordance by Doctrine, st. 287–288.

Sensuality, an embassador of Vice to Freewill, and an ally of Nature; Lydgate muses how he may make Sensuality and Reason to accord, st. 1; Sensuality is sent by Vice as embassador to Freewill, st. 144; sows evil seeds in Microcosm, st. 146–148, 153; is charged with corrupting Freewill, st. 176; taken prisoner by Sadness and brought to Virtue, st. 177; is placed under the guidance of Sadness, st. 180–181; his liberty plead for by Nature, st. 182; is denied freedom in Microcosm, st. 183; guarded by Reason, st. 187; meets with Residivation but can do no evil, st. 193, 194; his evil weeds cut down by Reason and Sadness, st. 195; enters with Reason the School of Doctrine to clear up Lydgate's doubt, st. 276–279; agrees with Reason as to the fear of Death, st. 281; vanishes, st. 283; interpretation of the concord by Doctrine, st. 287–288.

IN THE SCHOOL OF DOCTRINE, st. 211–290.

(A FOUR-SQUARE ARBOR).

Wytte, chief porter, st. 212.
Teachers of the people=
    Dame Doctryne, st. 213–214, st. 229–231; as interpreter, st. 232–288.

Holy Texte, st. 215.
Glose, st. 215.
Moralyzacion, st. 215.
Scrypture, st. 215, the Scribe.

PICTURED ON THE WALLS:

1ST AND 2D WALLS: TIMES OF DEVIATION AND REVOCATION.

(The false gods are not here described).

Adam, 1521.

Eue, 1521, holding an apple.

Noe, 1522, in a ship.

Abraham, 1522, holding a flintstone.

Isaac, 1523, bound on a mount.

Iacob, 1524, sleeping by a ladder.

Ioseph, 1526, in a cistern.

Moyses, 1527, with two tables.

Aaron, 1528,
Vrre, 1528, } supporting Moses' arms.

Ely, 1529, in a burning car.

Elyze, 1530, clad as a hermit.

Dauid, 1531, with a harp and stone sling.

Ieremy, 1532.

Ezechiell, 1532.

Danyell, 1533, in a lion's den.

Abacuc, 1534.

Mychee, 1534.

Malachy, 1534.

Ionas, 1535, coming out of a whale's body.

Samuell, 1536, in a temple.

Zakary, 1536, by an altar.

Osee, 1538,
Iudyth, 1538, } conspiring the death of Holofernes.

Salamon, 1539, dividing a child with his sword.

Melchisedech, 1543, offering bread and wine.

Ioachym, 1545,
Anne, 1545, } at the golden gate.

Iohn Baptyst, 1547, in a desert.

Sodechy, 1549,
Amos, 1550, } with faces toward Sophony.

Sophony, 1551.

Neemy, 1552.

Esdras, 1552.

Ioob, 1553, as an impotent.

Thoby, 1554, as patient.

3D WALL=TIME OF RECONCILIATION.

Petyr, 1562, with keys.

Poule, 1563, with a sword.

Iames, 1563, with a scallop.

Thomas, 1564, with a spear.

Phylyp, 1565.

Iames the lesse, 1566.

Bartylmew, 1567, all flayn.

Symon, 1568.

Thadee, 1568.

Mathy, 1569,
Barnabe, 1569, } drawing lots.

Marke, 1570, a lion holding his book.

Mathew, 1571, like an angel.

Luke, 1573, a calf holding his book.

Iohn, 1574, with a cup and palm in his hand, an eagle holding his book.

Gregory, 1576,
Ierome, 1576,
Austyn, 1576, } as doctors.
Ambrose, 1576,

Bernard, 1578.

Anselme, 1578.

Thomas of Alquyn, 1579.

Domynyk, 1579.

Benet, 1580.

Hew, 1580.

Martyne, 1581.

Iohn, 1581.

Crysostom, 1582.

Beede, 1583.

Orygene, 1584.

Sybyll, 1589.

Andrew, 1595, with a cross.

4TH WALL=TIME OF PILGRIMAGE, OR DANGEROUS PASSAGE, OR OF WAR.
(See the battle of the vices and virtues.)

DAME DOCTRINE.

Dame Doctrine, interpreter of the vision, summons Lydgate to draw near, st. 231–232; interprets the imprisonment of Eolus = unbridled wealth increases misrule, st. 233–234; Minos =Judge of Cruelness, st. 235; the complaint of Diana and Neptune= the blindness of fools, st. 235–236; the dismissal of the court=forgetfulness of fools, 237–239; the gods at the banquet = false idols, st. 240–249; the Time of Deviation, st. 241–249 =from Adam to Moses; the poets and philosphers=feigners of fables, st. 249; Time of Revocation = from Moses to Christ, st. 250–251; Time of Reconciliation=time of Grace, st. 251–252; Time of Pilgrimage=time of war, st. 255; (the present battle between Vice and Virtue, st. 256); the complaint of Atropos=the constraint of friendship (Discord and Death) st. 257–260; the battle between Vice and Virtue=the moral struggle in the human soul, st. 261; Microcosm = the world of man, st. 262; Perseverance = continuance of good living, st. 263; Prescience and Predestination=rewarders of vice and virtue, st. 264; the five keys given to Morpheus = the five inward wits, st. 265; Residivation=return to sin, st. 266; the accord of Reason and Sensuality=in the fear of Death, st. 275–288; Doctrine vanishes, st. 290.

OTHER NAMES.

God, 1293, 1333, 1410, 1497, 1640, 1685, 1748, 1754, 1818, 2065, 2088; Lord God, 1930; Lord, 1819; 2093, Lord of Glory, 2098; Fadyr, 2104; Alpha and Omega, 1158, 1176.

Ihesu, 1121, 2105; Cryst, 1103, 1752, 1775; Son of Man, 1755; Crystyn, 1764.

Mary, 2105.

Devyll, 21, 1818, 2080.

Peleus, feast of, 413.

Phebus, the sun, 1, 361.

Pictagoras, 3.

CATALOG OF PLACES.

A lake, st., 1.

Lydgate's habitation, st., 2.

The Court of Minos in Pluto's realm, st., 4.

The Palace of Apollo, st., 27, 36, 107, 192.

The Palace of Virtue, st., 187.

The field of Microcosm, st., 134, 135.

The school of Doctrine, a four-square arbor, st., 212.

Fantasy, 35, the dwelling place of Morpheus.

Synay, Mount of, 1747.

GLOSSARY.

(For a fuller explanation of many words see the Notes.)

Abew, 1063. See *bewe*.

Abhominable, adj., 711, abominable.

Aboorde, 248. See *borde*.

Abusion, sb., 660, abuse.

Abydyng, sb., 34, dwelling place.

Abyte, vb., 194, abides, remains.

Accusement, sb., 160, accusation.

Adryomancy, sb., 869, (Aero-? or Hydro-?) divination by air (or water).

Adulacion, sb., 644, flattery.

Afore, adv., 1120, before.

Afray, sb., 729, battle.

Aftyr, prep., 76, in accordance with; *aftyr*, adv., 1024, afterwards.

Agayn, prep., 100 and often, against. See *ayene*.

Aldyrs, 490, 579. gen. pl. of all, *althrys* 599.

Allyaunce, sb., 991, alliance.

All be, conj., 476, al-be-it.

Aloft, adv., 101, in the air, on high.

Altherlast, 186, last of all.

Aly, sb., 1810, ally.

Ambidextres, sb., 707, double dealing persons.

Ambyguyte, sb., 1012, ambiguity.

Anone, adv., 14, 1615, soon.

Apply, vb., 485, incline.

Aray, sb., 282, 296, dress.

Arere, adv., 962, to the rear.

Armure, sb., 931, armor, weapons.

Arow, 763 = a row, host.

Asaute, vb., 588; sb., *assawte*, 1049, assault.

Asay, vb., 980, try.

Asondre, adv., 66, asunder.

Aspyed, vb., 1368, spied.

Astert, vb., 1267, escape.

Astonyed, vb., 1311, astounded, dismayed.

Astyrlabes, sb. pl., 1896, instruments for taking altitudes of the sun and stars (astrolobes).

Ateynt, vb., 362, disgraced, afflicted with sorrow.

Atwene, prep., 2006, between.

Atwyx, prep., 1966, between.

Auaunce, vb., 954, advance; imper., *avaunt*, 1121.

Auauntage, sb., 727, 1033, advantage.

Auauntours, sb., 711, boasters.

Auaylyd, vb., 19, helped; *avale*, vb., 360, bow down — perhaps = to have force.

Auenaunt, adj., 885, agreeable, handsome.

Auentur, sb., 944, chance, adventure.

Auoutry, sb., 649, adultery; *auouterers*, 711.

Avowe, sb., 983, vow.

Auyse, vb., 860, advise; sb., 1352, advice.

Auysment, sb., 140, deliberation.

Awayters, sb., 1741, waiters.

Awter, sb., 1537, altar.

Ax, vb., 520, ask; *axyd*, 1383.

Ay, adv., 119, 256, 966, ever.

Ayene, prep., 19, and often, against. See *agayn*.

Ayeyn, adv., 63 and often, again.

Bake, sb., 1905, back.

Balaunce, sb., 1012, scale, decision.

Bankes, sb., 105, shores of the sea.

Banket, sb., 188 and often, banquet.

Batayll, sb., 753, 1010, etc., battle.

Baudys, sb., 700, bawds.

Bawdryk, sb., 285, belt.

Bayll, sb., 1259, bailiff.

Baytys, sb., 596, lures.

Be, vb., 115 and often, been.

Bedene, adv., 277, together, in order, or perhaps an expletive.

Beforn, adv., 819 ; *before,* 1792, before.

Begoon, vb., 441, suffered.

Begylyd, vb., 571, diverted.

Beheste, sb., 481, promise.

Behoue, sb., 1260, advantage.

Beleue, sb., 1679, belief.

Bende, sb., 1172, band, company.

Benedycyte, 1594, bless ye, equivalent to thank God.

Benygne, adj., 1224, gracious, benignant.

Beseene, vb., 275, 823, bedecked adorned.

Beseke, vb., 1929, beseech.

Beset, vb., 297, beset, studded with ornaments.

Beshut, vb., 1169, shut up.

Bespreynt, vb., 258, sprinkled.

Bestadde, vb., 1106, placed, sorely imperilled.

Besy, adj., 563, 746, 1811, busy, anxious.

Bettyr, sb., 882, better.

Betyn, vb., 105, beating (?) or beaten.

Bew, adj., 1063 (beu) good, fine.

Blere, vb., 1299, make dim.

Blyn, vb., 1860, cease from.

Blyue, adv., 941, quickly.

Bone, adj., 720, ready ; *bowne,* vb., 716, prepared.

Boorde, sb., 1242, conversation ; *boorde* 388, table ; *aboorde* 248.

Boote, sb., 1351, help, succor.

Borow, vb., 1167, bail out, secure.

Boystous, adj., 127, 156, boisterous, noisy.

Brayde, vb., 499, started up.

Breched, vb., 325, dressed with breeches.

Breede, vb., 599, grow, breed.

Brennyng, vb., 1529, burning.

Brokers, sb., 702, receivers of stolen goods.

Brybores, sb., 673, robbers, beggars.

But yef, conj., 89, 490, unless.

Caltrop, sb., 773, an iron instrument scattered in battlefields to impede cavalry.

Carders, sb., 696, card players.

Carnall, adj., 1381, worldly, fleshly.

Carpe, vb., 402, play, speak ; *carpyng,* 439.

Castaway, sb., 1274, something of no value.

Caytyffys, sb., 705, caitiffs.

Certeyne, adv., 112 and often, certainly.

Chamelet, sb., 320, camlet, a woven fabrik of wool and cotton, or of goat's hair and silk.

Chare, sb., 506, car.

Chases, sb., 58, open hunting grounds.

Chaunse, sb., 996, chance.

Chere, sb., 263, 284, face, countenance ; greeting, 418, 423.

Chese, vb., 882, chose.

Chyders, sb., 693, scolds.

Chyne, vb., 536, to open in cracks or fissures.

Chyst, sb., 1300, chest.

Claterers, sb., 684, tattlers.

Clause, sb., 136, proviso.

Cloke, sb., 1503, cloak.

Closshers, sb., 696, " closh "-players.

Clowte, sb., 1274, clout, rag.

Cofres, sb., 273, coffers for money.

Coloppys, sb., 697. See note.

Columbyne, adj., 374, dovelike, like the flower (?)

Comfort, sb., 65, 532, pleasure ; 206, confidence ; 488, help, support ; *comfortyd,* vb., 761.

Comon, adj., 1938, familiar.

Compace, sb., 1881, space.

Conceyte, sb., 1989, thought, idea.

Concordaunce, sb., 2005, agreement.

Condescendyd, vb., 1974, agreed.

Condycyons, sb., 322, states, circumstances.

Confound, vb., 506, destroy ; 1042, ? pass ; *confounders,* 916.

Coniecture, sb., 1694, opinion.

Coniugatoures, sb., 915, uniters.

Constreynyd, vb., 49, urged, compelled.

Context, adj., 1503, woven firmly.

Contumacy, sb., 638, resistence to authority.

Corner, sb., 35, secluded place.

Correccion, sb., 91, 486, correction, fine.

Cost, sb., 119, coast ; 952, region.

Costlew, adj., 296, costly.

Couerture, sb., 1723, covering, concealment.

Coueyte, vb., 1476, covet.

Counterfete, vb., 212, construct.

Cowchyd, vb., 287, 308, inlaid, laid in order.

Craft, sb., 1710, business, 1134 craftiness.

Crakers, sb., 676, braggarts, noisy fellows.

Croppe, sb., 620, stem of a plant.

Cropyn, vb., 1953, crept.

Cruell, adj., 41, 471, harsh, severe, cruel; *crewelnes,* sb., 1643.

Crysmatory, sb., 1444, a vessel for chrism.

Cryspe, adj., 374, fresh.

Culuer, sb., 1608, dove.

Curas, sb., 345, cuirass, breastplate.

Cure, sb., 59, 455, care.

Cure boyle, 617, hard leather; v. note.

Cyrcute, sb., 757, circuit.

Cysterne, sb., 1526, cistern.

Dalyaunce, sb., 1509, talk.

Dampnacion, sb., 1844, damnation.

Darkyd, vb., 1193, lay hid.

Dastard, sb., 1886, coward; pl. 703.

Date, sb., 425, date, time. See note.

Daungere, sb., 96, 527, 543, 2084, power; 165, 445 refusal.

Debonayr, adj., 1441, gentle.

Defaute, sb., 460, default; ? vb., 782.

Dele, vb., 146, deal, distribute; *deele,* 1634, have dealings.

Dell, sb., 1333, part; *dele,* 1027.

Deme, vb., 1068, think, judge.

Demenyng, sb., 269, demeanor.

Deputate, vb., 1641, appointed.

Dere, vb., 600, injure.

Dereygne, vb., 612, set in order, fight.

Desert, sb., 1288, merit.

Desperate, adj., 28, causing despair.

Desyreth, vb., 138, demands.

Disclaundyr, sb., 658, slander.

Disport, sb., 531, pleasure.

Do, vb., 54 and often, done.

Dolour, sb., 735, grief.

Domynacion, sb., 1911, domination.

Doole, sb., 487, dole, portion.

Dotyng, adj., 1394, foolish, childish.

Dowte, sb., 761, 1001, 1321, 1929, doubt; vb., 523.

Dowty, adj., 792, brave.

Draught, sb., 1232, drawing, move at chess.

Dresse, vb., 534, direct, reach, prepare; myn ey gan I dresse, 1512.

Dryuylles, sb., 703, idiots.

Dubbyd, vb., 974, conferred knighthood.

Dure, vb., 1777, last, extend; *duryd,* 751.

Duresse, sb., 1270, restraint.

Dynt, sb., 487, dint, stroke.

Dyscordyd, vb., 1973, differed.

Dyscrese, vb., 232, decrease.

Dysdeynyd, vb., 168, refused.

Dysgysyd, vb., 343, dressed, tricked out.

Dysport, sb., 67, 531, 671, pleasure, recreation.

Dyspurueyde, vb., 723, unprepared.

Dysseyte, sb., 647, deceit.

Dysvsyd, vb., 1400, disused, out of use.

Effecte, sb., 1617, 1916, conclusion, meaning.

Efte, adv., 560, again.

Eftsones, adv., 1007, immediately.

Egall, sb., 154, equal.

Eke, adv., 247, also.

Elles, adv., 33, else; *ellys,* 161.

Enbrowderyd, vb., 332, embroidered.

Enforme, vb., 783, inform.

Enhaunse, vb., 999, increase, raise.

Entent, sb., 108, purpose; 451, attention, effort; *thentent,* 1904.

Entresse, sb., 1941, interest.

Equyte, sb., 495, justice.

Er, Ere, adv., 8, 1558, before.

Eschew, vb., 901, avoid.

Estate, sb., 27, 424, state, place, rank.

Euerychoon, 1806, each one.

Euesdroppers, sb., 691, eves-droppers.

Euyll, adv., 38, in an evil manner.

Evyn, adv., 102, at the time; 202, evenly; adj., 886, even.

Execute, vb., 53, bring to bear.

Exorte, vb., 1488, teach, advise.

Fade, vb., 70, wither, decrease.

Fall, vb., 230, fall; 10, fallen, pp.; 124, befall; 558, happen; *fell.* 530, happened; *fyll,* 367, was fitting.

Fande, vb., 131, found.

Fantasy, sb., 35, 2050, fancy; *fantasyes,* pl., 1854.

Fare, vb., 810, proceed.

Fasers, sb., 674, hypocrites (facers).

Fauset, sb., 357, faucet.

Fawchon, sb., 283, falchion.

Fawcon, sb., 803, falcon.

Fayne, adj., 11, inclined, desirous.

Fee, sb., 995, domain.

Feere, sb., 1952, fear.

Feet, sb., 1064, deed.

Fell, adj., 434, cruel (many ?).

Fendes, sb., 1412, fiendes.

Fenyx, sb., 810, phœnix.

Fere, 52, *in fere*=in company.

Ferre, adv., 102, 1613, 1627, 1913 far; *ferther,* 1932.

Feruent, adj., 1448, vehement.

Fet, vb., 544, bring, fetch.

Feynt, adj., 80, 359, weak, lacking color and energy.

Finaunce, sb., 1242, fine, forfeiture.

Flayn, vb., 1567, flayed.

Foly, sb., 1631, 2097, foolishness, sin.

Fone, sb., pl., 1748, foes.

Foom (?), sb., 104, foam.

Forteresse, sb., 187, palace; 303 figuratively as strong-hold.

Forse, sb., 1057, matter, consequence, *no forse*=no matter.

Forsothe, adv., 211, 581, in truth.

Foryete, vb., 239, forgotten.

Fowtyn, vb., 1826, fought.

Foyson, sb., 408, abundance, plenty.

Frese, sb., 325, a cloth.

Froward, adj., 1816, ungovernable; *frowardness,* 640.

Fructuous, adj., 900, fruitful, profitable.

Fury, sb., 53, judgment.

Fygure, sb., 1725, form of speech.

Fyn, adv., 1463, very.

Fysenamy, sb., 870, physiognomy.

Gaderyd, vb., 760, gathered.

Galaunt, adj., 296, splendid, gay.

Gall, sb., 1614, nut-gall.

Gan, vb., 202, 534, began, and used as auxiliary=did.

Gape, vb., 1316, desire, stand in expectation of.

Garnysshyd, vb., 377, adorned.

Gastes, sb., 754, guests, (cf. Lat. hostis) followers.

Gate, vb., 1836, won.

Gawdy, adj., 320, gaudy, perhaps dyed with weld.

Geere, sb., 886 ? riches (or ? jeer).

Genalogy, sb., 854, lineage.

Geomansy, sb., 868, divination by earth.

Gesse, vb., 1386, think, suppose.

Get, sb., 1678, 1657, fashion.

Getters, sb., 693, ? swaggerers or ? thieves.

Gladyd, vb., 383, made glad.

Glosyng, adj., 2081, flattering; *glosers,* sb., 683, flatterers.

Go, vb., 1396, gone.

Gonnes, sb., 1038, guns.

Goostly, adj., 852, spiritual.

Gramercy, 575, many thanks.

Greefe, sb., 47, harm; 216, sorrow.

Grogyng, sb., 217 (grochyng) grumbling, malice.

Grounde, sb., 304, reason, agency, 1690, place.

Gryffyng, sb., 1718, grafting.

Guerdoun, sb., 2087, reward.

Guy, vb., 1720, guide.

Guytornes, 970, (? guydons) cavalry flags.

Gyldyn, adj., 367, golden.

Gymlot, sb., 357, gimblet.

Gyse, sb., 1965, manner.

Habundaunce, sb., 1714, abundance.

Habylyte, sb., 1247, ability.

Habytacle, sb., 11, habitation.

Happyd, vb., 419, chanced.

Hasardoures, sb., 696, gamblers.

Haunt, sb., 1295, dwelling; *hauntyd,* 119.

Heede, sb., 10, head.

Heede, sb., 1815, care.

Hele, sb., 1853, health.

Hem, pr., 1636 and often, them.

Her, pr., 47, 65, 1635, their.
Herber, sb., 1479, arbor.
Hermyne, sb., 266, ermine.
Herowde, sb., 719, herald.
Heuynesse, sb., 186, slowness, 10 heaviness.
Heynous, adj., 962, hateful, reprehensible.
Hit, pr., 62 and often, it.
Hogy, adj., 1095, huge.
Holly, adv., 2014, wholly.
Hoole, adj., 967, whole.
Houyd, vb., 1608, hovered.
Howe be hit, conj., 1081, how-be-it.
Hulke, sb., 88.
Hy, vb., 765, hie; *hyghyd,* 941, hied.
Hydyr, adv., 604, hither.
Hygh, adj., 73, great.
Hygh-weyes, sb., 1460, high-ways.
Hyghyd, vb., 941, hastened.
Hym, pr., 128 and often, them; also him.

Impotent, sb., 1553, sick man.
Inconuenyent, sb., 415, inconvenience.

Iape, sb., 525, jest, mockery.
Iugement, sb., 161, the court sentence.
Iurysdyccion, sb., 1111, power.
Iust, vb., 1099, joust.

Karyk, sb., 88, cark, a kind of ship.
Kendall, adj., 356, describing a kind of cloth.
Keruell, sb., 87, caravel.
Knowleche, sb., 529, knowledge.
Knyt, vb., 991, united; *knet,* 1186; *knette,* 2008.
Konnyng, sb., 854, wisdom.
Krany, vb., 536, crack into fissures.
Krauers, sb., 534, crevice.
Kynde, sb., 1647, nature; 1544, kind.
Kyrtyll, sb., 332, an outer garment.

Lak, sb., 369, lack.
Langoure, sb., 1853, languor.
Lappyd, vb., 120, wrapped.
Large, sb., 1239, liberty.
Largely, adv., 1637, freely.
Largesse, sb., 1327, liberty.

Lastyuyous, adj., 686, lascivious.
Laurer, sb., 791, laurel.
Lawe, vb., 404, laugh.
Leese, vb., 1100, lose.
Leme, sb., 1609, light.
Lere, vb., 887, learn.
Lerne, vb., 957, teach.
Lesynges, sb., 687, lies.
Let, vb., 1130, hinder: 251, avoid, neglect; 529, given; 956, let; sb., 319, hinderance.
Lewde, adj., 403, worthless, perhaps loud; sb., *lewdenesse,* 1633, free action.
Loft, see *aloft.*
Longeth, vb., 1327, belongs.
Loore, sb., 2074, wisdom, lore.
Lore, vb., 1309, lost.
Loselles, sb., 714, worthless fellows, lorels.
Lothe, adj., 881, loath.
Lowte, vb., 1089, 1430, 1925, bow, yield.
Lurdeyns, sb., 686, block-heads.
Luskes, sb., 714, lazy fellows.
Lust, sb., 1307, strength, desire; 1277, wish.
Lyeftenaunt, sb., 1254, lieutenant, representative.
Lyght, adv., 1201, lightly.
Lyke, vb., 225, please.
Lyklynes, sb., 1066, probability.
Lyst, vb., 1007, wished; 1291, wish.
Lythe, vb., 105, lies.

Mace, sb., 476, mace.
Malapert, adj., 503, impudent, forward.
Males, sb., 686, pockets.
Manaces, vb., 61, threatens.
Maner, sb., 69, kind of; on a *maner,* 5; any *maner* wey, 1735.
Marre, vb., 556, destroy.
Mastresse, sb., 243, mistress, governess.
Mawgre, prep., 1381, in spite of.
Mede, sb., 756, merit.
Medewes, sb., 259, meadows.
Mekyll, 92, "in as mekyll as"; mochyll, 1813.
Mene, sb., 1195, mediator; adj., 946, mean.
Mene, adj., 1720, mean, low.
Merueyle, sb., 103, marvel, wonder.

Messe, sb., 257, plate, table.

Mesure, sb., 84, degree, *out of mesure=* beyond due degree or bounds.

Meuyd, vb., 145, proposed; *meve,* 431, propose.

Meynt, vb., 361, mingled.

Meyny, sb., 853, followers, army; *meyne,* 774.

Monacorde, sb., 7, agreement.

Moo, 863, 1600; *more,* 1606, *moore* 1791.

Mood, sb., 1571, manner.

Mortall, adj., 732, 1450, deadly.

Mowte, vb., 1951, been able.

Mowthe, sb., 2060, mouth.

Multyplyers, sb., 371, 681, money makers.

Murre, sb., 329, murre, a cold in the throat.

Muryd, vb., 1460, enclosed, walled.

Myscheue, vb., 523, do harm; sb., *myschyef,* 620.

Myddes, sb., 934, midst.

Myte, sb., 1607, 1814, mite, thing of no value.

Ne, 1197 and often, not.

Nere, adv., 1, nearly.

Newe, adv., 562, newly.

Next, adj., 551, nearest.

Noonys, 502, nonce.

Nouelte, sb., 1705, new thing.

Noy, vb., 774, annoy.

Nygromansy, sb., 867, divination by the dead.

Obstacle, sb., 9, hinderance.

Odoryferous, adj., 336, fragrant.

Offyce, sb., 494, employment.

On, sometimes written *oo,* 117, one.

Onwarde, adj., 162, further.

On lyue, 1851, alive.

Oon, 6 and often, one.

Oonys, adv., 1127, once.

Opteygne, vb., 1353, obtain.

Or, conj., 752, ere.

Ordynatly, adv., 203, in good order.

Ordynaunce, sb., 245, decision, law.

Ornomancy, sb., 869, divination by birds.

Ospray, sb., 813, the fish hawk.

Ost, sb., 668, host; *hooste,* 1124, cf. Fr. ost.

Othes, sb., 502, oathes.

Ouches, sb., 297, jewels.

Outher, conj., 33, either; *owther,* 480.

Overstert, vb., 1593, ? overlooked.

Oweth, vb., 91, is under obligation, followed by an objective clause introduced by an infinitive, with *to,* as in Chaucer.

Pak, sb., 368, company.

Panter, sb., 822, panther.

Parable, sb., 1987, parable.

Parciall, adj., 153, partial.

Parde, 619, 1275, (par Dieu).

Party, adj., 316, partial, favoring one party.

Pase, sb., 632, step, way.

Passyd, vb., 368, surpassed.

Patent, sb., 496, written bond of office.

Pauyse, vb., 1640, used reflexively—bring to pause.

Pawmestry, sb., 870, divination by the hand.

Paynym, adj., 1679, pagan.

Penowns, sb., 970, small banners.

Pere, sb., 808, equal.

Perfyte, adj., 1491, perfect.

Permyssyue, adj., 1731, permitted.

Perpetuell, adj., 899, constant.

Pesecoddys, sb., 493, pea-pods.

Pety, adj., 827, inferior.

Peyne, sb., 746, 1811, pain, trouble.

Plenteuous, adj., 408, plenty, cf. O. F. plentevous.

Plesaunce, sb., 798, pleasure; *plesere,* 197.

Plyght, vb., 1473, pledge.

Polytyk, adj., 1742, wise.

Ponderously, adv., 9, heavily.

Posternes, sb., 1296, 1849, gates.

Poudryd, vb., 266, powdered.

Praters, sb., 674, trifling talkers.

Precept, sb., 1682, command.

Predicament, sb., 1329, in logic = a general class.

Prefyxyd, vb., 549, appointed.

Preparate, vb., 1467, prepared.

Presse, sb., 256, throng; 1755, torment.
Prima facie, 157, at first view.
Prophetyssa, sb., 1580, prophetess.
Proue, vb., 1728, test, determine.
Prykeryd, adj., 328, prick-eared.
Prynte, vb., 1784, impress.
Pryse, sb., 1354, contest.
Pseudo-prophetes, sb., 708, false prophets.
Purfylyd, vb., 266, trimmed.
Purpur, sb., 306, purple garments.
Purseuaunte, 776, messenger.
Puruey, vb., 75, provide; 946, *prevydyd;* 1029, *purveyde.*
Puruyaunce, sb., 956, 1433, provision, plan.
Put, vb., 761, 1090, bring to a condition of; *put out,* 1481, expel.
Pyke, vb., 1348, betake.
Pylary, adj., 608, pillory.
Pylow, sb., 12, pillow. Cf. Chaucer's *pilwe.*
Pylyons, sb., 1577, priests' hats.
Pyne, sb., 216, punishment.
Pyromancy, sb., 869, divination by fire.
Pyry, sb., 126, storm of wind.

Quelmers, sb., 709, killers, (infanticides).
Quod, 1477, said; 1210, quoth.

Rancour, sb., 235, enmity, malice.
Ray, sb., 550, striped cloth.
Recorde, vb., 272, remember.
Recouer, vb., 769, ? cover over, win.
Recreaunt, adj. 1256, defeated.
Redolence, sb., 1611, fragrance.
Reft, vb., 564, deprived.
Reherse, vb., 83, relate.
Reioyse, vb., 532, make glad.
Rekke, vb., 560, care, reck.
Relese, vb., 883, rehearse.
Reproche, sb., 71, reproach.
Rerewarde, sb., 1094, rear gaurd.
Resorte, vb., 63, return.
Respyte, sb., 170, postponement.
Resydyuacion, sb., 1340, back-sliding.
Retourne, vb., 100 (active), turn back.
Reuers, sb., 688, robbers.
Reyne, vb., 2086, reign.

Roode, sb., 1040, cross.
Route, sb., 388, 438, company.
Rought, vb., 1197, reached.
Rowne, vb., 12, consult with; *rownyd,* 142, consulted with; *rownyd,* 421, whispered; *rowners,* sb., 687, whisperers.
Russet, adj., 325, coarse.
Rybaudy, sb., 648, ribaldry.
Ryght, adv., 101, very.
Rynde, sb., 66, bark (tree).

Sabatouns, sb., 346, sabbatons, armorial coverings for the feet.
Sad, adj., 270, 390, 1561, earnest, serious.
Safe, conj., 402, except.
Safecondyte, sb., 89, 490, safe-conduct.
Sakcloth, sb., 290, sackcloth.
Sanctuary, sb., 1446, a sacred place.
Sauns, prep., 1858, without, (v. Nares' Glos.).
Sauerys, sb., 336, odors.
Sauoryd, vb., 338, smelled.
Scalop, sb., 1564, scallop-shell.
Scisme, sb., 411, division.
Se, pr., 376, she.
Secte, sb., 895, sect, kind.
See, sb., 365, seat.
Seere, adj., 1459, dry, withered.
Seethe, sb., 97, restoration.
Sekerly, adv., 787, surely.
Sentence, sb., 136, 458, decision; 1863, truth.
Sequelys, sb., 871, followers.
Sercote, sb., 276, surcoat, outer coat.
Sesyd, vb., 1744, ceased.
Sesyne, sb., 1455, possession (a law term).
Set, vb., 2016, settled.
Sew, vb., 219; *su,* 238, entreat; *sewyd,* 1198.
Sewe, vb., 1023, sowed.
Sewerte, sb., 449, surety.
Sewre, adj., 524, sure.
Shakerles, sb., 675 (?).
Shaueldores, sb., 675 (?).
Shent, vb., 1092, destroyed, shamed.
Shoures, sb., 322, gifts; *shoure,* 732, struggle.

Slepyr, adj., 1026, 1069, slippery.
Smokke, sb., 377, smock.
Sobre, adj., 1233, sad ; 1660, sober.
Sodomytes, sb., 708, fornicators.
Soort, sb., 619, troop, company ; *sorte,* 1489.
Soot, sb., 618, soot.
Sore, adv., 341, greatly.
Sothe, sb., 1226, truth.
Sotyll, adj., 1694, 1701, subtle.
Sought, vb., 788, went.
Sownde, vb., 1688, sound.
Sowneth, vb., 1302, tends, inclines; *sowyd,* 1987, seemed.
Spere, sb., 3, sphere; *speres,* pl., 1698.
Spreynt, see bespreynt.
Stadde, see bestadde.
Stale, vb., 2040, stole.
Stant, vb., 1887, stands.
Stede, sb., 340, place ; 1129, steed.
Steuyn, vb., 824, proclaim, announce.
Stoute, adj., 313 — said of eyes ; 430 — said of words: haughty, resolute, bold.
Strayte, adj., 45, strict ; adv., 539' narrowly.
Strechers, sb., 674, ? liars.
Stremes, sb., 1855, streams.
Streyngthe, vb., 751, strengthen.
Streytyd, vb., 1633, restricted, put in bonds.
Styrt, vb., 566, started.
Superfluyte, sb., 1824, superfluity.
Superfyciall, adj., 538, pertaining to the surface.
Sustynaunce, sb., 336, support, living.
Sy, vb., 1058, saw.
Sygne, sb., 1442, miracle.
Sykerly, adv., 270, surely.
Sylogyse, vb., 19, reason, contend, argue.
Symonyakes, sb., 680, simonists.
Synderesys, sb., 937, syneresis.
Syngler, adj., 71, special.
Syth, conj., 1354, since.
Sythe, sb., 127, time.
Swage, vb., 1038, ? discharge.
Swemfully, adv., 1223, sorrowfully.
Swet, sb., 104, 2044, sweat. In 2044 said of body.

Take, vb., 59 and often, taken; *takyn* 1626.
Tane, vb., 2013, taken.
Tayll, sb., 754, company, number.
Teche, vb., 1701, teach; *taught,* 1231.
Tendre, vb., 135, consider, have a care for.
Tenebrus, adj., 1169, dark.
Than, adv., 89 and often, then.
The, pr., 52 and often, thee.
Then, conj., 1607, than.
Tho, pr., 447, those.
Thorough, prep., 70, on account of (preceded by where) ; *thorow,* 2061.
Thought, sb., 1234, 1360, 2051, anxiety, care ; 1991, thought.
Thryd, 1776, third.
Thynne, adj., 1591, thin.
To, adv., 511 and often, too.
Tong, sb., 367, tongue.
Tonne, sb., 1807, tub.
Trapure, sb., 815, trappings.
Traunse, sb., 15, trance.
Trauayll, sb., 1971, work.
Trayne, sb., 773, snare.
Tregetours, sb., 685, jugglers.
Trespase, sb., 221, injury, offense.
Triumphall, adj., 2087, triumphal.
Trouthe, sb., 1473, troth.
Trow, vb., 957, believe; 1386, know *trowyd,* 432.
Try (out), vb., 2071, separate.
Tryacle, sb., 12, a medicine, (cf. treacle).
Tryfyls, sb., 1854, trifles, cheats.
Trypartyte, adj., 1031, divided into three parties.
Tryphelers, sb., 685, cheaters.
Tweyne, sb., 1966, two.
Tyburne, sb., 697. See note to this line.
Tyde, sb., 334, time.
Tylthe, sb., 1710, cultivation.
Tyne, 1063, tiny (generally preceded by little, as here)..
Tytyuyllys, sb., 694. See note on line 694.

Vnbrydelyd, vb., 1630, unrestrained.
Vnderlowte, sb., 1273, servant.

Vndyrtake, vb., 233, 1390, 1411, be surety, promise.
Vnkynde, adj., 1023, unnatural, cruel.
Vnlustes, sb., 713, idle men.
Vre, sb., 1448, use, practice.
Vsyd, vb., 117, was accustomed to do.
Vtter, adj., 594, absolute.

Valewyng, vb., 1607, valuing.
Varyaunce, sb., 244, difference, dispute.
Vaward, sb., 602, van.
Verrey, adj., 918, 2002, true.
Veryly, adj., 2042, truly.
Vouchesafe, vb., 2019, granted.

Walewyng, vb., 557, wallowing.
Wanton, adj., 378, sportive; 1230, reckless; sb., *wantones*, 1362, 1635.
Ware, adj., 128, aware.
Wede, sb., 377, garment.
Wedyr, sb., 530, weather.
Welde, vb., 670, wielded.
Wele, sb., 56, 210, weal, prosperity.
Wende, vb., 739, 1623, go; see *wene*.
Wene, vb., 278, 985, think, suppose; *wenyng*, 1651, 1713; *wend*, 239; *wende*, 1344.
Weryd, vb., 379, wore.

Wetewoldes, sb., 710, tame "cuckolds."
Wex, vb., 1369, 1415, grow.
Whan, conj., 1, when.
Whedyr, conj., 24, whether.
Whereas, adv., 118, where.
Whereon, adv., 48, whereof.
Whew, sb., 1316, 2049, hue.
Whore, adj., 400, white; *whore-berdyd*= hoar-bearded.
Whyle, sb., 129, time.
Wood, adj., 1314, mad (also *mad* 347).
Woote, vb., 621, knows; *wote*, 1011.
Wrapped, vb., 1383, wrapped.
Wrethe, sb., 417, wrath.
Wrought, vb., 1882, done.
Wrythers, sb., 674 ?
Wyght, sb., 987, 1034, man.
Wyre, sb., 1872, doubt.
Wyse, sb., 51, manner.
Wysshe, vb., 1384, direct, recommend.
Wyt, sb., 896, wisdom.

Ydiote, sb., 1963, idiot.
Yef, conj., 56, 63, etc., if.
Yeue, vb., 17, 77, give.
Yuy, sb., 355, yew.
Ywys, adv., 879, 1056, certainly.

All and some, 192, each and all, the whole matter.

In especiall, 116, 1445, 1599, especially.

By and by, 202, then; 302, 800, one after the other.

More and lesse, 306, 536, more or less; 1264, altogether.

Lest and moost, 766, 784, high and low degree. *Most or leste*, 480.

To or fro, 24.

Fer and wyde, 626.

Make and marre, 556.

For feyre or foule, 475.

For the nonnys, 502, for the nonce.

Out of mesure, 84, 102, beyond measure or reason.

What in the deuyllys date, 425, exclamatory.

Howe a deuyll way, 1317, exclamatory.

Croppe and roote, 620, the whole of anything.

Roote and rynde, 66, the whole tree.

Kepe noon in store, 151, keep nothing in reserve.

Not worth a peere (pear), 597.

Then a myte, 1007; *nat a myte*, 1814, *myte* a small thing.

Rekke nat a strawe, 500.

Nat yeue two pesecoddys, 493.

Bryght as glas, 276.

Breched lyke a bere, 325.

Grene as any gresse, 334.

Here shone as wyre of goold bryght, 373.

As a goste came in wyndyng shete, 420.

Tomblyng as a ball, 557.

Harde as glas, 614.

Hard as horn, 618.

Blakker then soot, 618.

Slepyr as an yele, 1026.

As a castaway or a shoo clowte, 1274.

Close as in a chyst, 1300.

Coloryd as a crystall, 1603.

Darke as a myste or a feynyd fable, 1988.

Wyt ys oute where hyt went ynne, 1999.

Dreuyn to her wyttes ende, 1665.

My wyt ys so thynne, 1997.

Ferre ys fro the wytte and ferther good mende, 1932.

Thy wytte stant acrooke, 1887.

For feere I lookyd as blak as a coole. I wold haue cropyn in a mouse hoole, 1952 53.

Howe the game gooth, 426, how the matter stands.

Ledeth by the sleue, 1680, causes to follow submissively, cf. *loke me by the sleve* 14, 2033.

Cast in a boon (of contention), 1805.

Hit hyng in hys balaunce, 1012, it depended upon his decisions.

Of all maner greynes she sealyd the patent, 202; cf. "wenyng in her honde had leyn all power of cornys habundaunce" 1713-14; v. 440, ye seelyd my patent.

Take the mantell and the ryng, 267, vow perpetual widowhood.

Varyaunt Fortune, 318.

Taught to drawe another draught, 1232, taught to make another move—to do differently.

Lerne hem a new daunce, 957, teach them a new motion.

Fro poost to pylour was he made to daunce, 1147, he was driven from one thing to another without purpose.

Made her beerdys on the new gete, 1657, changed their minds.

The bende of your bowe begynneth to slake, 1243-44.

Put in prese, 1755, enter into torment.

He must nedys go that the deuell dryues, 21.

Where vertew occupyeth must nedys well grow, 1372.

A false myrrour deceyueth a mannys look, 1727.

Bettyr late then neuer, 1204.

Bettyr be dede than a lyve, 518.

He ys nat as he doth apere, 2083.

As good ys ynowgh as a gret feste, 2035.

Such as ye haue sowe must ye nedes reepe, 1244-45.

Bettyr were a chylde to be vnbore then let hyt haue þe wyll and for euer be lore, 1308-9.

Wealth unbrydelyd encreseth mysrewle, 1631.

Fooles ouercome ay wyse men, 1661.

Try out the corne clene from the chaff, 2071 "take the best and let the worst be," 2070.

14 DAY USE

RETURN TO DESK FROM WHICH BORROWED

LOAN DEPT.

This book is due on the last date stamped below, or
on the date to which renewed.
Renewed books are subject to immediate recall.

OCT 28 1968 1 9	
REC. CIR. JUN 21 '76	
REC. CIR. JUL 1 1977 Jun 20 '77	
FEB 4 '79	
REC. CIR. OCT 14 '80